Christ, History and Apocalyptic

THEOPOLITICAL VISIONS

SERIES EDITORS:

Thomas Heilke
D. Stephen Long
and C. C. Pecknold

Theopolitical Visions seeks to open up new vistas on public life, hosting fresh conversations between theology and political theory. This series assembles writers who wish to revive theopolitical imagination for the sake of our common good.

Theopolitical Visions hopes to re-source modern imaginations with those ancient traditions in which political theorists were often also theologians. Whether it was Jeremiah's prophetic vision of exiles "seeking the peace of the city," Plato's illuminations on piety and the civic virtues in the Republic, St. Paul's call to "a common life worthy of the Gospel," St. Augustine's beatific vision of the City of God, or the gothic heights of medieval political theology, much of Western thought has found it necessary to think theologically about politics, and to think politically about theology. This series is founded in the hope that the renewal of such mutual illumination might make a genuine contribution to the peace of our cities.

PUBLISHED VOLUMES:

Stanley Hauerwas and Roman Coles
Christianity, Democracy, and the Radical Ordinary: Conversations Between a Radical Democrat and a Christian

Bryan C. Hollon
Everything Is Sacred: Spiritual Exegesis in the Political Theology of Henri de Lubac

Gabriel A. Santos
Redeeming the Broken Body: Church and State after Disasters

Christ, History and Apocalyptic:

The Politics of Christian Mission

Nathan R. Kerr

CASCADE *Books* · Eugene, Oregon

CHRIST, HISTORY AND APOCALYPTIC
The Politics of Christian Mission

Theopolitical Visions 4

First published in Great Britain in the Veritas series, by SCM Press, 13–17 Long Lane, London EC1A 9PN, England.

First U.S. edition published by Cascade Books under license from SCM Press.

Cascade Books
A Division of Wipf and Stock Publishers
199 W. 8th Ave., Suite 3
Eugene, OR 97401
www.wipfandstock.com

ISBN 13: 978-1-60608-199-0

Cataloging-in-Publication data:

Kerr, Nathan R.

Christ, history and apocalyptic : the politics of Christian mission / Nathan R. Kerr.

xvi + 206 p. ; cm. —Includes bibliographical references and index.

Theopolitical Visions 4

ISBN 13: 978-1-60608-199-0

1. Christianity and politics. 2. History—Philosophy. 3. Troeltsch, Ernst, 1865–1923. 4. Barth, Karl, 1886–1968. 5. Hauerwas, Stanley, 1940–. 6. Yoder, John Howard. I. Title. II. Series.

BR115. P7 K41 2009

Manufactured in the U.S.A.
Typeset by Regent Typesetting, London, UK.

Contents

Preface

This book is an exercise in ideology critique, though of a very
ambivalent kind. It is meant theologically to address a peculiarly modern philosophical idea: 'history'. Most acutely, however,
it is this as an attempt to address modern theology's temptation
to root its work (and particularly is socio-political work) in its
own historical presumptions. Whether by way of 'world historical' achievement or 'ecclesiological fundamentalism' (warned
against so presciently by Donald MacKinnon over 40 years
ago), such presumptions inevitably take the Church's experi-
ences within history to be self justifying.

That this book unfolds unmistakably as a kind of story,
however, forbids the illusion that there is a perspective outside
the space of what we call 'history' from which to critique its
abuses. Though this work is not simply a story or genealogy,
then, it is even less a philosophy or for that matter a theology
of history. It is rather written out of the conviction that the only
way to exceed our own assumptions as to what is historical is
to imagine an altogether different way of acting *in* history. It
is furthermore written out of the conviction that such an imagination must be the gift of arrival of one who acts as coming
from *beyond* and as one who *interrupts* what we presume to be
given to us historically. It is this conviction that has led me to
address the question of history by speaking of 'Christ' and of
'apocalyptic'.

If the theologian is to risk speaking in this way, then perhaps the best she can do is to insinuate herself into a discourse,
to write herself into it in such a way as to be unapologetically
open to an act and event of such unexpected newness that it

vii

cannot but occur outside the writing and reading of a text – outside of and beyond the two covers of a book. To do that is my most humble ambition in *this* book.

Nathan Kerr
Pentecost 2008

Acknowledgements

I gladly take this opportunity to thank Conor Cunningham and Pete Candler, who have been unwavering in their support of this project from the beginning. They have given me and my work the gift of unfailing encouragement, generosity and trust. As well as a friendship. Many thanks also to Thomas Heilke, Steve Long, and C. C. Pecknold, who have graciously welcomed this book into the series they edit, as well as to all at Cascade Books, among whom I am glad to say my work has found something of a "home."

Thank you to Natalie Watson and Mary Matthews, who worked so hard to bring this book to print. Also, thank you to Charlie Collier, Jim Tedrick, Diane Farley, and James Stock, as well as to all those at Cascade whom I can't name but who have worked indefatigably on behalf of this book. Their excitement about this project has truly been a grace. Peter Andrews, my copy-editor, did wonderful work proofreading and correcting the text, and made the book stronger as a result.

Thank you also to my colleagues and students at Trevecca Nazarene University, whose willingness to put up with a too absent-minded (and sometimes just plain 'absent') professor during the final stages of this work has made its completion possible.

Thank you to the following for the ways in which each has contributed to this book and my work: Paul DeHart, my doctoral supervisor, from whom I have learned more than I can express; Doug Meeks has accepted my work with faith and a generosity of vision. Also: John Thatamanil; Melissa Snarr; Jamie Smith; Dan Barber; Tim Eberhart; Mike Gibson; Aaron Simmons; Adam Kotsko; Dave Belcher; and Josh Davis and

Acknowledgements

Craig Keen, who have been my two closest friends along the way. I cannot express sufficient thanks to my parents: Bucky and Sandi Kerr, who I know where up and awake praying for this book as often as I was up and awake writing it.

If there is a soundtrack to this book, it is thanks to my daughter Zoë Grace. All those hours we spent 'rocking out' to the Pixies when I 'should' have been working taught me one thing: It is something like a father's love for his daughter that gives life to projects like these.

This work is as much my wife's as it is mine. The way she has given herself to live with me through this project convinces me that she understands what it is about in ways that I never will. I trust she understands also what it means when I say that this book is a gift 'for Kristina.'

Guide to Abbreviations

The following abbreviations will be used for frequently cited titles:

Works by Troeltsch

ACHR *The Absoluteness of Christianity and the History of Religions*, trans. David Reid (Richmond, VA: John Knox Press, 1971).

CF *The Christian Faith*, trans. Garrett E. Paul (Minneapolis: Fortress Press, 1991).

CT *Christian Thought: Its History and Application* (New York: Meridian Books, 1957).

DH *Der Historismus und seine Probleme. I. Buch: Das Logische Problem der Geschichtsphilosophie*, in *Gesammelte Schriften*, vol. 3 (Tübingen: J. C. B. Mohr, 1922).

ET *Ernst Troeltsch: Writings on Theology and Religion*, trans. and ed. Robert Morgan and Michael Pye (Atlanta: John Knox Press, 1977).

PP *Protestantism and Progress: A Historical Study of the Relation of Protestantism to the Modern World*, trans. W. Montgomery (Boston: Beacon Press, 1958).

RH *Religion in History*, trans. James Luther Adams and Walter F. Bense (Minneapolis: Fortress Press, 1991).

Abbreviations

STCC   *The Social Teaching of the Christian Churches*, 2
       vols, trans. Olive Wyon (New York: Harper Torch-
       books, 1960).

Works by Barth

CD   *Church Dogmatics*, eds, G. W. Bromiley and T. F.
       Torrance, 4 vols, 14 parts (Edinburgh: T. & T. Clark,
       1956–77).
ER   *The Epistle to the Romans*, 6th edn, trans. Edwyn
       C. Hoskyns (Oxford: Oxford University Press,
       1968).

Works by Hauerwas

AC   *After Christendom? How the Church Is to Behave
       If Freedom, Justice, and a Christian Nation Are Bad
       Ideas* (Nashville: Abingdon Press, 1999).
AN   *Against the Nations: War and Survival in a Liber-
       al Society* (Notre Dame: University of Notre Dame
       Press, 1992).
BH   *A Better Hope: Resources for a Church Confronting
       Capitalism, Democracy, and Postmodernity* (Grand
       Rapids: Brazos Press, 2000).
CC   *A Community of Character: Toward a Constructive
       Christian Social Ethic* (Notre Dame: University of
       Notre Dame Press, 1981).
CCL   *Character and the Christian Life: A Study in Theo-
       logical Ethics* (Notre Dame: University of Notre
       Dame Press, 1994).
CET   *Christian Existence Today: Essays on Church,
       World, and Living in between* (Durham, NC: Laby-
       rinth Press, 1988).

Abbreviations

DFF   *Dispatches from the Front: Theological Engagements with the Secular* (Durham, NC: Duke University Press, 1994).

IGC   *In Good Company: The Church as Polis* (Notre Dame: University of Notre Dame Press, 1995).

PF   *Performing the Faith: Bonhoeffer and the Practice of Nonviolence* (Grand Rapids: Brazos Press, 2004).

STIT   *Sanctify Them in the Truth: Holiness Exemplified* (Nashville: Abingdon Press, 1998).

TPK   *The Peaceable Kingdom: A Primer in Christian Ethics* (Notre Dame: Notre Dame University Press, 1983).

VV   *Vision and Virtue: Essays in Christian Ethical Reflection* (Notre Dame: University of Notre Dame Press, 1981).

WGU   *With the Grain of the Universe: The Church's Witness and Natural Theology. Being the Gifford Lectures Delivered at the University of St. Andrews in 2001* (Grand Rapids: Brazos Press, 2001).

WW   *Wilderness Wanderings: Probing Twentieth-Century Theology and Philosophy* (Boulder, CO: Westview Press, 1997).

Works by Yoder

AE   'Armaments and Eschatology', *Studies in Christian Ethics*, 1.1 (1988), pp. 43–61.

CWTS   *The Christian Witness to the State* (Scottdale, PA: Herald Press, 2002).

DPR   *Discipleship as Political Responsibility*, trans. Timothy J. Geddert (Scottdale, PA: Herald Press, 2003).

EE   'Ethics and Eschatology', *Ex Auditu*, 6 (1990), pp. 119–28.

FTN   *For the Nations: Essays Public and Evangelical* (Grand Rapids: William B. Eerdmans, 1997).

Abbreviations

HHRN 'How H. Richard Niebuhr Reasoned: A Critique of *Christ and Culture*', in Glen H. Stassen, D. M. Yeager, and John Howard Yoder, *Authentic Transformation: A New Vision of Christ and Culture* (Nashville: Abingdon Press, 1996), pp. 31–89.

JCSR *The Jewish-Christian Schism Revisited*, ed. Michael G. Cartwright and Peter Ochs (Grand Rapids: William B. Eerdmans, 2003).

KBPW *Karl Barth and the Problem of War and Other Essays on Barth*, ed. Mark Thiessen Nation (Eugene, OR: Cascade Books, 2003).

OR *The Original Revolution: Essays on Christian Pacifism* (Scottdale, PA: Herald Press, 2003).

PJ *The Politics of Jesus: Vicit Agnus Noster*, 2nd edn (Grand Rapids: William B. Eerdmans, 1994).

PK *The Priestly Kingdom: Social Ethics as Gospel* (Notre Dame: University of Notre Dame Press, 1984).

PT *Preface to Theology: Christology and Theological Method* (Grand Rapids: Brazos Press, 2002).

RP *The Royal Priesthood: Essays Ecclesiastical and Ecumenical*, ed. Michael G. Cartwright (Scottdale, PA: Herald Press, 1998).

Apocalyptic is the mother of theology.
Ernst Käsemann

Jesus Christ will not live in history in any other
way than as Jesus Christ.
Søren Kierkegaard

Errata

Concerning p. 41, at the beginning of the section entitled, "Politics and Mission: The 'Constantinian Temptation' and the Triumph of Ideology":

My reading of Troeltsch, and of *The Social Teaching of the Christian Churches* in particular, in this and the previous section is heavily indebted to the work of J. Alexander Sider. Although my reading of Troeltsch is not identical to his, I owe some of my way of putting things to J. Alexander Sider, 'To See History Doxologically: History and Holiness in John Howard Yoder's Ecclesiology' (Ph.D. diss., Duke University, 2004), ch. 2, 'Seizing Godlikeness: Ernst Troeltsch and the "Constantinian" Syntheses', pp. 82–133.

Concerning pp. 137ff.

For some of the terminology employed here, as well as for some of the ways of putting things in this and the next section, I am dependent upon Daniel Barber, 'The Particularity of Jesus and the Time of the Kingdom: Philosophy and Theology in Yoder', *Modern Theology* 23.1 (January 2007), pp. 63–89.

I

Introduction

The Question

The question which prompts the following essay is this: what mode of thinking about history and the historical character of human action renders the 'truth' of the earliest and most straightforward Christian confession, that of Jesus Christ's 'lordship' – *kurios Iesous* – for our world today? By confessing that 'Jesus is Lord', Christians thereby confess that in Christ's life, death, and resurrection we are confronted not only with the definitive disclosure of God in history but also by the fact that, as such, Jesus of Nazareth in his very historicity is the one in whom we are to discern the locus of the meaning, or 'truth', of history. Only as we refuse to grant history a status or meaning apart from the interruptive event of Christ's cross and resurrection, and only as this event itself perpetually conditions history as the site of the apocalyptic arrival and inauguration of God's coming reign, can the confession that 'Jesus is Lord' be considered true for us today. Hence the title proper of this work: *Christ, History and Apocalyptic*.

The subtitle of this work, however, *The Politics of Christian Mission*, signals a refusal to grant that either this confession or the truth of Christ's lordship for history are in any sense merely parochial matters, as a matter of 'the church's' intra-ecclesial (or, ecclesiocentric) constitution vis-à-vis 'the world'. As the truth of history, Christ's lordship is neither a privilege nor a possession, but rather a *political* and *missional* vocation. In the most straightforward sense, this vocation is political insofar as the apocalyptic inbreaking occurs as a uniquely *sovereign* act.

From the very beginning, the confession of Christ's lordship meant nothing less than that Jesus Christ, having suffered rejection on the cross at the hands of the powers and principalities of history, had been raised up by God as victorious over those powers.

And yet, as the author of Hebrews so clearly affirms, Jesus is uniquely the *apostolos*, the one who is *sent* into the world, precisely in order that he might *give* himself to the world for the sake of the world's own *transformation* – the world's own *freedom* from the powers. As a matter of such transformation, the inbreaking of God's reign is made real and available only as a way of *life*, a concrete *practice*, a mode of historic *action*, which 'way of life', 'practice', and 'action' constitutively and fundamentally concur as this world's *conversion*. Furthermore, if the church itself is to be understood as the gathering of that people whose very existence is to be a sign and a parable of the incursion of God's coming reign into this evil age that is passing away, then this missionary vocation must be considered equally constitutive of *ecclesia*. The 'church' only ever exists, *ecclesia* only ever 'is', as the occurrence of a people which, like Jesus himself, is *sent* into the world, a people whose very life is the gift of participation in this world's liberation and transformation. Thus, this essay arises out of a deep conviction that what is now needed in Christian theology is an account of Christian 'politics' which is rooted firmly in a conception of 'the church' – *ecclesia* – that is irreducibly and constitutively *missionary*.

In short, the ultimate aim of this work is to seek out and to expound *a vision of history that at once calls for and is empowered by an apocalyptic politics of mission*.

Modernity and the Historicist Problematic

This work thus amounts to a defence of Christian apocalyptic as a mode of taking seriously the intrinsically political character of the church's mission. However, to take up such an inquiry today, under the pressures of late modernity, does not allow us to select our starting point. The complexities of what Charles Taylor calls 'the modern identity'[1] do not leave us free simply to frame our hypothesis concerning Christian apocalyptic and then to proceed as if such a project were not itself conditioned and determined at least in part by our awareness of the fact that 'living in history' is a peculiarly modern sentiment. As is well known, the edifice upon which the modern identity is constructed is thoroughly historical: the pervasiveness and inescapability of 'the historical' is a reality which, within the modern *ethos*, comes finally to be recognized as universally valid.[2]

Furthermore, as Pierre Manent has shown, the belief that 'all is historical' and 'history is irreversible' achieves with modernity for the first time the status of a *political* authority.[3] Particularly since Hegel, but even as far back as Montesquieu, it has been assumed that genuine political sovereignty – the freedom of Absolute Spirit – must engender itself, and must itself be engendered, by and through the processes of historical and institutional development. True freedom – 'liberty' – can be achieved only as the result of these processes.[4] The 'authority of history' thus assumes a politically *ideological* function: history becomes the artifice which produces, and thus protects and encourages, the endurance of that institution which alone guarantees the attainment of freedom: the nation state. 'History' has itself come to be recognized as 'sovereign'. Humanity's very freedom assumes the sovereignty of

1 C. Taylor, *Sources of the Self: The Making of the Modern Identity* (Cambridge, MA: Harvard University Press, 1989).

2 L. Dupré, *Passage to Modernity: An Essay in the Hermeneutics of Nature and Culture* (New Haven: Yale University Press, 1993), pp. 145–64.

3 P. Manent, *The City of Man*, tr. M. LePain (Princeton: Princeton University Press, 1998), pp. 11–49.

4 One thinks here of Hegel's oft-repeated refrain that the goal, the 'end', of history is the self-realization and awareness of freedom. See G. W. F. Hegel, *The Philosophy of History*, tr. J. Sibree (New York: Dover Publications, 1956), pp. 17–19, 48–51, 55–6, 59, 63.

the historical process, a sovereignty which itself requires, and includes, nothing from beyond or outside its own immanent circulation.

Given these assumptions, the status of Christian apocalyptic, which stresses that, in a singular historical event, God has acted to inaugurate the reign of God by making real and present an eschatologically perfect love in the middle of history, has – to say the least – been something of a contended issue in modern theological thought. For apocalyptic calls into question the very presuppositions of modern philosophical historicism: it challenges the many explanations of history as an immanental, self-contained sphere of contingent yet analogous happenings, which are nonetheless related in the intrahistorical development towards a single unified *telos*; its unabashed insistence upon singularity troubles the universalist aspirations of modern religious thought. Where history is seen as a universal nexus of distinct yet analogously related events which are relativized in their absoluteness by way of reference to a shared *telos*, then to portray Jesus of Nazareth as a unique, unsubstitutable event of the inbreaking of God's eschatological kingdom within history becomes incomprehensible. It thereby becomes necessary to relativize claims to Christ's absoluteness by submitting Jesus of Nazareth to the rigorous canons of modern historical reason and by assessing his significance as it arises from within the rational structures of historical development itself. So it is that we have learned to 'translate' apocalyptic into categories comprehensible to the modern mind. We have learned to historicize apocalyptic itself, to circumscribe it within the thought-world of a distant day, to demythologize and then to reconceptualize it as a way of fitting it into our own historical, intellectual, and political categories.

Of course, I have indulged here in something of a sweeping historical generalization. The modern 'historicist problematic' is much more difficult when one begins to look at the details, and we shall indeed make recourse to these details as this study progresses. Nevertheless, suffice it to say at this point that, in what follows, I seek to commend Christian apocalyptic

4

as a way *not* of evading but rather of confronting and taking seriously the several difficulties that history and modern historical inquiry pose for Christian faith, at the levels especially of Christology, eschatology, and Christian mission. In what follows, I shall not be concerned with whether there is an easy way to assert the universality, uniqueness, or absoluteness of Christianity in such a manner as to keep Jesus Christ, or for that matter anything about the faith, elevated above the waves of historicity. I shall rather insist, with Lessing, that we still yet reside on the near side of that wide ditch that separates the contingencies of history from the universal truths of reason.[5] That we can remain awash in our historicity and yet proclaim that 'Jesus is Lord' thereby confirms theology in its original condition: praise of God rooted in the fact that God has come to this side of the ditch, that God has chosen to confront us in a localizable, contingent, and singular historical event, and that this event itself frees us in our own localizable, contingent, and singular histories to participate in the coming reign of God.

What this study interrogates, then, is the difference between two contrasting theological 'historicisms':

1 that which assumes the modern historical consciousness, for which the relativities of history give way to a universalizing tendency by which talk of eschatology and the Kingdom of God comes unhinged from the singular historicity of Jesus Christ and attains an ideological-critical function, as a way of navigating the unresolved tension between the relativities of a historical immanentism and the intrahistorical development towards a rational, subjectively, and universally realized *telos*;

---

5 G. E. Lessing's famous image of the 'broad ugly ditch' that separates the 'accidental truths of history' from the 'necessary truths of reason' might be taken as something of a short-hand symbol for the problem of modern historicism as I shall be describing it in this essay. See G. E. Lessing, 'On the Proof of the Spirit and of Power', in *Lessing's Theological Writings*, tr. Henry Chadwick (London: A. & C. Black, 1956), pp. 51–6.

2 that of a renewed Christian apocalypticism which maintains that here, on this side of the ditch, our only hope is to
remain immovably fixed alongside Christ in his irreducible
singularity because, with this singular history of a Nazarene
rabbi crucified under Pontius Pilate, our own singular histories and our openness to (and participation in) the coming
reign of God uniquely coincide.

Constantinianism and Ideology

Of crucial importance to this work will be the argument that
not only do the assumptions of modern historicism play an important ideological-critical function within modern political
thought but also that this has important implications for how
one conceives of the socio-political dimensions of the Christian
existence. In the course of this argument, I shall draw heavily upon John Howard Yoder's analysis of the 'Constantinian'
nature of modern historical reason and its correlative politics of
'effectiveness'. It will thus prove helpful at the outset to define
what Yoder means by 'Constantinianism', as it is a term that
will appear with some frequency, as well as with some shifting
nuances, throughout what follows. The point of this summary
of Constantinianism is not necessarily to vindicate Yoder's
analysis, nor is it to hedge my own constructive proposal for
the politics of Christian mission on the authority of Yoder's
own anti-Constantinian stance. My point is to foreground the
sense in which 'Constantinianism' loosely names a certain set
of ideologically bound theological assumptions that perennially recur as ongoing temptations to Christian socio-political
thought. In fact, the nature of this temptation will lead me
to explore the 'limits of anti-Constantinianism' as a matter of
course. But even here the constructive primacy of articulating
an apocalyptic vision of history as the basis for a politics of
Christian mission will remain the focus of this study.

So to begin with, Constantinianism most fundamentally
names a certain orientation toward the political meaning of

history which is rooted in a heretical eschatology based upon a misconception of the relation of Christ to history. Most importantly, Constantinianism proceeds as if what happened in the cross, resurrection, and ascension of Jesus had not profoundly altered history, and it provides for the church a way of acting politically in history which is not entirely determined by the lordship of Jesus Christ. Yoder sums all of this up in a particularly rich passage:

> The apostolic church confessed Jesus Christ as Lord; risen, ascended, sitting at the right hand of the Father, i.e., ruling (1 Cor. 15:25ff.) over the not yet subdued *kosmos*. The principalities and powers, though not manifestly confessing His Lordship, could not escape from His hidden control or from the promise of His ultimate victory. In ways that took account of their rebelliousness He denied them free reign, using even their self-glorifying designs within His purpose. A later term for this same idea was 'Providence.' But with the age of Constantine, Providence no longer needed to be an object of faith, for God's governance of history had become empirically evident in the person of the Christian ruler of the world. The context of the millennium was soon pulled back from the future (whether distant or imminent) into the present. All that God can possibly have in store for a future victory is more of what has already been won.[6]

Four key points can be made by way of commentary upon this passage. First, Constantinianism describes the setting in which the normative locus for determining the meaning of political action in history is assumed to be the ordered structures of a given society rather than the kind of God-active-in-history of which the Bible speaks in its narrative of Israel, Christ, and the Church. It becomes axiomatic that 'civil government is the main bearer of historical movement', such that the 'civil sovereign' is now God's privileged political agent

---

6 Yoder, PK, pp. 136–7.

within history.[7] Consequently, the church itself is 'politicized' according to the terms of 'the state', the civil sovereign, the powers and principalities of this world. The church understands itself as a servant of the given structures of social and political development within this world.[8]

Second, Constantinianism idealizes the politically charged concept 'Kingdom of God'. Such idealization occurs variously, as the Kingdom is made into a transhistorical political ideal which is being worked out concretely but fragmentarily through the various human political constructions within history, or as it is spiritualized and personalized as a metaphysical ideal with no outward empirical referent. What such idealizations share is the denial that God has acted decisively and concretely in Jesus of Nazareth to inaugurate God's reign as a socio-political reality in the middle of history, in favour of either political 'realism' or religious 'personalism'.

According to this idealization of the Kingdom, Christian 'mission' in the sense of commending Jesus Christ to the world as its true Lord must be redefined.[9] On the one hand, belief in and confession of Christ as Lord is interiorized and individualized, such that what matters ultimately is the particular religious stance of one's soul. On the other hand, dependent as it is upon its interpretation of the human soul as being a priori oriented to the religious, this notion of mission must necessarily come to think of Christianity as being on some level a true and universally valid 'religion'. There is thus an exterior dimension to mission within Constantinianism, which requires of the Christian that she align herself with those social, political, and cultural movements which make possible the propagation of the Christian faith to all peoples within history, whether that be the expansion of the Roman Empire, as in early medieval Christendom, or the Europeanization of non-Western countries, as in modern Christian colonialism. In any case, the

---

7 Yoder, PK, pp. 138–9, 143; cf. Yoder, RP, pp. 198–203.
8 Yoder, PK, p. 138; Yoder, RP, pp. 198–9.
9 Yoder, PK, p. 137.

idealizing of the Kingdom of God leads to a situation in which the politics of Christian mission is dually 'compromised', in that Constantinianism trades upon an interior/exterior tension which leads it at once to locate the ultimate meaning of religion within the soul, and to conceive of Christianity as universally 'true' in such a manner as to compel it to sanctify certain structures and movements within a given society.[10]

Third, Constantinianism presupposes a conception of history and the *eschaton* that is at odds with a properly biblical and Judeo-Christian eschatology. Constantinianism foregoes an interpretation of history in terms of an overlapping of the 'two ages' or as a tension between the 'already' and 'not yet' and instead identifies the *eschaton* as the teleological working-out and development of certain immanental historical processes.[11] History is thought of primarily in metaphysically immanentist terms: the very conditions of historical existence require that there be a *telos* that both impels and grows out of the totality of history itself. The only way to relate to the *eschaton* within history is as a metastatic, transhistorical ideal that works through its relation to various intrahistorical forces and concepts: evolution, process, causality, organic development, etc.

Politically, this idea of the *eschaton* assumes the function of what we might today call an 'ideology', in the basic sense of the term: it orients history towards very specific political and social purposes by serving as a necessary postulate to secure the development of history towards its proper *telos*. Thus, fourth, Constantinianism assumes that the dominant norm for right political action is that of the 'effectiveness' of our actions in moving history towards the desired future end.[12] Furthermore, alongside effectiveness, '"responsibility" . . . becomes an autonomous moral absolute'.[13] Once 'history' is defined by

---

10 Yoder, RP, pp. 89–101.

11 Yoder, PK, pp. 136–8; Yoder, RP, pp. 144–67.

12 Yoder, PJ, pp. 228–33.

13 John Howard Yoder, 'Reinhold Niebuhr and Christian Pacifism', *Mennonite Quarterly Review* 29 (April 1995), pp. 101–17, p. 113; Yoder, CWTS, pp. 66–9; Yoder, RP, pp. 161–7.

its presumed determinate future, the church itself is conceived as *responsible* for aligning with those movements, institutions, and powers that are most likely to bring about the future that is envisioned. Constantinianism thereby underwrites an ideological politics of 'technique', which amounts to the strategic functional ordering of the powers and institutions of a given society.

Finally, Yoder sees in this ideological politics of 'technique' or 'effectiveness' a supreme instance of *idolatry*. Constantinianism is literally a matter of 'disavowal and apostasy'. In claiming 'for itself the authority from God to represent the cause of history', the powers of the nation, the state, the empire – and the church in collusion with them – are involved in an explicit structural denial of Christ's Lordship and his victory over the powers.[14] For Constantinianism basically represents the attempt 'to take into human hands the work that will be done by the Word of God at the end of the age – the final victory of the church and defeat of evil'.[15] Such attempts represent the very denial of the 'gospel substance': the shape and pattern of Christ's own lordship, as that of *kenosis*, of suffering servanthood, of the powerlessness of the cross.[16] Whereas the powers see 'equality with God' as a matter of being in control of the course of events, Christ is God and Lord precisely insofar as he 'renounced the claim to govern history'; it is precisely in Christ's cruciform 'renunciation of lordship, his apparent abandonment of any obligation to be effective in making history move down the right track', that the earliest Christians come to confess him, paradoxically, as *the* Lord of history.[17] Thus: 'What the churches accepted in the Constantinian shift is what Jesus had rejected, seizing godlikeness, moving *in hoc signo* from Golgotha to the battlefield.'[18] Constantinianism represents not just a failure of political strategy, but rather rep-

---

14 Yoder, RP, p. 155.
15 Yoder, RP, p. 156.
16 Yoder, PK, p. 145.
17 Yoder, PJ, p. 233–7.
18 Yoder, PK, p. 145.

resents, precisely *as* a kind of political strategy, a failure of *doxology*.

To sum up: Constantinianism is symptomatic of a heretical eschatology and a concomitantly heretical view of history. For the purposes of this book, it is this 'new view of the meaning of history' that is the real challenge of the Constantinian shift: 'the level on which the shift matters the most' is the question 'how does God work in history'?[19] Thus, in what follows I intend to deploy Yoder's analysis and critique of Constantinianism heuristically, as a way of accepting and addressing the challenge of modern historicism, and for the purposes of foregrounding the theological issue that is, in terms of the present work, logically and constructively prior to the critique of Constantinianism and modernism. This problem is that of retrieving for our time a biblically eschatological, apocalyptic perspective on history, for the sake of conceiving Christian mission as a distinctively political mode of ecclesial existence rooted in and flowing out of the doxological confession that 'Jesus is Lord'.

Christian Apocalyptic: A Thematics

The term that is most central to this book is perhaps the most elusive of definition: 'apocalyptic'. It does not make matters any easier that interest in apocalyptic has enjoyed not only a wide but diverse re-emergence in the theological disciplines over the past half-century, but in the humanities more broadly as well, especially within the disciplines of sociology, political theory, history, and philosophy. A central conviction of this book, however, is that at a time when 'apocalyptic' has taken on the status of what Jacques Derrida calls 'a certain tone' in contemporary culture and thought,[20] some account must be

---

19 Yoder, *Christian Attitudes to War, Peace, and Revolution: A Companion to Bainton* (Elkhart, IN: Goshen Biblical Seminary, 1982), pp. 42–3.

20 J. Derrida, 'On a Newly Arisen Apocalyptic Tone in Philosophy',

given of the difference that *Christian* apocalyptic makes for how we see and live in history today.

The point of this work, then, is not to provide an overview and account of the idea of 'apocalyptic' as such, but rather to work inductively and genealogically in such a way as to articulate a distinctively *Christian* apocalyptic vision, as well as to articulate the decisiveness of this vision for how we conceive the 'truth' of history and of the meaningfulness of Christian action within history.

What I should like to do, then, at the outset of this essay, is to offer a general 'thematics' of 'Christian apocalyptic', so as to provide a broad outline of the themes that will govern my use of the term 'apocalyptic' and its cognates in what follows. Because the purpose of this book is to ally these themes in such a way as to offer a compelling portrait of history and of the politics of Christian mission as rooted in an apocalyptic Christology, each theme can here be set forth in an initially general way, to be arranged properly in relation to the others in the chapters that follow, so as eventually to allow this portrait to be seen in its fullness and concreteness. How these themes come together in this way is not deducible from the themes as such, but is a cumulative case that is to be made over the course of the book as a whole.

1 Christian apocalyptic stresses *the otherness and the priority of God's action*. This first theme is most clearly dependent upon the conceptual framework inherited by early Christianity from Jewish apocalyptic. As John Collins has demonstrated, the Jewish apocalyptic 'genre' is first of all a literature that stresses radical contrasts, especially the contrast between God and the world.[21] Apocalyptic thus stresses a God who is utterly

---

tr. J. Leavey, Jr., in *Raising the Tone of Philosophy: Late Essays by Immanuel Kant, Transformative Critique by Jacques Derrida*, ed. P. Fenves (Baltimore: Johns Hopkins University Press, 1993), pp. 117–71, pp. 123, 167.

21 J. J. Collins, *The Apocalyptic Imagination: An Introduction to Jewish Apocalyptic Literature*, 2nd edn (Grand Rapids: Eerdmans, 1998), pp. 1–42.

different from this world, who breaks into this world from beyond, and who is revealed – *apocalyptai* – there precisely as *other*. Apocalyptic displays the otherness of God as a kind of commentary upon, but also a *showing* of, God's 'invasive action' with relation to the world.[22] 'Apocalyptic' thus names the particular operation of God's *transcendence*, conceived according to the prior inbreaking of God's Kingdom into history from beyond.

2 Christian apocalyptic has its 'centre of gravity'[23] in *the history of Jesus Christ*. As Douglas Harink puts it, for Christian apocalyptic, 'God's action and the history of Jesus Christ are both one and singular'.[24] That is to say, God's interruption of history in Jesus Christ is that of a *singular historicity*. Christian apocalyptic precludes any perspective on reality, any world-view, historical system or mythical framework, any principle, or idea, or metaphysic, which evades or abstracts from the concrete flesh-and-blood reality of that crucified Jewish peasant of Nazareth. The action of God by which the Kingdom breaks into this world is the singular event of Jesus Christ's historicity, with all the contingency and complexity that such historicity involves.

3 Christian apocalyptic is *cosmic* and *historical* in scope. The heart of the apocalyptic reality is that God, in Jesus Christ, has inaugurated a new cosmos, which is brought about through the liberation of the whole of creation from its enslavement to the powers of this evil age, which liberation is the work of Christ's own 'independence' from the powers and principalities. But

---

22 I am borrowing the language of 'invasive action' from J. L. Martyn, 'The Apocalyptic Gospel in Galatians' , *Interpretation* 54 (2000), pp. 252–60; Martyn, *Galatians: A New Translation with Introduction and Commentary* (New York: Doubleday, 1997), pp. 97–105.
23 D. Bosch, *Transforming Mission: Paradigm Shifts in Theology of Mission* (Maryknoll, NY: Orbis, 1991), pp. 142–3.
24 D. Harink, *Paul among the Postliberals: Pauline Theology beyond Christendom and Modernity* (Grand Rapids: Brazos Press, 2003), p. 69.

the inbreak of God's reign in Christ is only cosmic *as* historical. That is, Jesus' own apocalyptic historicity is *cosmically*
unintelligible apart from its operativity (qua apocalyptic)
within the ongoing contingencies and complexities of history.
The 'cosmic' significance of God's apocalyptic action in Jesus
Christ must be conceived as at one with what God is doing to
transform the contingencies and realities of ongoing history
in relation to the reign of God inaugurated in Christ. As such,
God's apocalyptic action is cosmic and historical and also
pneumatological. For the Spirit's work is truly that of making
Christ 'present' to us in the contingencies of ongoing history,
making us genuine participants in the mode of divine life that
is the singular apocalyptic action of Jesus of Nazareth.

It is this pneumatological aspect of apocalyptic which expresses the complex sense of the tension between the 'already'
and the 'not yet' of God's reign. History is inscribed or en-
coded as the Spirit-inspired dynamic movement between these
two foci: Christ's future 'second coming', his *parousia*, and
Christ's 'first' advent, his life, death, and resurrection. This
in-between time is the time within which Christ's own cosmic victory over the powers is *performed* (through the power
of the Spirit) with respect to the contingencies and particularities of our own histories. It is by way of this performance
that Christ's apocalyptic historicity is made real and visible as
constitutive of the very meaning, or 'truth', of history itself.
Christian apocalyptic articulates history itself as nothing less
than the time of the Spirit's ongoing focal disclosure in our
lives of Jesus Christ's death and resurrection, of his cosmic
'independence' from the powers and principalities, until this
world's final consummation in glory.

4 Christian apocalyptic is constitutive of *the meaning and
shape of Christ's lordship*. Conceived according to the terms
of Christian apocalyptic, the 'meaning' of Christ's lordship is
that of his *giving* of himself, in service and in radical love, to
the work of the Spirit in history. That is, Christ is Lord as he
gives *himself* – his very own 'identity,' his *person* – as a reality

to be embodied amid the *here and now* of our own contingent
localities. The apocalyptic nature of Christ's lordship is thus
at once *prophetic* and *priestly*. It is prophetic, in that Christ's
cross and resurrection represent not only a *challenge to* but
also a *victory over* the powers and principalities that hold this
world in bondage to their presumed political and historical
ideologies. But this victory is a priestly operation, in the sense
that, in giving himself on the cross, what Jesus gives is the
very *agape* of God. Such a love is real and present only as an
embodied *work*, a *way of life*, which cannot be captured or
accounted for on the basis of any of the assumed categories by
which the powers of this world seek to control and manipulate
the meaning of human life and death. Apocalyptic is thus constitutive of Christ's lordship insofar as 'apocalyptic' is another
name for the grace by which we are made participants in the
radical love which sent Jesus to the cross, and in the power of
the Spirit by which he was raised to new life. That is, Christ
is Lord according to that grace by which we are made participants in his very own prophetic and priestly work.

5 Christian apocalyptic is *doxological* and *missionary*. Christian apocalyptic is that divine action by which creation, in its
being made new and transformed, is converted to the *praise*
of Christ as Lord. Indeed, the 'church' – *ecclesia* – occurs precisely as that people that has been gathered into Christ by the
Spirit and has been made 'to turn to God from idols, to serve
a living and true God' (1 Thess. 1.10). Apocalyptic is doxological, however, insofar as it is our very *participation in* the
lordship of Jesus that leads us to acknowledge a slain lamb as
alone worthy to be praised. In other words, doxology is itself
a modality of God's apocalyptic action, as our own mode of
participation in the singular, apocalyptic historicity of Jesus
of Nazareth.

It is in this sense that apocalyptic is doxological as *missionary*. As Louis Martyn puts it, 'God's apocalypse of Jesus
Christ . . . was the birth of the gospel mission'.[25] Just as the

---

25 Martyn, *Galatians*, p. 99.

apocalyptic inbreaking of God's new creation is a matter of God's *sending* his Son into the world 'in the fullness of time' (Gal. 4.4), so also does the church occur as *sent* into the world through Christ, in the power of the Spirit, who gathers this people as a sign of God's *conversion* of the world to the coming of God's reign. What emerges from within an apocalyptic perspective, then, is the requisite existence of a people who celebrate Christ's lordship by sharing in his mission, by being broken for the world as he was broken, by being poured out in sacrificial love for others. Furthermore, the church *is* this mission as that people for whom Christ's lordship over history is not an assumed and static *given*, but a dynamic *gift*, to be received everanew in the mode of engaged and embodied action. It is precisely by way of such missionary reception that a certain Spirit-empowered *politics* of mission emerges as a sign of the gift and reality of God's ongoing apocalyptic action in Christ.

If, then, I am to offer a genuinely Christian apocalyptic perspective on history, it will have to be offered as an everrenewed exercise in articulating the primacy of God's action in Jesus Christ for the salvation of the world, through the explication of what Louis Martyn calls an 'evangelical, cosmic, history-creating Christology'.[26] Furthermore, this apocalyptic perspective on history will have to give way to a certain vision of *ecclesial* existence, oriented around the questions of *mission and politics*, in such a way that neither is conceivable as extricable in any way from the other. It will articulate Christ's relationship to the church, as well as the church's relationship to the world, as an operation of Christ's lordship in history. And it will articulate the lived embodiment of this lordship as a sign of the Spirit's ongoing conversion of history to the

---

26 Martyn, 'Events in Galatia: Modified Covenantal Nomism Versus God's Invasion of the Cosmos in the Singular Gospel: A Response to J. D. G. Dunn and B. R. Gaventa', in *Pauline Theology*, vol. 1, *Thessalonians, Philippians, Galatians, Philemon*, ed. J. Bassler (Minneapolis: Fortress Press, 1991), pp. 160–79, p. 165.

coming reign of God. In this way, I shall have succeeded in demonstrating God's apocalyptic action, in its many facets, as at the heart of the Christian evangel, and as the deepest 'truth' of history itself.

The Approach of this Work

The core of this book is divided into five chapters. Chapters 2–5, on Ernst Troeltsch, Karl Barth, Stanley Hauerwas, and John Howard Yoder, are structured in such a way as to provide the analytical and conceptual scaffolding for my own constructive suggestions for an apocalyptic politics of Christian mission in Chapter 6. What is offered in my readings of these four thinkers is a genealogy of sorts, which directs the progression of the next four chapters. There are two dimensions to this genealogy that I shall be isolating. First of all, Troeltsch, Barth, Hauerwas, and Yoder are genealogically related by way of their diverse understandings of the church's political life and of the task of Christian mission in the world, which are significantly underwritten by how they conceive of the nature and meaning of history generally, and in particular of the significance of the person of Jesus Christ for history. Barth's apocalyptic Christology is best understood as a sustained response to the crisis of modern immanentist historicism within Protestant liberal theology, of which he considers Troeltsch's work to be paradigmatic. Hauerwas's and Yoder's own conceptions of the political significance of apocalyptic are equally a matter of their respective critical appropriations of Barth's Christology for the sake of responding to the agenda-setting 'Christian realism' within twentieth-century American political theology, which Troeltsch's social teaching has from the beginning underwritten.

Second, I have chosen to engage these four thinkers for the way in which they help to isolate critical moments that represent the eclipse, re-emergence, failure, and promise of Christian apocalyptic within the narrative of twentieth-century theo-political encounters with the modern philosophical problematic of historicism. At the same time, these are moments which serve to reveal clearly the philosophical developments within and influences upon the dominant trajectory of twentieth-century liberal and postliberal theo-political thought that must be negotiated if the ideological presumptions at work in the genealogy I am tracing are to be confronted and overcome.

It will become clear to the reader by the end of the book that Yoder plays a distinctively more positive role for me than do Troeltsch, Barth, and Hauerwas. There are two reasons for this. First, it is primarily Hauerwas who has erected much of the conceptual scaffolding of the postliberal 'Barthian' response to the politics of modern liberalism. More than anything, Hauerwas's own particular narrative conception of the 'church-as-polis' has been used to police the supposed postliberal-liberal divide in theological politics. To which I argue: however illuminating 'narrative' might be as a broad, heuristic tool for arbitrating Christian 'identity' (and even here it is a tool that lends itself immediately to misuse), its use as a tool for ecclesial political formation is theologically misguided and, most importantly, circumscriptive of the church's missionary task. Second, the too easy assimilation of Yoder's project to that of Hauerwas has skewed interpretation of the former. Once the narrative, postliberal 'church-as-polis' optic has been abandoned as the primary lens through which to read his work, Yoder provides some powerful insights into the nature of Christian apocalyptic, history, and the ecclesial political and missionary vocation. Only in light of these insights do some of the insights and contributions of Troeltsch and Barth also show new promise, in spite of the flaws in their political thought which Hauerwas and others have so forcefully brought to the fore. In short, insofar as this book is designed not only to uncover and to dismantle the theologically and politically ideological presuppositions at work in the genealogy I shall be tracing but also, through this genealogy, to tell the story of the re-emergence of Christian apocalyptic as the way beyond ideology, the greatest balance of the verdict at the end of this investigation will fall in favour of a distinctively Yoderian vision of apocalyptic as providing the greatest resources for the recovery of the politics of Christian mission for twenty-first-century ecclesial life.

The plan of this book is thus as follows. In Chapter 2 I focus my attention on Ernst Troeltsch's life-long engagement with the logic and the crisis of modern critical historical thinking. I take Troeltsch as not only paradigmatic of this crisis, but also as most incisive in articulating both the limits and the challenge of modern thinking about history for Christian theo-political reflection, particularly with respect to the questions of Christology, eschatology, politics, and Christian mission. I shall seek to show how Troeltsch's attempt to provide a non-reductive historicism is underwritten by an idealist metaphysics that leads him to develop certain theological assumptions about the nature of the eschaton, the Kingdom of God, divine providence, and Christology, which at once *psychologize* and *idealize* their relation to the given, immanental processes of 'history'. As a result Troeltsch is unable to think the tasks of Christian politics and mission except in the Constantinian mode of 'compromise', as these tasks remain ideologically bound by an ethics and politics of historical 'construction' and 'control'. I argue that this failure is directly linked to an 'eclipse of apocalyptic' in Troeltsch's theological and metaphysical formulations, and conclude by suggesting, in conversation with Walter Benjamin, that what is needed in surpassing the universalist and immanentist logics of modern historicism is a reinvigoration of a certain 'Messianic' perspective on history via the articulation of a specifically Christian 'apocalyptic historicism'.

In Chapter 3 I turn to the work of Karl Barth, as representative of a key turning point in the genealogy I am tracing out. The chapter documents the development of Barth's apocalyptic and Christocentric theology of history, as it is shaped and determined by the very 'crisis of historicism' which he felt Troeltsch and modern liberalism had bequeathed to his generation as its central problematic. I shall argue that the progression from *Der Römerbrief* to the *Dogmatics* positively articulates for us the foundations of an 'apocalyptic Christology', which provides the point of departure for an alternative, 'cosmic-historical' account of Christ's relation to history. In the course of this exposition, however, I shall show that Barth's actualist ontology relies upon a residualist idealist metaphysic, which effects a twofold metaphysical abstraction with respect to Jesus' history and to ours, and leaves Barth unable adequately to address the modern historicist problematic. For this reason, Barth's turn to apocalyptic and his Christocentrism become the key loci for both the promise and the failure of his entire oeuvre for my project of constructing an alternative 'apocalyptic historicism'.

Chapter 4 focuses upon the explicitly 'political' supplementation of Barth's apocalyptic Christology with what has come to be known in contemporary theology as 'narrative ecclesiology', particularly as developed in the work of Stanley Hauerwas. My analysis will focus upon the way in which Hauerwas's ecclesiology deploys the logic of apocalyptic for the sake of developing a conception of the church as an alternative *polis* in opposition to modern political liberalism. My main concern will be to show how Hauerwas's apocalyptic-ecclesiological understanding of Christ's relation to history is negatively determined from the outset by Hauerwas's 'anti-liberal' agenda. Drawing parallels to the political theory of Carl Schmitt, I argue his postliberal concern to secure a certain fixed narratival and linguistic 'identity' for the church risks a structurally imperialistic and functionally ideological articulation of the church's political and missionary existence in the world. Hauerwas's narrative ecclesiology thus remains stuck within a kind of 'anti-liberalism'; he can *only* conceive the importance of Christ and of the church for history as overagainst a theological and political liberalism. In the end, Hauerwas's anti-liberal narrativalism itself harbours within it certain theological assumptions about the relation of Christ to the church and about the nature of the eschaton which leave him unable to think the relation of 'church' and 'politics' as genuinely *missionary*, that is, as a matter of an ongoing, multilayered, politically subversive *encounter* between 'church' and 'world'.

Chapter 5 endeavours to open up the space for such subversive political encounter, by expounding the logic of an
alternative 'apocalyptic historicity', in which the historicist
problematic is fully taken up and recapitulated from within
the Christian apocalyptic-eschatological idiom. By proffering
a new reading of Yoder's *The Politics of Jesus*, I shall argue that
this occurs as the apocalyptic political act of Jesus opens up
for us a Christological 'logic of singularity' which overcomes
the metaphysical fetishization of 'universality' as found in the
idealist heritage inherited and bequeathed to us by Troeltsch,
as well as a trinitarian 'logic of excess', which takes up key trajectories of Barth's apocalyptic Christology in a manner that
surpasses the metaphysical idealism of Barth's Christocentrism. The relation of Jesus to history thus emerges into view
as that of a *crucified Logos*, the logic of which is the cruciform
interruption of history and its radical exposure to the excessive life of the Spirit that is the power of the resurrection as the
sign of the reign of God – a reign that is now the 'truth' of all
of life's radically contingent historicity as the 'truth' of Jesus'
own apocalyptically contingent life as God.

In Chapter 6, I extend my reading of the apocalyptic politics of Jesus by articulating the rudiments for 'an apocalyptic
politics of Christian mission'. Such a politics is only possible,
I argue, insofar as the apocalyptic historicity of Jesus foregrounds *doxology* as the basis for faithful and transformative political action. Doxology compels us to move beyond the
ontologization of the church-as-*polis* and requires us to think
of mission as that which alone 'makes' the church. As such, I
shall argue (via a critical mode of engagement with the work
of Michel de Certeau) that the politics of mission is one in
which *ecclesia* occurs as a mode of dynamic and dispossessive
liturgical action, which action occurs as *a work of exile*, via
the reimagining of Jesus and the church through the medium
of Jewish diasporic existence. 'Liturgy' and 'diaspora' thus
provide the conditions for a new form of ecclesial political life.
'Ecclesia' is a work of missionary encounter with the world,
and is only ever visible as a *people* of dispossession, a *sociality*

of shared poverty in which our lives are thrown together with 'the poor', as a matter of our ongoing conversion to the transformative and liberating inbreak of God's coming reign.

2

Ernst Troeltsch: The Triumph of Ideology and the Eclipse of Apocalyptic

This chapter elaborates the logic of modern theological historicism and traces its ideological underpinnings, through an analysis and critique of the work of Ernst Troeltsch. Thus, I aim to do two things: first, to present Troeltsch's work as the culmination – 'the final and fullest expression'[1] – of modern theological historicism as it entered the twentieth century, in a way that accentuates the metaphysical, religious, and ethico-political crises that historicism engendered; and second, to examine how the metaphysical and theological assumptions at work in Troeltsch's historicism function ideologically, so as to give way to a structurally 'Constantinian' construal of the church's political and missionary tasks. The ultimate goal of this chapter is to show how the 'universal historicism' of Troeltsch effects an ideological 'eclipse' of Christian apocalyptic understandings of the eschaton and of Christ's relation to history, as well as to begin to articulate the conditions for constructing an alternative 'apocalyptic historicism'.

'The Crisis of Historicism'

In the foreword to his *Social Teaching of the Christian Churches*, Troeltsch stated that he was responsible as a

---

1 S. Davaney, *Historicism: The Once and Future Challenge for Theology* (Minneapolis: Fortress Press, 2006), p. 56.

theologian 'to think through and formulate the world of Christian thought and life in frank relation to the modern world'.[2] As Mark Chapman has noted, this involved Troeltsch from the outset in a twofold task:

1 the ongoing assessment and analysis of the underlying currents of modern thought and life; and
2 the analysis of the ways in which these currents condition Christian social ethics.[3]

In his 1922 retrospective essay 'My Books', Troeltsch put his understanding of this twofold task in the form of a question: 'To what extent are the appearance, the development, the modification, and the modern impasse of Christianity sociologically conditioned, and to what extent is Christianity itself an actively formative sociological principle?'[4] For Troeltsch, answering this question meant first of all coming clear on how it is that the 'modern impasse of Christianity' is of a piece with what he called 'the crisis of historicism', and then of coming to understand the way in which this crisis is constitutive of genuinely new 'politico-social conditions of life'.[5]

What Troeltsch calls 'historicism' is of a piece with what he thinks is a uniquely modern *Weltanschauung*, by which we come to interpret all spheres of human life and culture in terms of their historical development out of the past: it marks 'the fundamental historicizing of all our thinking about human being, its culture, and its values'.[6] As Troeltsch puts it:

The word 'historicism' . . . signifies the historicizing of our entire knowledge and experience of the spiritual world . . .

---

2 Troeltsch, STCC, p. 19.
3 Mark D. Chapman, *Ernst Troeltsch and Liberal Theology: Religion and Cultural Synthesis in Wilhelmine Germany* (Oxford: Oxford University Press, 2001), p. 8.
4 Troeltsch, RH, p. 372.
5 Troeltsch, DH, p. 9.
6 Troeltsch, DH, p. 102.

Here we see everything in the stream of becoming, in end-less and always new individualization, in determination by the past towards an unrecognizable future. The state, law, morality, religion, and art are dissolved in the flow of his-torical becoming and are comprehensible only as ingredients of historical development.[7]

For Troeltsch, any 'modern' theology worth the name must build radically upon this historicist basis:[8] it must begin with the basic presupposition that the very contingencies and stream of happenings that we experience as natural life themselves provide an inner duration and continuity by which we might find identity, coherence, and meaning in relation to all that has come before, and all that is yet to occur.

Throughout his life and work, Troeltsch never tired of get-ting clear on the internal 'logic' of historicism. Troeltsch's earli-est writings were an attempt to come to grips with the key issue in all modern philosophy of history as he had come to understand it through the writings of Hegel and the German idealists: 'the relationships of the historically relative and the substantially absolute'.[9] From the outset, then, Troeltsch under-stood the problem of history as one of how logically to relate the absolute to the relative, and of how to speak of the univer-sal in the particular and contingent:

[W]ithin the individual and the non-recurrent, there is something universally valid – or something connected with the universally valid – which makes itself known at the same time. The problem is to hold these two elements together in the right relation . . . Thus the problem is to define the scope of the relative and individual with ever increasing exactness and to understand with ever increasing comprehensiveness

7 E. Troeltsch, 'Die Krisis des Historismus', *Die Neue Rundschau* 33 (1922), pp. 572–90, p. 573. Unless otherwise noted, all translation from works cited by their German titles are my own.
8 Troeltsch, RH, pp. 12, 16.
9 Troeltsch, RH, p. 370.

the universally valid that works teleologically within history. Then we will see that the relative contains an indication of the unconditional. In the relative we will find a token of the absolute that transcends history.[10]

These early investigations were Troeltsch's means of laying the groundwork for and delineating the need to do theology 'within the context of the most comprehensive whole', that is, to think of 'universal history' as the primary locus of all theological and metaphysical thought.[11] For Troeltsch,

[T]his is how the historical method works. It relativizes everything, not in the sense that it eliminates every standard of judgement and necessarily ends in a nihilistic skepticism, but rather in the sense that every historical structure and moment can be understood only in relation to others and ultimately to the total context, and that standards of values cannot be derived from isolated events but only from an overview of the historical totality. This relativism and respect for the historical totality belong together, as indeed they are always conjoined in the practical application of the method.[12]

Herein lies the important point: the primary consideration of the particularity and relativity of all events is that of their recounting within the largest possible 'total context', such that these events might be understood primarily for what they allow us to glimpse of the universal, absolute reason which underlies them and provides them with their coherence and meaning.

This essentially Hegelian, Idealist conception of the formal 'logic' of modern historicism remained operative throughout Troeltsch's life work.[13] Troeltsch never gave up on his sense

10 Troeltsch, ACHR, p. 106.
11 Troeltsch, RH, pp. 15, 19.
12 Troeltsch, RH, p. 18.
13 See G. Yamin, Jr., *In the Absence of Fantasia: Troeltsch's Relation to Hegel* (Gainesville: University Press of Florida, 1993).

that the always new 'individualizations' of history are 'embed-ded in what is universal';[14] the construction of something like a 'universal history' remained necessary for any true philosophy of history.[15] At the same time, however, Troeltsch came in-creasingly to believe that the dominant strands of nineteenth-century critical-historical thought had led in his time to a *crisis* within historicism. Troeltsch felt as if such attention had been given to discerning the abstract *principles* by which universal history is governed – whether dogmatic, ethical, or metaphysi-cal – that the dominant philosophies of history had interpreted the relation of the absolute to the relative, the universal to the particular, in such a way as to lead ultimately to a measure of abstraction from the individualities and contingencies of his-torical becoming. In all of this, the modern philosophical con-sciousness threatened to run aground. For, as Troeltsch put it:

> The modern idea of history knows no universal principle on the basis of which the content and sequence of events might be deduced. It knows only concrete, individual phenomena, always conditioned by their context and yet, at bottom, un-derivable and simply existent phenomena. For this reason the modern understanding of history knows no values or norms that coincide with actual universals.[16]

At this point in particular, Troeltsch is clearly following the path laid out by David Friedrich Strauss, and his critique of Schleiermacher's and Hegel's evasions of a fully *wissen-schaftlich* understanding of history.[17] Troeltsch's point is that the nature of history itself, its very *reality*, relativizes all claims to absoluteness within history. And so history disallows any

---

14 Troeltsch, DH, p. 199.

15 E. Troeltsch, 'The Ideas of Natural Law and Humanity in World Politics', in O. Gierke, *Natural Law and the Theory of Society, 1500–1800*, trans. Ernest Barker (Boston: Beacon Press, 1957), pp. 201–22, pp. 217–18.

16 Troeltsch, ACHR, pp. 66–7.

17 Troeltsch, ACHR, pp. 78, 90, 115.

abstract footing from which to deduce absolute norms and universal standards of value, outside of the contingencies of the individualities of history itself.

The 'crisis of historicism', however, had another side to it. For if it is the case that a false prioritizing of the absolute can lead to ahistorical abstraction, it is equally the case that the stress upon radical historicity, and the relativizing of claims to universally valid norms, can lead to what Troeltsch calls 'unlimited relativism', in which all attempts to arrive at agreed criteria for value judgments within history are disallowed.[18] The 'crisis' that Troeltsch is concerned to address, then, is that of the possibility of deriving 'historical values' from among the radical historicizing of our thought about the absolute and the universal, with relation to the relative and particular. Troeltsch thus comes to understand the crisis of historicism as essentially that of 'how the way to valid cultural values is to be found when one starts with the historically relative'.[19] For Troeltsch, this meant nothing less than the construction of a new *metaphysics of history*, a new conception of the relation of the relative to the absolute, of the particular to the universal which, against all attempts to retire behind an a prioristic or dogmatic conception of the absolute, insists upon a relation to the absolute and the universal within history that is rooted in and grows out of the contingencies and particularities of real historical facticity.[20] It is this more historicist metaphysics, Troeltsch thought, that will ultimately provide us the means to discern the norms and values by which to construct the conditions for ethical, social, and political life in the present.

---

18 Troeltsch, DH, pp. 68, 102; see S. Coakley, *Christ without Absolutes: A Study of the Christology of Ernst Troeltsch* (Oxford: Clarendon Press, 1988), pp. 5–44.

19 Troeltsch, RH, p. 374.

20 See B. A. Reist, *Toward a Theology of Involvement: The Thought of Ernst Troeltsch* (Philadelphia: Westminster Press, 1966), pp. 68–76.

Metaphysics, Eschatology, Ethics

Troeltsch's concern to address the crisis of historicism was never merely academic; he was never interested in history for history's own sake, but rather for the purpose of analysing how one's intellectual awareness of belonging to history shapes one's conception of ethical and political activity.[21] That is to say, as *ethical*, the central problem of modern historicism was a *constructive* one, a question of crafting a mode of contemporary thought and life adequate to the relativities and contingencies of modern social life. This ethical 'idea of construction' lies at the heart of Troeltsch's attempt to address directly the 'crisis of history' that is modern historicism:[22] the task of the philosophy of history is nothing less than that of 'damming and controlling the historical stream of life' for the sake of 'shaping' a better socio-political future.[23]

For Troeltsch, however, this constructive ethical task was consequent upon a specific metaphysics, for only by discerning the proper metaphysical backdrop did Troeltsch think one could cultivate normative values from history. As we have already seen, such a metaphysics of history will involve one in the conscious pursuit of relating the particular to the universal, and the individual to the absolute, a pursuit which lies at the very heart of the crisis of the modern historical consciousness. For Troeltsch, the question of metaphysics is one of resolving the tension between a radical historicity, in which the individualities of history are awash in contingency and relativity, and an absolute that by nature lies beyond history, but which also can be partially related to from within the contingencies and particularities of history.

---

21 Troeltsch, DH, p. 9.

22 Troeltsch, DH, pp. 695–703. See T. Yasukata, *Ernst Troeltsch: Systematic Theologian of Radical Historicality* (Atlanta: Scholars Press, 1986), pp. 126–32, 151n. 27; B. A. Gerrish, 'Ernst Troeltsch and the Possibility of a Historical Theology', in *Ernst Troeltsch and the Future of Theology*, ed. J. Clayton (Cambridge: Cambridge University Press, 1976), pp. 100–35, pp. 123, 125–6, 134.

23 Troeltsch, CT, p. 115; cf. Troeltsch, DH, pp. 118, 169.

This tension is resolved for Troeltsch according to a *teleologico-eschatological* conception of the absolute, which is related to the individualities of history in the mode of intrahistorical *development*. For Troeltsch, only as the absolute is conceived teleo-eschatologically can the meaning of the 'universal-historical' be secured for ethical and political thought and action. For precisely as an eschatological *goal*, a *telos*, the absolute is a *transhistorical* reality which stands *beyond* history, yet works as a force *within* history. On a most basic, descriptive level, the absolute functions as an expression of the metaphysical belief 'that history is not a chaos but issues from unitary forces and aspires toward a unitary goal'.[24] 'True history is teleological history.'[25] Within this teleological framework, the 'eschaton' thus names a certain *transhistorical reality*, which, though by nature *beyond* history, constitutes the conclusion and horizon of all history. By allowing this teleo-eschatological horizon to emerge into view, Troeltsch thinks, we have a way of conceiving our relation to the absolute that is limited by the recognition that this relation as such always occurs historically, in a manner *relative* to the intrahistorical whole.

Troeltsch thus posits *development* as the only mode of intrahistorical continuity fitting a teleo-eschatological conception of the absolute. The importance of this 'teleological law of development'[26] comes especially into view in Troeltsch's last great work, *Der Historismus und seine Probleme*. There, without giving up on the idea of a metaphysical 'All-life' (*Alleben*), participation in which constitutes the perfection and goal of all things, Troeltsch insists even more radically upon the *individualities* or *particularities* of history and upon the fact that our participation in this universal goal cannot be known in advance, but must rather be seen as arising anew out of each unique historical situation. Thus, while the fundamental

---

24 Troeltsch, RH, p. 27.
25 Troeltsch, 'Ideas of Natural Law', p. 218n.
26 Troeltsch, ET, p. 117.

object of the philosophy of history for Troeltsch remains that of the unity of the whole, this object itself is *historicized*, as it 'belongs to a continuous flow of becoming and must be so placed'.[27] The idea of development thereby allows Troeltsch to conceive of the individualities of history as coalescing in a final unity *beyond* history, which coalescence is simply the result of each individuality 'adhering to its own course' *within* history.[28] Historical development has to do finally with the immanent unfolding of the individualities of history.[29] Troeltsch puts it thus:

> [T]herein lies the important logical result, that the continual becoming of historical things, insofar as it is in truth continual, cannot be purely causally presented in a ranging together of definable particular events, but that the particular events are fused (*verschmolzen*) into a developing unity (*Werde-Einheit*), in which the particular events are interweaving and dissolving into each other and thereby continually producing just this developing unity. This may be described logically only with great difficulty, but to see and feel it is the essence of the historical sense.[30]

It is in this sense, finally, that a system of values can be arrived at and *related to as absolute* from within history, namely, via the immanent unfolding of the unique historical individualities themselves.

With this idea of teleo-eschatological development, Troeltsch felt as if he had hit upon the metaphysical perspective which would allow him to affirm (without absolving) the tension between a transhistorical absolute which we relate to as a goal that resides outside of and beyond all history and a modern immanent historicism, which necessitates that we relate to the absolute by way of remaining with and in the particularities

---

27 Troeltsch, DH, p. 54.
28 Troeltsch, DH, p. 58.
29 Troeltsch, DH, p. 657.
30 Troeltsch, DH, p. 55.

and relativities of our historical individualities. By suggesting that we relate to the absolute on the basis of such individualities alone, he indeed felt as though he had articulated a notion of the 'life-process of the absolute in which the absolute itself can be grasped and shaped from every point of view and in a fashion corresponding to each point of view'.[31] Furthermore, he thought that such a relation to the absolute via the development of historical individualities could also serve as an effective critique against the claim of any one individuality to have attained 'universal applicability, timelessness or absoluteness' within history.[32] Thus, Troeltsch appears to have retained what is best about the Idealist understanding of history, via an extremely subtle inversion of Hegel's notions of the 'Absolute' and of historical 'development'. An alternative, inductive metaphysics of the absolute has been articulated, and a positive account of the relation between the relative and the absolute, the particular and the universal, has been reached 'by other logical and methodological paths', namely, by beginning with the a posteriori facticity of history's individualities.[33] Moreover, by insisting upon a notion of development on the basis of this idea of historical individuality, Troeltsch seems to have preserved attention to the particular in such a way that the idea of universality is not given up, but properly contextualized as a matter of the interrelation between individualities.

But we must remember at this point that the underlying impetus for Troeltsch's metaphysics of history is *ethical*. Troeltsch's teleo-eschatological metaphysics is an attempt to return the historical subject to the realm of practical rationality. In this attempt, Troeltsch is led to hang his metaphysics of history on a neo-Kantian frame, which becomes 'theologically' deter-

---

31 Troeltsch, DH, p. 212.

32 Troeltsch, DH, p. 166. See T. Rendtorff and F. W. Graf, ' Ernst Troeltsch', tr. S. Coakley, in *Nineteenth Century Religious Thought in the West*, vol. 3, ed. N. Smart, J. Clayton, P. Sherry, and S. T. Katz (Cambridge: Cambridge University Press, 1985), pp. 305–32, pp. 310–11.

33 See Troeltsch, ET, p. 117.

minative of his metaphysics at certain decisive points. What
I mean by this is that Troeltsch combines his subtly Hegelian
metaphysics of history with an equally subtle version of Kant's
moral subject, which perceives the individual human being as
somehow 'transcending' the relativities of history on the basis
of an a priori transcendental relation to the absolute.[34] This
Kantian element forces Troeltsch into a dualistic conception of
history as that of humanity's 'entrapment' between the brute
givens of pure 'nature' and the essentially sublime realm of
'spirit'. In turn, this leads Troeltsch into an ethic of 'mastery'
and 'control', an ethic in which the human being is responsible
for constructing the shape of the future out of what we know
of the past in the present moment.

Let me articulate the contours of this, before moving on to
consider its implications for Christian politics and mission. It
is clear from his latest works that Troeltsch assumes an understanding of the 'moral conscience' which foregrounds the direct
and immediate relation of the individual to the absolute.[35] On
the basis of such immediacy, says Troeltsch, it is metaphysically
necessary that 'history goes . . . in its borders back to a mystical background of All-Life (*Alleben*)', 'an inner life-movement
of the All or of divinity'.[36] Herein lies our 'metaphysical faith,'
which constitutes 'the conclusion and horizon of all history'[37]:
namely, a 'belief in immediacy', that is, faith in the irreducibil-
ity and particularity of the individual soul's relation to God,
which yet respects 'the universal connectedness and continuity
of all things'.[38]

This line of thought is traceable to Troeltsch's articulation of
the need for a religious a priori as the 'goal' of history and of
the importance such an a priori has for the grounding of ethics

34 See P. C. Hodgson, *God in History: Shapes of Freedom* (Nashville: Abingdon Press, 1989), p. 132; Chapman, *Ernst Troeltsch*, pp.
83–6.
35 See esp. Troeltsch, CT, pp. 67–93.
36 Troeltsch, DH, pp. 87, 175.
37 Troeltsch, DH, p. 176.
38 Troeltsch, CF, p. 215; cf. Troeltsch, ACHR, p. 99.

within history.[39] With this concept, Troeltsch was seeking to show that the formation of religious ideals was grounded in the structure of human reason; human consciousness as such is aboriginally anchored in the 'absolute substance' as the goal toward which the individual consciousness in history is always striving.[40]

Three points concerning the religious a priori should be noted here. First, there is an underlying 'subjectivism' at work in this concept, for Troeltsch. The religious a priori is validated at the level of the 'personal consciousness'; it registers on the level of the individual's experience of its own participation in the 'Absolute Life'.[41] The a priori refers to 'an active presence of the absolute spirit in the realm of the finite', and it does this by understanding the absolute as 'an activity of the universe . . . in individual souls'.[42] Second, the religious a priori is constitutive of a 'universal inner necessity'.[43] By this, Troeltsch means to say that one's own experience of participation in the absolute substance is intuitively felt and described as the unconditioned impulse of *all* historical individualities toward 'inner unity' with the absolute as their 'ultimate and supreme goal'.[44] Third, then, this recognition of the universality of the religious a priori is what constitutes the 'most intimate secret of the urge to know history'; it is the recognition of subjective, individual participation in the absolute as such that finally delivers to us the 'value-constructs' by which to chart the logical continuity and intrahistorical development of all individualities, on the basis of which we refer these individualities to an 'absolute purpose'.[45] To say this is to say that the true metaphysical back-

---

39 See Chapman, *Ernst Troeltsch*, pp. 111–37.

40 Troeltsch, ET, pp. 115–17. Cf. E. Troeltsch, 'Empiricism and Platonism in the Philosophy of Religion – to the Memory of William James', *Harvard Theological Review* 5 (1912), pp. 401–22, pp. 407–8.

41 Troeltsch, RH, pp. 67–8.

42 Troeltsch, RH, p. 41.

43 Troeltsch, RH, p. 67.

44 Troeltsch, RH, p. 59.

45 Troeltsch, RH, pp. 295, 302; see also p. 41.

drop of modern historicism is what Troeltsch elsewhere calls an 'emancipated individualism', which functions according to a 'universal vision' of the maximum participation of each individuality in the absolute ground of life and which stresses the 'continuity and the intrinsic vital unity' of the individualities of history for the sake of such participation alone.[46]

What is interesting here is the way in which Troeltsch's articulation of the 'ultimate goal', the *eschaton*, is driven and determined by this understanding of the religious a priori. For it is with 'the religious idea itself' that we experience a sense of the '"last things"; that is, of ultimate realities and values that are absolute and unconditioned, uniform and inherently necessary, in contrast to the finite realities and values that are relativized more and more by reflexion'.[47] On these terms, Troeltsch must conceive of the eschaton in a quasi-monistic and individualistic fashion, as a final stage wherein the self or the soul is 'consumed', 'returns to God', and is 'absorbed' into the divine life, there coming to rest in its 'consummate blessedness'.[48] At the same time, it is on the basis of this radical individualism (Troeltsch calls it a 'superindividualism') that a genuinely universal 'common spirit' emerges among human beings.[49] Every individual *in her very individuality* is, as such, an end in-herself, insofar as the question of the end of each is nothing but the possibility of her own subjective and personal absorption into the absolute substance, a merging of her own individual finite will into the final, 'Universal Will' that is God.[50] Troeltsch's development of the 'morality of conscience' thus relies upon the identification of a supposedly 'pure' sphere of religion, which concerns the sanctity of the will – one's own 'pure will and devotion to an ideal world' – by which the individual makes a final personal decision for the absolute.[51]

---

46 Troeltsch, RH, pp. 271–2.
47 Troeltsch, RH, p. 146.
48 Troeltsch, RH, pp. 154–5.
49 Troeltsch, CT, pp. 123–46.
50 Troeltsch, RH, pp. 146–58.
51 Troeltsch, CT, pp. 67–93.

However, precisely because this is an *eternal* and *ideal* end, it is an end that by nature transcends and exceeds the temporal and the finite. Furthermore, we have no means of conceiving this end in abstraction from the contingencies and relativities of history. For this reason, Troeltsch insists, 'The Beyond can be conceived only as a result of the Here. Only that which here is already directed toward the consummation can achieve it in the beyond.'[52] In other words, Troeltsch's metaphysics of history, while still allowing him to affirm a pure, ideal realm of the absolute to which we are immediately related, commits him also to affirm the contingencies and particularities of history as the stuff of 'reality', a reality apart from which our relation to the ideal is unthinkable.

Troeltsch holds these affirmations together on the basis of a nature/spirit dualism. There are two sides to this dualism. The first side, which we have already been examining, is the assumption that we are oriented spiritually to a goal which resides beyond and transcends history. The second side, or underside, of this dualism is the assumption that history as such is empirically and naturally 'tragic', a matter of breaks and (dis-)continuities with no clear dominant direction, in which new realities arise in order to mature and eventually decay.[53] Troeltsch presupposes that the underlying structure of nature is basically agonistic: 'We can and must frankly acknowledge the natural process with its consequences, the struggle for existence, natural selection, and the formation of power, as the natural order.'[54] This spirit/nature dualism thus becomes the means by which to affirm 'history as a whole' as 'the form of a struggle between flesh and spirit', 'as the upward struggle of spirit against matter, enabled by the self-communication of God'.[55] The metaphysics of history is thus itself a structural means of affirming the freedom of the human spirit overagainst

---

52 Troeltsch, CF, pp. 287–8.
53 Troeltsch, DH, pp. 171–4, 188; see Hodgson, *God in History*, p. 137, for this way of wording the matter.
54 Troeltsch, RH, p. 200; cf. Troeltsch, ACHR, p. 64.
55 Troeltsch, CF, pp. 253, 256.

this underlying structure of nature, as a way of also affirming the natural struggle for existence as 'a positive ordinance of God based on the very nature of things'.[56] Accordingly, what we call 'universal history' is just the God-ordained imposition of value and order on the given and contingent 'stuff' – the bare 'facticity' – of nature in its tragic fluctuation.

Thus we come to the ethical upshot of all this; it is at this point, at last, that the 'ethical' task coincides with the constructive task of 'history'. The point of the metaphysics of history is finally to 'ethicize the struggles of life',[57] to imbue nature with an 'ethical spirit'.[58] We are 'ethical' insofar as we find ourselves responsible, in the here and now, in our own 'historical individuality', our own 'particular sphere of culture', for 'damming and controlling the historical stream of life' in order to create the possibilities for achieving the victory of the freedom of spirit over the tragic *data* of nature.[59] Furthermore, to take the religious, spiritualized goal of the eschaton as the 'ultimate goal' in which is found the 'unity of the human spirit'[60] as the basis of ethics is not a way of evading the vicissitudes of history, but rather of recognizing therein the concrete intertwining of nature and spirit, and so the concrete site for ethical work. Ethics is the means of penetrating the vicissitudes of history, of discovering within each historical individuality its particular *élan*, its spiritual vitality, which is then exploited as the 'criterion of value' for its own proper development, by which history is advanced towards the future, through evernew cultural syntheses of spirit and nature. It is in this regard that Troeltsch describes the task of ethics as one of 'perpetual struggle' and 'perpetual creation', which is of a piece with the 'controlling and conquering of mere nature'.[61]

---

56 Troeltsch, RH, p. 200.
57 Troeltsch, CF, p. 256.
58 Troeltsch, RH, p. 200.
59 Troeltsch, CT, pp. 118, 115.
60 E. Troeltsch, 'Geschichte und Metaphysik', *Zeitschrift für Theologie und Kirche* 8 (1898), pp. 1–69, pp. 40–2.
61 Troeltsch, CT, p. 88.

Ethics is the work of 'controlling' the forces of nature and history, so as to 'use' history as a means by which to prepare for the 'end' of the soul's participation in God.

The main point to iterate here, in summing up this section, is that in identifying the crisis of historicism as an essentially *ethical* crisis, Troeltsch is led by a number of manoeuvres into articulating a metaphysic by which history's ultimate 'value' resides in the embodiment of a religious and ethical ideal which lies *beyond* this world and *beyond* the bare 'facts' of history. Yet in this turn to the metaphysical, the a priori nature of Troeltsch's relativism has become increasingly visible. It is not so much that Troeltsch *discovers* history to be a realm of essentially tragic contingency; his concentration upon history's relativity as such is derived from his Idealist commitments, which are most clearly evident in his reflections upon the 'ideal' and the 'real', 'nature' and 'spirit', 'freedom' and 'transcendence', etc.

Troeltsch's conceptual use of the eschaton as marking out the realm of an absolute 'ideal' is illustrative of this. For Troeltsch, the appeal to eschatology turns out to be a means of re-affirming his prior commitment to the canons of modern historicism and to historical relativity: because present history is no place for such an ideal, historical realities exist in their bare givenness, to be exploited and manipulated by the moral will for the sake of a better future.[62] Thus, by way of this 'volitional teleology',[63] Troeltsch appears to convert the Kantian appeal to practical reason into something like the view that it is only within the historically tragic and relative that we know ourselves as free ethical subjects, as free by way of relation to an absolute, transhistorical goal, at which point freedom brings us up against the limits of our historical moment and context.[64] When our own historical limitations cannot deliver

---

62 Troeltsch, RH, p. 272.

63 Troeltsch, DH, p. 112.

64 See Troeltsch, RH, pp. 146–7. I. Kant, *Critique of Practical Reason*, tr. L. Beck (Indianapolis: Bobbs-Merrill, 1956), pp. 126–8; Kant, *Groundwork of the Metaphysics of Morals*, tr. M. Gregor (New York: Cambridge University Press, 1997), pp. 37–40.

to us the values by which to act, we then discover ourselves as transcendent subjects able to rise 'above' our 'natural' situatedness, on the basis of our free creations of a 'higher reality'. It is this subjective freedom which provides the basis of a universal 'morality'; to be moral just is to *act* everywhere on behalf of 'the attainment and the defence of a free personality'.[65]

These last observations raise for me a critical question, though, which has to do with the way in which Troeltsch *psychologizes* the eschaton and history's relationship to it. The question is whether Troeltsch's transhistorical idealization of the eschaton does not unwittingly disambiguate history within immanence, in such a way as to betray and subvert the true nature of 'historicity'. Is it possible that this psychological-historical understanding of the eschaton actually represents a failure to do justice to the real contingencies, complexities, and singularities of history? That is, does Troeltsch's eschatological spirit/nature dualism succumb after all to the problem of what Walter Benjamin called the triumph of 'homogeneous, empty time' in modern historicism,[66] whereby all *particular* events, though distinct within the concatenation of immanental, 'natural' development, are interchangeable with respect to the soul's *universal*, transcendental goal?

It could be argued that this problem is endemic to what Troeltsch early on in his work calls the 'omnipotence of analogy' within the modern historical consciousness:

> The observation of analogies between similar events in the past provides the possibility of imputing probability to them and of interpreting what is unknown about the one by reference to what is known about the other . . . This omnipotence of analogy implies the similarity (in principle) of all historical events.[67]

---

65 Troeltsch, CT, p. 77.

66 W. Benjamin, 'Theses on the Philosophy of History', in *Illuminations: Essays and Reflections*, ed. H. Arendt, tr. H. Zohn (New York: Schocken Books, 1968), pp. 253–64, p. 262.

67 Troeltsch, RH, pp. 13–14.

By this principle of analogy Troeltsch means to stress the intrinsic integrity of each particular and contingent event, while at the same time relativizing each event with relation to the 'total context' of 'universal history'.[68] Yet crucially, as Troeltsch comes more and more to psychologize the eschaton as the realm of the absolute and of 'spirit' as overagainst 'nature', the relativization of history which the analogical principle effects appears more and more to be a means of privileging the universal as *overagainst* the particular. In the face of the crisis of relativism which Troeltsch feared, does it not become necessary to isolate historical events as discrete particularities, precisely as a way of 'damming and controlling' the contingencies and relativities of history? Does not the 'similarity (in principle) of all historical events' now privilege a kind of analogical interchangeability of all immanent (intrahistorical) *particularities* with respect to a shared, transcendent (transhistorical) *universal telos*? And would this not turn out to be the real failure of the modern historical method as Troeltsch has represented it: not to *discover* history to be irreducibly the emergence of ever-new contingencies and difference, but rather to *posit* history as a realm of *given* contingencies and differences, for the sake of 'comprehending' those differences in their relation to 'the most comprehensive whole'?[69]

There is, of course, another side to all of this, which is that Troeltsch's psychologization of the eschaton prohibits conceiving the eschaton as itself a cosmic-historical *event* of God's coming Kingdom that is at once both an intervention into and qualitative determination of history itself. Troeltsch's historicist logic disallows such an event precisely to the extent that it would amount to a 'miracle' which remains untouched 'by real history'.[70] But could such an event perhaps not be considered otherwise? Might not such an irruptive event be conceived according to a kind of 'cessation of happening'[71] – an inter-

68 Troetlsch, RH, pp. 18–19.
69 Troetlsch, RH, p. 15.
70 Troeltsch, DH, p. 14.
71 Benjamin, 'Theses', p. 264.

ruption of the 'universal' historical 'process' – which is not untouched by the contingencies and relativities of history, but rather a kind of *intensifying* of them, an event that is determinative of history precisely as an event which is all the more *contingent*, all the more *complexifying*, all the more *differentiating*, and all the more *historicizing* of history itself?

That these questions can be answered in the affirmative, by way of recourse to a very particular kind of 'apocalyptic historicism', is the key wager of this essay. Indeed, I shall argue, it is only as the eschaton is conceived as precisely this kind of cosmic-historical, apocalyptic event that we are able to think the truth of history in its real contingency and difference and to think this truth in such a way as to free us for the kind of singular political action by which we are delivered from the ideological bonds of 'universal history' as such. But first, I need to show how modern historicism as embodied by Troeltsch and the theological assumptions which underlie it give way to an understanding of politics that is still too ideologically bound. I shall do this by examining and explicating the 'Constantinian' framework within which Troeltsch conceives of the tasks of Christian political responsibility and mission in the world.

Politics and Mission: The 'Constantinian Temptation' and the Triumph of Ideology

So far I have been analysing the logic of Troeltsch's own metaphysics of history. In this section, I want to show how this metaphysics informs and shapes Troeltsch's understanding of the dual task of Christian politics and mission. I shall argue that these tasks are inconceivable for Troeltsch except as structurally and ideologically 'Constantinian'. In making this argument, however, I shall draw out further some of Troeltsch's theological assumptions about the essence of Christianity and especially about the political nature of the Kingdom of God and of God's action in history that themselves must be questioned for the way in which they condition how the Christian political and missionary tasks must be conceived and carried out in light of certain historicist commitments.

Politics

John Howard Yoder has argued that political Constantinianism arises from the 'temptation . . . of the church to establish symbiotic relations with every social order'.[72] For if, as Constantinianism assumes, 'the locus of meaningfulness' is to be found 'in the course of the history of a society or of the world at large', then politically the church's task is to discern within that history the structural means for a future 'better society', and to join in the work supporting those socio-political structures by which that future is most effectively to be brought about.[73] It is in this sense that Troeltsch succumbs to the 'Constantinian temptation', for in seeking to develop an ethic adequate to the relativities and contingencies of modern society, Troeltsch affirms a mode of Christian political engagement which has compromise for the sake of stabilization of the dominant order as its first task.

Take, for example, *The Social Teaching of the Christian Churches*. While many interpretations of this work have focused on the famous church-sect-mysticism typology as descriptive of a set of options available for Christian social engagement, it is clear that Troeltsch saw this historical work from the outset as being constructively prescriptive, as a way of working toward a normative ecclesiological ideal capable of addressing the specifically modern socio-political and historical crisis.[74] *The Social Teaching* is thus driven by a twofold thesis: on the one hand, Troeltsch believed that Christian social thought throughout history is best understood as the church's development and adaptation of itself to the specific nature of social problems as they arise; on the other hand, he believed

---

72 Benjamin, 'Theses', p. 202.
73 Yoder, RP, pp. 90–5.
74 Troeltsch, STCC, p. 1009.

that the political and social situation of Western Europe was such that the institutional form of Protestantism had become sufficiently inadequate to this task to warrant a new cultural synthesis of Christian faith and secular society. Thus, the ultimate question which drives his investigations throughout is this: 'How can the Church harmonize with these main forces [of secular state and society] in such a way that together they will form a unity of civilization'?[75] As Troeltsch is well aware, to put the question this way is to make Christian social teaching dependent upon the dominant political and cultural structures of its time, and to concede that there is no manner in which the Christian can think and act politically apart from a measure of 'compromise' with these structures.[76]

Yet crucially, what ultimately necessitates Christian sociopolitical engagement taking the form of compromise is Troeltsch's assumed dualism between the ethico-religious and the historicist embeddedness of political, social, and economic institutions. As Duane Friesen has shown, the 'normative factor' underlying the text of *The Social Teaching* is the tensive dual commitment Troeltsch makes to think religion according to a non-mediated a priori 'ideal', which refers to a 'transcendental realm beyond the relativities' of history, and also to think that ideal as it arises and is expressed from within the very development of historical individualities.[77] Thus, we see how Troeltsch's metaphysics of history, and particularly the ethical impulse which drives that metaphysics, sets the terms for Christian socio-political thought. Troeltsch sets up the problem in such a way that there is, on the one hand, a monolithic sphere of 'politics' structured by the state (and

75 Troeltsch, STCC, p. 32.

76 See Troeltsch, RH, p. 218.

77 D. Friesen, 'Normative Factors in Troeltsch's Typology of Religious Association', *Journal of Religious Ethics* 3 (Fall 1975), pp. 271–83, p. 273; Friesen, 'A Critical Analysis of Troeltsch's Typology of Religious Association', in *Studies in the Theological Ethics of Ernst Troeltsch*, ed. M. Meyers and M. LaChat (Lewiston, NY: Edwin Mellen Press, 1990), pp. 73–118, pp. 74–5.

various other natural, social, economic, and political forces) which is coterminous with the 'historical' sphere and operates according to the 'realistic' natural law paradigm, while on the other hand there is an ideal sphere of 'pure religion' that manifests itself within history at various degrees of entanglement and confrontation with these purely 'natural' forces.[78] Meant to be free by essence from entrapment in the socio-political forces of history, yet unable by the natural law of development to reject these forces, religious values are bound to work on these forces spiritually, to penetrate them, and to aid these forces in directing history towards the future and, ultimately, towards God. In other words, the purpose of political 'compromise' for Troeltsch is none other than this: to maintain the ethico-religious ideal of Christianity within the contingencies of history, by way of 'compromise' with the naturally given socio-political powers, as the structural means by which the ideal itself is carried forward in history.

The question underlying *The Social Teaching* as a whole, then, is quite simply that of how the idealistic ethic of Christianity can be related to the world as a whole in its 'universal-historical' development.[79] Yet once the problem is set up in this way, it becomes impossible to think of Christian socio-political engagement as anything other than a compromise with the natural political forces of this world, as the basis for establishing the 'cultural syntheses' from which emerge the dominant values by which the religious truth of Christianity is carried into the future. Indeed, Troeltsch reads the history of the church's political teachings as nothing less than the ongoing search for new compromises and syntheses with the cultural, political, and economic forces of history.[80] Thus, as Troeltsch says, 'The Church only reached her full development . . . when, in the days of Constantine, she became a state Church. Only then was it possible for her to realize her universal and absolute

---

78 Troeltsch, STCC, p. 31.
79 Troeltsch, STCC, p. 25.
80 Troeltsch, STCC, pp. 999–1000.

unity and supremacy, which . . . then enabled her to subdue the State itself to the unity which had been gained with the help of the State'.[81] It is as an extension of this synthesis that Troeltsch understood the church of the Middle Ages to have created 'a Christian unity of civilization', and it was on the basis of the need for a new such synthesis that Troeltsch believed the ascetic ethic of Protestantism had arisen as a distinct 'sociological type'.[82] What motivated Troeltsch's work was his conviction that the ecclesial forms which had secured this synthesis had broken down in the face of Enlightenment subjectivity and the emergence of the modern democratic state, such that now a new synthesis was needed, as a way of carrying Christianity forward into the future and relating it anew to the emerging world-historical situation.

The point is that it is through such syntheses of the emergent Christian-ethical ideal of the Kingdom of God with the 'brute facts' of history that Christianity as a religion has learned 'to control the world-situation in its successive phases',[83] and it is by way of the ongoing search for an ever-new synthesis that the particular cultural, economic, and political forces to which Christianity is wed will be driven onward towards a future religious unity. And hence, one sees the sense in which the Christian socio-political work of 'compromise' and of the creation of ever-new 'cultural syntheses' becomes for Troeltsch the concrete means by which to 'master' historical relativism, to seek the 'universal' in the 'individual' and thus the means of discharging our ethical 'duty'.[84]

Mission

We can gain a clearer view of the ideological nature of such politics by noting the way in which this politics is convergent with Troeltsch's particular conception of the task of Christian

81 Troeltsch, STCC, p. 463.
82 Troeltsch, STCC, pp. 461–5.
83 Troeltsch, DH, p. 111.
84 See Troeltsch, DH, pp. 111–13.

mission, and especially of the way in which this conception of mission trades upon the interior/exterior dialectic of 'spirit' and 'nature', of 'religion' and 'politics'.

At the end of his *Glaubenslehre* lectures, Troeltsch defines the task of mission as 'the establishment of the religious unity of the human race'. Such is, he goes on to say, 'an ideal which Christianity demands'.[85] Furthermore, it is clear that for Troeltsch this task is to be theorized and defined as in line with the nature and function of the religious a priori: that is, the 'ideal' of 'religious unity' is to be understood ethico-metaphysically in terms of the human spirit's striving for the higher reality in 'resistance to the merely natural world' and a growing affirmation of the 'unconditioned worth of the inner man' on the basis of a relation to the absolute which lies 'beyond earthly history'.[86] As such, the task of Christian mission has to do with displaying what is *essential* to Christianity in relation to that which is universally and a priori ethico-religious. As Troeltsch comes to conceive of it, Christianity's primary claim to 'universal validity' as a religion, and thus its fundamental missionary impulse, lies especially with its particular expression of the ethico-religious 'concept of personality', which has to do essentially with the metaphysical 'end' of the soul's participation in the divine substance.[87] Thus, as a means of propagating the ideal of Christian 'religious unity', Christian mission is simply a matter of understanding and expressing our shared 'common ground in the Divine Spirit', the individual soul's 'ultimate union' with which is the universal goal of all persons.

What is important about this understanding of Christian mission is not so much the particular 'missiology' entailed therein. Rather, what is important is the way in which Troeltsch's understanding of Christianity's universal religious validity is determined by his teleo-eschatological metaphysic of history.

---

85 Troeltsch, CF, p. 299.
86 Troeltsch, ACHR, pp. 99–100.
87 Troeltsch, CT, pp. 54–63; Troeltsch, PP, pp. 35–8.

This can be seen especially in the way in which Troeltsch psychologizes the idea of the Kingdom of God in a way consistent with his transhistoricization of the eschaton. What Christianity offers with its idea of 'the Kingdom' is a particular expression of the soul's elevation to and inward union with God.[88] The Kingdom of God as an eschatological reality is and remains a matter of 'the final personal decision and sanctification' of the individual soul.[89] As such, the Kingdom of God 'just because it transcends history, cannot limit or shape history': that is, as the particular way in which Christianity conceives the universal ethico-religious phenomenon of 'the eschaton', the Kingdom of God lies outside of all history and cannot be related to from within history 'except in the form of devout anticipations of the Hereafter' – that is, as the direction of the individual's gaze 'beyond the bounds of history'.[90]

Yet we only have this idea of the Kingdom, Troeltsch consistently maintains, as it arises a posteriori out of the development of the spirit's struggle with nature *within* history. Christian mission is thus also of a piece with the primary ethical task of relating to 'the historical stream of life' as in need of 'damming and controlling'. And here especially does the task of Christian mission coincide with the task of sociopolitical compromise for Troeltsch: insofar as Christianity's validity as a religion turns upon the emergence and ongoing availability within history of its particular perspective on the universal, eschatological goal of all 'religion', such validity can only continue on into the future on the basis of evernew syntheses and compromises of Christianity's own eschatological ideal with those *given* social, political, and economic processes which have conditioned and given rise to this ideal in history. Materially, this turns out for Troeltsch to require an ongoing compromise and synthesis of the Christian eschatological ideal with the historical processes and development of Western

---

88 Troeltsch, ACHR, p. 145; cf. Troeltsch, CF, p. 96.
89 Troeltsch, CT, p. 93.
90 Troeltsch, CT, pp. 93, 146.

European Christianity. Thus, Troeltsch comes in his later work to ally the task of mission and the expansion of the Christian religion with his proposed solution to the crisis of historicism, namely, a 'universal history of Europeanism'.[91] Herein lies the Constantinian upshot: precisely because its religious essence of Christianity has to do with the 'universality' of its perspective on that eschatological ideal which lies *beyond* history, an ideal which cannot itself 'shape' history but which must yet be related to from *within* history,[92] Christianity's ongoing validity as a religion *requires* its compromised alliance with whatever *given* political and historical process afford the Christian faith the widest possible perspective on the total development, or 'world history'.

With this, we see clearly how the tasks of Christian mission and of Christian socio-political thought come together for Troeltsch: namely, at the point of Christianity's compromise and synthesis with those particular cultural and political developments from which it has emerged as a valid religious perspective on the whole, as well as at the point of discerning within the socio-political developments of modernity those syntheses and compromises by which Christianity might be sustained as such into the future. The critical point to be made here is simply this: to claim that it is of the nature of Christianity to provide us with a perspective on the eschatological *beyond* of history, which perspective must yet (in theory) be made universally available *within* history, is already to have chosen a particular provincial vantage point, whereby the given, 'natural' structures of power are de facto bound to form

---

91 See Troeltsch, DH, p. 725. As John Milbank has pointed out, this particular *Universalgeschichte des Europäismus* leads Troeltsch to read the history of the Germanic peoples as the 'metanarrative' coming-to-be of the Christian eschatological and spiritual ideal, in such a way that Western European Christianity is *always already* 'Protestant-liberal', and thus politically and religiously 'modern', whether it recognizes it or not. J. Milbank, *Theology and Social Theory: Beyond Secular Reason* (Oxford: Blackwell, 1990), pp. 92–8.

92 See Troeltsch, CT, pp. 93, 145–6.

Christianity's 'political' constituency and 'historical' meaning system.

But here I want to be clear. Given all that has just been said, what is at stake here *theologically* is not simply a certain set of assumptions about the nature of 'history', as such. Rather, what is really at stake here theologically is the nature of the eschatological reality of the Kingdom of God itself, and whether or not the church can relate to that Kingdom *as a reality within history* and engage the world in mission and politically on the basis of that reality in any way that does not succumb to the Constantinian temptation to allow the prevailing social order to set the terms for such engagement. What I am suggesting is that this is something that Troeltsch's metaphysic of history cannot abide, not so much because of its (historicist) commitment to take seriously the contingencies and particularities of history (which is a commitment I am wanting to applaud and carry forward), but because it harbours fundamental theological assumptions which stand in the way of any sustained alternative account of the Kingdom of God and of God's providential action in history that might proceed in a way no less committed to remaining with the concrete, contingent, and singular nature of historical reality.

The most basic of these assumptions, simply put, is that the Kingdom of God, inaugurated in the person of Jesus Christ, is not in itself political. By definition, the Christian gospel is apolitical; Jesus did not leave the church with a political agenda to be enacted in secular society.[93] In accordance with the spirit/nature and religion/politics dualisms that his metaphysics of history presumes, Christian social witness must always occur at a point at least once removed from the gospel or what Troeltsch calls 'pure religion'. Because 'the main problem of the Christian Ethos' remains, for Troeltsch, that of the 'transworldly' ideal of the Kingdom of God, the Christian ethic must be aided and supplemented by 'an ethic of civilization'

---

93 Troeltsch, STCC, pp. 51–3, 58–61.

– a politics – reconcilable with that ideal.[94] Christianity needs must look elsewhere than the gospel (its own 'pure religion') if it is to be engaged in 'politics' as such.

Thus, when Troeltsch talks of the church needing to develop a 'social philosophy', he means specifically a Christian philosophy about the secular state and the natural order of political, economic, and cultural forces, all of which maintain, even in their orientation toward the eschatological 'goal', a measure of autonomy that de facto involves these forces in pursuing their own distinct ends. A corollary to this is that, insofar as these forces operate on the basis of a 'natural' agonistic process as part of the bare struggle for existence, politics as such is conceived primarily as the *formation of power*: 'Power is the fundamental condition of political life'.[95]

Once this point is conceded, politics reduces to the 'maintenance and consolidation' of power; politics has as its goal the simple task of present social stability for the sake of a possible better future. This leads almost inevitably to the insistence that the Christian political task must be compatible with the demands of secular politics and its goal of sustaining historical order. Any given major religion, as Troeltsch puts it, is socially responsible for deploying its 'indestructible moral idea' as a means of determining, as far as possible, the state's 'possession and use of power'.[96] As such, the church not only loses the gospel as its political locus but also ceases to act on the basis of any political reality that is not itself finally assimilable to the broader society.

All of this leads Troeltsch to associate God's providence in history with the forces and control of this socio-political power. The theological assumption at work here is that providence is embodied in the sum of the forces operative in nature and society. In his understanding of divine providence, Troeltsch assumes the political sovereignty of 'the state' across the entire

---

94 Troeltsch, STCC, pp. 1001–2.
95 Troeltsch, RH, p. 175.
96 Troeltsch, RH, p. 176.

universal-historical whole. Providence resides in the hands of the state as the instrument of social stability and control, which allows for people to be drawn to the higher world of religion. Troeltsch further describes the German political (and military) apparatus as a primary instrument of divine providence in history, asserting that belief in the Kingdom of God means believing also in the earthly political means God uses to fulfill his will: 'God – through his governance of the world – protects and asserts the national incarnations of the divine spirit.' Thus, Troeltsch can declare 'love for state and fatherland as the embodiment of the divine thought in the German essence', and conclude by saying, 'We hear God's voice in this, our struggle imposed by fate, and follow it with strong faith, innerly at one with fate's will, which is imposing these fights on us. We will stay and remain as it [i.e., fate's will] does'.[97]

What is important about these statements is the kind of appraisal Troeltsch puts on the state as the political 'sovereign' in history and the way in which he credits this state sovereignty to the workings of divine providence. While such language is in part meant to *free* true religion from its entanglement in the violent vicissitudes of nature by providing for the kind of social stability that will allow the growth and propagation of the religious ideal, it disallows the idea that the church might recognize *another* sovereign in history, one that might allow it to conceive of politics and its political vocation *otherwise*. Once it is conceded that providence works primarily through the structures of society-wide political order, then Christianity must accept as its primary political task the joining of its religious ideal with the economic, cultural, and social forces in moving history toward the common future to which the very developments of history have determined it should be directed.

---

97 Troeltsch, *Deutscher Glaube und Deutsche Sitte in unserem groen Kriege* (Berlin, 1914), pp. 25, 28–30. Cited in A. Rasmusson, 'Historicizing the Historicist: Ernst Troeltsch and Recent Mennonite Theology', in *The Wisdom of the Cross: Essays in Honor of John Howard Yoder*, ed. S. Hauerwas, C. Huebner, H. Huebner, and M. T. Nation (Grand Rapids: Eerdmans, 1999), pp. 213–48, pp. 228–9.

In the final analysis, then, it is hard to resist the conclusion that the key socio-political function of Christianity within the paradigm of modern historicist thought, as laid out by Troeltsch, is fundamentally *ideological*. Indeed, what Troeltsch seems really to be interested in with his account of both Christian politics and mission is an understanding of Christianity which can assist in 'the creation of a new sociological matrix for ideology, animated by a fresh spiritual insight', which allows us better to control the political and economic forces of history for the sake of a better, more thoroughly 'modern', future.[98] It seems as if the developments within Christian social thought that Troeltsch traces out serve especially as indices of a providential process which affirms the emergence of modern historicist consciousness as of a piece with the modern (liberal) socio-political problematic. Troeltsch's own attempt to salvage the project of historicism thus turns out not only to be a means of identifying and addressing a crisis within the critical practice of history, but also a means of isolating the metaphysical structures and figures – a certain relation of the absolute to the relative, of the ideal to the real, of the religious to the socio-political, of the eschatological to the historical, etc. – that spur all political and historical development, as well as the political and economic structures and figures – the nation state, capitalism, personalism and individualism, etc. – by which alone the modern liberal project might go forward in history. Faced with the vacuity of the crisis of Western historicism, then, we turn to Christianity as 'the only firm religious capital that we have',[99] and we turn inevitably to the missionary and political strategies of 'synthesis' and 'compromise' as the means of deploying and exploiting that capital by investing in the future of the 'modern spirit'.[100]

But this, ultimately, is just what 'Constantinianism' in its many guises is: the 'capitalization' of Christianity; religion in the service of ideology.

---

98 Troeltsch, DH, p. 771.
99 Troeltsch, CF, p. 38.
100 See Troeltsch, RH, pp. 237–72 *passim*.

The Nature of Christ's Lordship

To this point, I have concentrated upon the way in which the metaphysics of history that underwrites the 'triumph of ideology' in modern theological historicism (as represented by Troeltsch) can be analysed and critiqued in terms of a fundamentally *eschatological* failure. In this section, I want to suggest that this eschatological failure is bound up with a second *Christological* failure. Troeltsch's teleo-eschatological assumptions regarding the sovereignty of the processes of historical development are politically ideological as also theologically reductive of the cosmic-historical significance of the figure of Jesus Christ. The question I want to ask, then, is to what extent is the triumph of ideology in modern historicism dependent upon a refusal to acknowledge the cosmic-historical – and to that extent *apocalyptic*-eschatological – truth of the Christian confession of Christ's lordship?

Troeltsch's own modern historicist commitments, along with his dualistic metaphysics of history, always served as an a priori into which the Incarnation fitted very awkwardly, if at all. Whatever else might be said about the importance of Jesus for faith, the modern historicist methodology has left Jesus with no 'special metaphysical position' at all;[101] there can be no question of Jesus' 'cosmic significance' as the 'centre of the entire history of all of mankind', or of the transfer to him of 'the role of a universal world-redeemer traditionally assigned by the church'.[102] 'One thing . . . the believer will have to forego', says Troeltsch, '– namely, to construe Jesus as the centre of the world or even of human history and to base his essential significance on this construction.'[103]

But what then does this mean for the relationship of Jesus to history? In 'The Significance of the Historical Existence of Jesus for Faith', Troeltsch argues for the need to develop an alternative, 'historicist' account of Jesus for faith; he wants to

101 Troeltsch, RH, pp. 72–3.
102 Troeltsch, RH, p. 348.
103 Troeltsch, RH, p. 349; cf. Troeltsch, ET, p. 189.

discern 'the effect of historical criticism upon faith in Christ'.[104] That is, Troeltsch thinks that whereas 'the primitive Christian community had already taken him out of history and made him Logos and God', Jesus must be 'returned . . . to history where all is finite and conditioned'.[105]

In order thus to reconceive the historic importance of Jesus for faith, Troeltsch draws upon a certain set of psychological- and social-historical criteria.[106] *Psychologically*, Troeltsch interprets Jesus' significance in terms of a kind of 'Christ-mysticism', one in which Jesus' significance 'will refer rather to the transformation of souls through Jesus' impact on them'.[107] Christ's person, on this scheme, refers to 'an inward spiritual principle, felt in every stirring of religious feeling, present in every influence of the Divine Seed and the Divine Spark; this mystical Christ . . . can only be recognized and affirmed in inward spiritual experience; this principle therefore agrees with the "hidden ground" of the Divine Life in man'.[108] This 'Christ-mysticism' should therefore be understood as of a piece with Troeltsch's metaphysical predilections for 'Spiritual Religion' (which he understood to be intrinsically related to 'modern Idealism').[109]

But as has become clear, we cannot for Troeltsch properly think religion in its primary importance for the individual without understanding how the individual is nourished in her faith by the 'universal-historical', that is, without understanding how this faith arises as a matter of *development* within history. To articulate this historicist dimension, Troeltsch describes Jesus' psychological significance for Christian faith in a manner that is also *social*. Troeltsch delineates this social dimension by stressing the centrality of the cultus for the Christian community. The main point is that it is in the Christian cultus

---

104 Troeltsch, ET, p. 182.
105 Troeltsch, ET, p. 182.
106 See Troeltsch, ET, pp. 190–207.
107 Troeltsch, CF, p. 89.
108 Troeltsch, STCC, pp. 994–5.
109 Troeltsch, STCC, p. 996.

that Jesus is understood as a 'living, many-sided and . . . elevating . . . personality', a 'living . . . indefinable personal life'.[110]
In the cultus, the Church interprets 'the picture of Christ very
freely and flexibly, using everything that flowed into him and
everything which in the course of thousands of years has been
accommodated and loved in him'.[111] It is through this 'development' and 'self-production' of Jesus' personality in the cultus
that Christian faith is mediated to the individual soul in history.[112] Furthermore, it is in the cultus that we generate 'devotion to the historical totality of life which has its point of departure in Jesus', through which 'historical totality of life' we
gain that perspective on the 'absolute values' of the soul and
of the human person which allows us to overcome relativism
by orienting us teleologically towards the moral goal of 'the
temporal development of the human spirit'.[113]

All of this talk of the cultus, then, and of the importance
of the ecclesial structures which support its communal practice, turns upon the psychological element in Troeltsch's
Christology, his 'Christ-mysticism'.[114] Christ here is recognized as 'Head' of the Christian community, *not* on the basis
of his being the *cosmic* Lord of history, but rather on the
basis of his being *psychologically* Lord over human souls.[115]
Take, for example, Troeltsch's christological discussion in the
Glaubenslehre. Troeltsch organizes his discussion around the
tradition of Christ's three offices – prophet, priest, and king
– and stresses especially the 'Kingly' office (Christ's reign,
or 'lordship') as most important, as it is here that Christ
is understood as a 'unifying point' for the community, as
'the central and foundational personality' of the Christian

110 Troeltsch, ET, pp. 202, 213.
111 Troeltsch, ET, p. 201.
112 Troeltsch, CF, pp. 63–4.
113 Troeltsch, RH, pp. 351, 353.
114 Troeltsch, RH, p. 351.
115 B. Gerrish, 'Jesus, Myth, and History: Troeltsch's Stand in
the 'Christ-Myth' Debate', *Journal of Religion* 55 (1975), pp. 13–35,
p. 24.

revelation.[116] But (and here is the key) such a community exists only as 'the *correlate of redemption*', which 'aims at separating the elevated, spiritual human self from the natural human self'.[117] 'Redemption' as such is not a *cosmic*-historical event, but rather a *psychological*-historical event, a transformation of the soul of the believer as mediated by the various specific religious developments of world history. Consequently, to confess Jesus as Lord, on this basis, the community 'will never be able to speak in terms of cosmic or metaphysical transformations, but will refer rather to the transformation of souls through Jesus' impact on them. In particular, the only meaning that can be attached to his suffering and death will be historical and psychological – the effect it has on believing souls'.[118] The result is an ecclesial community formed upon the basis of an entirely 'voluntary' conception of Christ's lordship.

What I would like to point up here is that in severing the confession of Christ's lordship from any notion of Jesus' redemptive work as 'cosmic-historical', Troeltsch also severs this confession from its original *political* meaning and from the significance this confession once had as the basis and content of Christian *mission*. To consider again the cosmic-historical nature of this confession, in our own day, as the point of departure for Christian mission and politics in their inseparability, is the constructive burden of this essay. For now, it is enough to note that Troeltsch and modern theological historicism cannot abide such a cosmic-historical understanding of Christ's person precisely insofar as their immanentist and universalist metaphysics of history will not allow for the kind of eschatological event of God's action which would occur as an event which is paradoxically *within* history as an interruption and transformation *of* history. It is thus that the 'triumph of ideology' in modern theological historicism

---

116 Troeltsch, CF, p. 89.
117 Troeltsch, CF, pp. 291–2.
118 Troeltsch, CF, pp. 291–2.

goes hand in hand with an 'eclipse of apocalyptic'. For apart from the idea that the person of Jesus Christ occurs as an inbreaking arrival of the transcendent God, and thus as the inbreaking of God's Kingdom within history itself, the very historicity of Jesus Christ (like all discrete historical events) will assume the status of a given *datum*, and the confession of his 'lordship' will only signal the reduction of his 'person' to a kind of psychological ideal that is analogous (though univocally so) to the religiously universal ideal that that undergirds all socio-political development within history. By contrast, only a renewed emphasis upon Jesus of Nazareth's historicity as the singular event of God's apocalyptic action will genuinely free the contingencies and particularities of history from the 'omnipotence of analogy' by which all discrete historical events are disambiguated within immanence for the purpose of teleo-ideological political construction.

Conclusion and Forecast: 'The Messianic Cessation of Happening'

Before moving on to a close reading of Karl Barth, whose work represents the re-emergence of 'apocalyptic' within the genealogy I am tracing out, I wish to conclude this chapter by returning to the work of Walter Benjamin, whose 'Theses on the Philosophy of History' constitutes one of the most important philosophical and political critiques of the kind of 'universal historicism' that Troeltsch so manifestly represents. What I would like to do is briefly to put forth Benjamin's 'Messianic' notion of history as 'time filled by the presence of the now [*Jetzt-zeit*]'[119] as providing a kind of philosophical propaedeutic for the particularly Christian apocalyptic historicism that I shall be constructing over the next three chapters. More specifically, the operative logic of the Messianic thematics of Benjamin's 'Theses' provides an important philosophical bridge between my critique of modern 'universal historicism' as represented

119 Benjamin, 'Theses', p. 261.

by Troeltsch and my analysis of the uniquely apocalyptic-eschatological perspective that Barth represents.[120]

Though notorious for its complexity, the text of Benjamin's 'Theses' is most profound at its most basic level, namely, in its dogged pursuit of the conditions for a single historical possibility. That single historical possibility is what Benjamin calls 'the time of the Messiah' or 'messianic time', which marks the irruption of that evernew and unforeseeable event whereby each historical particular is 'blasted out' of the 'continuum' of 'universal history' and 'redeemed' as an event of singular action on behalf of the Kingdom of God, which redemptive action Benjamin articulates in a number of ways as the eschatological liberation of the oppressed.[121] What is important for the purposes of this discussion, however, is the way in which Benjamin carries out a critique of the modern historicist notion of teleological 'development' and its ideological conception of 'progress', from within the construction of his own alternative, Messianic vision of history. So what I would like to do here is note three distinctive elements of this vision of history as a way of situating my own critique of Troeltsch and modern theological historicism more positively within the broader scope of the 'Christian apocalyptic' vision that I shall be constructing in the remainder of this book.

First, for Benjamin the Messianic 'now-time' is only possible as the time of an unmistakably *singular* instant. Whereas for modern historicism the progression of history can only occur in servile conformity to an ideologically constructed 'universal',

---

120 Here I am building upon the provocative suggestion of Jacob Taubes that it is possible to understand Benjamin's notion of 'the Messiah' from the point of view of Barth's *Epistle to the Romans* as a kind of non-dogmatic 'dialectical theology', a kind of philosophical 'lay-theologese', if you will. J. Taubes, *The Political Theology of Paul*, tr. Dana Hollander (Stanford: Stanford University Press, 2004), p. 75.

121 Benjamin, 'Theses', pp. 262–3, 253–4. On this liberationist reading of the 'idea of redemption' in Benjamin's 'Theses', see M. Löwy, *Fire Alarm: Reading Walter Benjamin's 'On the Concept of History'*, tr. C. Turner (London: Verso, 2005), pp. 29–40 and *passim*. See also Benjamin's 'Thesis XVIIa', in Löwy, pp. 96–7.

the 'Now-Moment' (*Jetztzeit*) of the Messiah's coming is only ever possible as an irreducibly singular and contingently unforeseeable event. Benjamin thus speaks of the Now-Moment as the 'Messianic cessation of happening',[122] the grinding to a halt of teleological development, which, following Taubes, we might call the irruption of immanental universality by the transcendent *prius* of singularity.[123]

Second, this singular event occurs also for Benjamin as the recapitulation and transformation of history itself. Thus, this 'cessation of happening' occurs also as the 'blasting open' of 'the continuum of history'.[124] This is what I take it to mean when he says the 'entire course of history' itself is 'preserved' in this irruption: what is conceivable for the universal historicist only as the 'homogeneous, empty time' of teleological development is now for the first time *heterogenized*, as 'time filled by the presence of the now'.[125] The Messianic event of singularity alone *differentiates*, as it alone renders history in its fullness, making of each contingent event a unique sign of the evernew possibility of the Messiah's inbreaking. Thus, every moment of history becomes 'the straight gate through which the Messiah might enter'.[126]

Third, the Messianic inbreaking occurs as an event of engaged and embodied *action*. The 'Messianic cessation of happening' is nothing less than the revolutionary critique and subversion of the real and material institutions that secure the appearance of assumed universality of 'historical continuity'. In other words, only an engaged and embodied action can *interrupt* – can 'blow apart' – the 'continuum of history', for the 'continuum of history' is itself a construction by real this-worldly power brokers who trade on the capitalization of ideals. It is significant that this action coincides for Benjamin with a critique of the neo-Kantian ideal of the Kingdom as an

---

122 Benjamin, 'Theses', p. 263.
123 Taubes, *Political Theology of Paul*, pp. 75–6.
124 Benjamin, 'Theses', p. 262.
125 Benjamin, 'Theses', pp. 263, 260.
126 Benjamin, 'Theses', p. 264.

'infinite [*unendlich*] task', as the 'final goal of historical progress'. For it is precisely as this ideal that the idea of the Kingdom functions ideologically: as this 'infinite task', the Kingdom
will never *arrive* in history but is rather upheld as that which
is to be 'progressed' towards via the gradual accumulation and
reforms of the always-already *givens* of history. Alternatively,
it is only by way a kind of a concretely revolutionary political
action, a definitive – 'ultimately [*endlich*] achieved' – *interruption* of 'the political' ideal, as such, that history reveals itself
to be what it truly is, namely, the *gift* of transformed, 'messianic time', which is to be received singularly, contingently, and
everanew in the mode of such action.

It is precisely in terms of something like this 'Messianic cessation of happening' – this singular, history-transforming mode
of political action – that I shall seek in what follows to render
the revolutionary logic of Christian apocalyptic vis-à-vis the
ideological logic of modern theological historicism I have critiqued as at work in Troeltsch. My aim will be to demonstrate
that there is within the primal Christological confession 'Jesus
is Lord' a way of thinking Christ's relation to history otherwise, on the basis of a cosmic-historic and apocalyptic understanding of the eschaton. This alternative conceives history's
contingencies and particularities as having been *transformed*
by a decisive, singularly irruptive act of the transcendent God,
such that now these contingencies and particularities are not
there as bare facts to be manipulated and controlled, but rather
as gifts given by God in Christ, to be returned in gratitude and
praise. History received in this way is history lived in such
a way that the tasks of Christian politics and mission come
together, so as to propel the church beyond political ideology
into a mode of political action rooted in doxology. If God's
reign really has broken into history, in such a way as to make
true our lived praise of Christ's cosmic-historical Lordship, as
the gift of a concrete political action rooted in the transformation of the world itself, then Christ must be concretely and cosmically Lord, not as one who hovers over or beyond history,
but as one who invades history and pervades it in such a way

as not to overwhelm its contingencies and singularities but to redeem them, making them truly to be signs of the coming of God's Kingdom on earth.

And yet it is at this point that the work of Troeltsch and the crisis of modern historicism will need to be read as *exceeding* the critique offered in this chapter, for this crisis comes to us as a challenge in itself. If the cosmic-historical and apocalyptic nature of Christ's lordship is to render the 'truth' of history, precisely by way of its concentration on the singular historicity of God incarnate in Jesus of Nazareth, such a truth must be communicable without betraying and evading the crisis and burden which Troeltsch and modern theological historicism has discerned and bequeathed to us. That is, if Christian apocalyptic is to resist and to move beyond the postmodern and theoretical temptation to reify apocalyptic according to a new 'Messianic ideal', in terms, for example, of what Derrida calls the 'universal structure' of a historical, 'quasi-transcendental' messianism of infinite deferral,[127] and is rather to insist that apocalyptic has to do with the singular act of *God's* decisive transformation of history in the historical reality that is the Messianic *arrival* of Jesus of Nazareth, then Christian apocalyptic must be able to take up the challenge of historicity and in doing so must give way to *its own distinctively theological historicism*, a historicism no less rooted in and committed to the complexities, contingencies, and disaccord of historical 'reality' than that of someone like Troeltsch.

It is this alternative, 'apocalyptic historicism', I shall argue, that gives way finally to the non-ideological politics of Christian mission after which I am seeking in this book. However, before I arrive there, I will need to trace the contours for an alternative, 'apocalyptic Christology' by means of exploring and critiquing the particular Christological and ecclesiological responses of Karl Barth and Stanley Hauerwas, respectively, to

---

127 J. Derrida, *Specters of Marx: The State of Debt, the Work of Mourning, and the New International*, tr. P. Kamuf (London: Routledge, 1994), pp. 210–12.

modern theological historicism and the politics of liberalism. For these explorations will constitute the fundamental bases for a more thoroughgoing apocalyptic historicism and demonstrate the necessity of such a historicism for overcoming the Constantinian 'triumph of ideology' in Christian politics and mission.

3

Karl Barth: Foundations for an Apocalyptic Christology

As I have argued in the previous chapter with regard to Ernst Troeltsch, modern theological historicism, in its primarily idealist-constructivist approach to historical processes, is hard-pressed to provide a way of thinking Christian mission politically without capitulating to ideological manipulation from the very outset. One key reason for this is that idealist language about the Kingdom of God has depoliticized Christian claims to Christ's lordship, relegating such claims to the 'psychological' register. In this chapter, I should like to begin to develop an alternative, 'cosmic-historical' understanding of Christ's lordship and of the Kingdom of God. This is best done, I shall be arguing, on the basis of an 'apocalyptic Christology'. I shall be seeking to locate and expound the 'foundations' for such an apocalyptic Christology in the theology of Karl Barth, by documenting the development of Barth's later Christocentric theology of history against the 'apocalyptic' backdrop of his second *Epistle to the Romans*. The 'apocalyptic Christology' which emerges from this development will provide the indispensable framework for the construction of an alternative 'apocalyptic historicism' in Chapter 5. If, as I shall argue, we shall need finally to move 'beyond' Barth in developing this 'apocalyptic historicism', it is because Barth's own formulations, vis-à-vis those of Troeltsch, compel us to reorientate 'apocalyptic Christology' according to its more 'historicist' dimensions and implications.

Der Römerbrief, History, and the Metaphysics of Apocalyptic

I begin this chapter by offering a reading of Karl Barth's second *Epistle to the Romans* (*Der Römerbrief*) as a text which is itself conditioned by the same 'crisis of historicism' that pre-occupied Troeltsch throughout his work and that reached a peak for Protestant theology in the wake of the First World War. Following F. W. Graf, I thus locate *Der Römerbrief* as at the heart of what he calls the 'anti-historicist revolution' of Protestant theology in the period of Weimar Germany.[1] In this sense, *pace* Jacob Taubes,[2] I take Barth's text to be a kind of theological antitype to Benjamin's entire oeuvre (especially his 'Theses') and thus the precise point at which to begin to address the theological-political predicament that modern theological historicism has created for us.

Der Römerbrief has long been recognized as representing Barth's unbridled attempt to begin to do theology anew from an altogether *apocalyptic* perspective. What is most important, however, is the way in which this unreservedly 'apocalyptic' text is itself shaped and determined by the very 'crisis of historicism' which occupied Troeltsch. Rudolf Bultmann was right to reckon with Barth's commentary as a vigorous rejection of all 'historicizing' and 'psychologizing' trends in modern theology.[3] What Barth was opposed to in all 'believing and unbelieving historicism and psychologizing' was the idea that God can somehow be intuited in such a way as to be submitted to our 'historical and psychological analysis', that is, in such a way as to be 'described historically' or 'treated pragmatically' on the basis of a certain historical magnitude or psychological

---

1 F. W. Graf, 'Die "antihistorische Revolution" in der protestant-ischen Theologie der zwanziger Jahre', in *Vernunft des Glaubens: Wissenschaftliche Theologie und kirchliche Lehre*, ed. J. Rohls and G. Wenz (Göttingen: Vandenhoeck & Ruprecht, 1988), pp. 377–405.

2 Taubes, *Political Theology of Paul*, p. 75.

3 R. Bultmann, 'Karl Barth's *Epistle to the Romans* in Its Second Edition', in *The Beginnings of Dialectical Theology*, ed. J. Robinson (Richmond, VA: John Knox Press, 1968), pp. 100–4.

givenness.[4] By refusing 'historicism' Barth was thus refusing those patterns of thought that made history itself the bearer of the truth of the world and the meaning of human existence. Historicism makes of Christianity a predicate of history; in so doing, however, it confuses Christianity with the totalism of the ideological worlds produced by modern reason. Christianity as such is impotent to criticize the limits of historical subjects and their plans to control the development of the world and life on the basis of the self-celebration of the power of historical reason.

(So it is precisely as a text written *against* modern theological historicism that *Der Römerbrief* is a text written *against* ideology.[5] The gospel – that 'question-mark set against all truths'[6] – is nothing less than the apocalyptic *krisis* by which God has judged religion, society, and its political ideologies and found them corrupt and sinful.)[7]

It is especially important to note, however, that in rejecting 'historicism' Barth is still attempting in his own way to deal with what Troeltsch recognized as the relative, transient, and contingent character of all history.[8] Barth acknowledges that the world and human history are moving in a 'secular and relative context', one which 'in itself is ultimately meaningless'.[9] History teaches us by its own logic that it has no inherent relation to the eternal, that it is unable to 'progress' or 'develop' towards the divine, and as such it pronounces judgment upon itself – taken in itself history is nothing but a chaos of meaningless

---

4 Barth, ER, p. 277. Bruce McCormack notes that 'historicism' and 'psychologism' are for Barth shorthand for the kind of liberal non-theology against whose 'No-God' Barth has set God as *God*, that is, as *Other*. B. McCormack, *Karl Barth's Critically Realistic Dialectical Theology: Its Genesis and Development 1909–1936* (Oxford: Clarendon Press, 1995), pp. 248–9.

5 See Timothy J. Gorringe, *Karl Barth: Against Hegemony* (Oxford: Oxford University Press, 1999), pp. 55–69.

6 Barth, ER, p. 35.

7 Barth, ER, p. 390.

8 Barth, ER, pp. 77, 85–7, 115–48.

9 Barth, ER, p. 107.

phenomena.[10] In this way, Barth acknowledges the nihilism of contemporary society and the ideological crisis of the Weimar Republic immediately following the Great War as his point of departure. *Der Römerbrief* is Barth's own attempt to develop a strategy with which to address the growing crisis of historicism that the events of his time signified.[11] Precisely thereby, Barth's agenda was to develop a theology which conceives of God's relationship to humanity and of the relationship between time and eternity in terms *other* than 'historical'.

The relationship Barth goes on to describe is indeed an 'apocalyptic' one, in that it stresses the otherness and priority of God's action, in a way that is interruptive of 'history' and of the ideological-constructive task of modern historicism. From the side of the historically contingent and the relative, the side upon which we as human beings inevitably reside, God's relation to humanity can only be one which is established *extrinsically*, by the initiative of God.[12] God's action is an action by which God exposes all false conceptions of the God-human relationship and grounds the God-human relationship in God's otherness alone. The character of this relation vis-à-vis 'the voice of history' is that of a 'miracle', of God's sheer freedom, power, and grace.[13] As apocalyptic rupture, grace thus accomplishes a primarily *negative* work in relation to the world – the event of God's grace happens as a tangent touching a circle, a crater resulting from an explosion, a signpost that points away to another destination.[14] So it is that apocalyptic is deployed by Barth so as to maintain the 'wholly otherness' of God, and the priority of God's *action*, as one who breaks into the world and history from the outside, and manifests Godself there, as *other*, and as the *krisis* of the world and history.

10 Barth, ER, pp. 85–90, 145.

11 See 'Barth and the Eschatology of Weimar: A Theology on Its Way?', in R. Roberts, *A Theology on Its Way? Essays on Karl Barth* (Edinburgh: T. & T. Clark, 1991), pp. 169–99.

12 Barth, ER, pp. 148, 187.

13 Barth, ER, pp. 115–26.

14 Barth, ER, pp. 30, 29, 88.

What is interesting here is that while Barth is unwilling to speak of the apocalyptic action of God as either 'human-historical' or 'temporal' – 'the action of God cannot occur in time; it can occur only . . . in eternity'[15] – Barth still thinks of that action in terms of the one 'Primal History' (*Urgeschichte*) that 'conditions all history'.[16] The point is that the idea of apocalyptic allows Barth so to consider the history of creation in its absolute fallenness, nihilation, and flux that the only metaphysical space left within which to consider the meaning-fulness of this history is that of an eternal event which occurs as a non-historical interstice of the temporal flux itself. Thus, by associating God's action with a primal source or ground, Barth is able to speak of the disclosure of a 'timeless, necessary reality in the longitude of time'.[17] This reality is characterized as follows: 'Between the past and the future – between the times – there is a "Moment" that is no moment in time. This "Moment" is the eternal Moment – the *Now* – when the past and the future stand still, when the former ceases its going and the latter its coming.'[18] This eternal 'Now-moment', in the words of Richard Roberts, thus creates a kind of 'temporal vacuum' within the order of time; it occurs, in other words, as a kind of actualistic non-temporality, a *nunc stans* in the midst of the flux of time and history, an 'intrusion of a timeless "Moment" "between" the successive stages in the temporal order'.[19] Barth considers this timeless, non-historical Moment as itself the basis of history's unity and meaning, as that which 'conditions all history' by making of 'historical occurrence it-self . . . the manifestation of the ground of knowledge and the power of creation'.[20]

---

15 Barth, ER, p. 435.

16 Barth, ER, pp. 140, 143.

17 Barth, ER, p. 116.

18 Barth, ER, p. 497.

19 R. Roberts, 'Karl Barth's Doctrine of Time', in *Karl Barth: Studies of His Theological Method*, ed. S. W. Sykes (Oxford: Clarendon Press, 1979), pp. 88–146, pp. 88, 99.

20 Barth, ER, pp. 140–1.

Crucially, what one sees here is Barth's *embracing* of the nihilistic description of bare 'historicity', such as we find in Troeltsch, for the sake of an alternative metaphysical reality, namely, an apocalyptic 'beyond' which breaks in vertically from above and puts an 'end' to history, by establishing each discrete moment in time in direct and contemporaneous relationship to the eternal event of God's own *Urgeschichte*. History taken in itself is indeed nothing more than a chaos of particular occurrences,[21] but the event of the timeless Moment happens in such a way as to render each of these occurrences in immediate relation to its primal source or ground. Thus, the gospel (as the 'seed of eternity') is 'the fruit of time, the meaning and maturity of history',[22] by testifying to what is true of all history, namely, its negation under the grace of God, by which 'history' as such collapses and all occurrences in their particularity are made to point away from themselves to their non-historical *Urgrund*. Human history is not so much done away with here as it is 'de-realized', given meaning only by way of its dialectical giving-way to a reality beyond and behind all history.

The key point of significance here is that Barth's response to the 'crisis of historicity' is that of his own mode of idealist eschatologico-metaphysical construction: his appeal to God's apocalyptic action as *Urgeschichte* is a retreat into a metaphysical 'eschatological' reality that is transcendentally 'beyond', and so always-already at one remove from, the messy complexity of 'human-historical' occurrence.[23] In speaking of the apocalyptic action of God negatively in relation to history as he does, Barth is attempting to base our entire existence upon

---

21 Barth, ER, pp. 145–6.

22 Barth, ER, p. 28.

23 This move is characteristic of what Bruce McCormack has called the 'consistent eschatology' of *Der Römerbrief* and of what Ingolf Dalferth names Barth's 'eschatological realism'. See McCormack, *Karl Barth's Critically Realistic Dialectical Theology*, pp. 207–323. Ingolf U. Dalferth, 'Karl Barth's Eschatological Realism', in *Karl Barth: Centenary Essays*, ed. S. W. Sykes (Cambridge: Cambridge University Press, 1989), pp. 14–45.

an eschatological reality which is 'positively not-given', that is, a reality uninferrable from the givenness of what is passing and transitory.[24] This eschatological reality is 'the Kingdom of God', which belongs to the sheer fact that 'God exists', and to which we stand in relation as our 'Origin' as also our 'Goal'.[25] Barth thus speaks of the eschaton as somehow always-already *realized*, such that what the eschaton names is that 'invisible and non-historical' power by which we endure the 'dissolution' of time through expectation of our return to the primal origin, which we experience 'here and now as the eternal future'.[26] Again, this is not to deny historical *occurrence*, but rather to insist that every such occurrence is relativized in such a way that it only obtains abiding *reality* in relation to this non-historical eschatological event of eternity, from which it comes and to which it returns.

On these terms, we might well describe the theology of *Der Römerbrief* as 'dialectically anti-nihilist'. It is marked by its drive to go 'beyond' the twin alternatives of historical be-coming and nihilation, by affirming a logically prior mode of realization. But dialectically, it must come to an awareness of the reality of what is positively 'not-given' through the 'de-realization' of that which is 'given', but which itself has no *being*. Such theology thereby must inscribe *Das Nichts* into its affirmation of the Absolute. In order to be 'ontologically affirmative' it must proceed according to an inescapable 'logic of negation'.[27] Such a de-realization of history is a common-place of a dialectically driven metaphysical Idealism. And it is helpful to think of Barth's eschatology as performing a kind of *Aufhebung* here, albeit one in which Barth replaces the Hegel-ian synthesis with a simple overcoming of an initial antithesis

---

24 See Dalferth, 'Karl Barth's Eschatological Realism', p. 22.

25 Barth, ER, p. 295. For a characteristically helpful discussion of the 'protological' character of Barth's 'consistent eschatology' in *Der Römerbrief*, see McCormack, *Karl Barth's Critically Realistic*, pp. 245–62.

26 Barth, ER, pp. 152, 186–7.

27 See Roberts, *Theology On Its Way?*, pp. 190, 193–6.

(historical time) by a stronger thesis (the 'absolute Moment').[28] So an initial *diastasis* is posed (time and eternity) so as to represent the *Urgeschichtlich* 'victory' of the latter over the former – 'time is swallowed up in eternity'.[29]

The 'apocalyptic eschatology' of *Der Römerbrief* thus amounts to something of another turning of the Idealist screw,[30] one which effects an inversion of Troeltsch's own 'teleo-developmental eschatology'. That is, precisely in setting out to dilute or to eliminate the destructive tendencies of Troeltsch's and others' developmental and immanental approaches to 'time' and 'history', Barth's own anti-historicism formally repeats, in my view, their fundamental methodological error by making recourse to a transcendent 'beyond' whose primary function is the eschatologico-metaphysical qualification of all moments in time. And so Barth demonstrates the difficulty of responding to the 'crisis of historicism' in a way that is not metaphysically determined by the very idealist presuppositions of that crisis itself.

This difficulty is exemplified by the way in which Barth's apocalyptic-eschatological metaphysics determines his early Christology, his understanding of the nature and importance of Jesus' historicity, and his characterization of Christ's 'lordship'. Barth famously wrote: 'If Christianity be not altogether thoroughgoing eschatology, there remains in it no relation whatever to Christ.'[31] This statement occurs within a long excursus on the nature of the 'resurrection', in which Barth expounds the resurrection as determining the 'eventiveness' of the eschaton and the 'truth' of Christ's reality.[32] The resurrection

---

28 For this way of putting things, see J. McDowell, *Hope in Barth's Eschatology: Interrogations and Transformations beyond Tragedy* (Aldershot: Ashgate, 2000), p. 88.

29 Barth, ER, p. 285.

30 On the idealist structure of *Der Römerbrief* see K. Sonderegger, *That Jesus Christ Was Born a Jew: Karl Barth's 'Doctrine of Israel'* (University Park: Penn State University Press, 1992), pp. 15–42.

31 Barth, ER, p. 314.

32 Barth, ER, p. 317.

is not a 'historical event' that may be placed 'side by side with other events', but is rather the '"non-historical" happening by which all other events are bounded and to which events before and on and after Easter Day point'.[33] It is this, furthermore, as the 'reversal' or the 'transformation' of the life of the historical man Jesus.[34] This 'life' is one that is interpreted through the cross as the supreme event of crisis between a Holy God and sinful humanity; the cross is that one point at which all human (and especially all 'religious') attempts at self-aggrandizement are shattered. The death and resurrection, respectively, are the bringing to an end of the 'old', whose power is the fallen one of 'history', and a bringing in of the 'new', whose power is not that of 'history' as such but of the Primal Origin, the *Urgrund*, which is nothing less than 'the Krisis within which all history stands'.[35] The resurrection is thus that apocalyptic action by which we are drawn into a life whose power is 'invisible and non-historical'.[36] As the resurrected one, Jesus Christ himself does not occur at a particular point in history, but as the 'crimson thread which runs through all history',[37] rendering every historical event contemporaneous with the eternal Now-Moment. Herein, then, lies the great genius of Barth's apocalyptic logic and the great *aporia* to which it leads: genuine life in Christ has its reality in the *action of God* alone, but as such it is de facto *dissociated* from history, as 'the action of God cannot occur in time'.

David Mueller has argued that Barth's point here, in developing an entirely eschatologized Christology, is to stress the union of God and humanity in Christ's particularity.[38] In Christ's resurrection the 'Last Things' are inaugurated, such

33 Barth, ER, p. 203.
34 Barth, ER, p. 203
35 Barth, ER, p. 146.
36 Barth, ER, p. 152.
37 Barth, ER, pp. 96, 117.
38 D. Mueller, *Foundation of Karl Barth's Doctrine of Reconciliation: Jesus Christ Crucified and Risen* (Lewiston, NY: Edwin Mellen Press, 1990), p. 11.

that a new covenant of union between God and humanity is made possible.[39] Yet what I want to stress here is that this union is one of being made 'contemporaneous' not with a God who has come into being in time (to borrow Kierkegaard's formulation), but with a certain transcendental metaphysical reality: God's eternal actuality. So far as this is the case, the *life* of Jesus of Nazareth ceases to be the key for the relationship between time and eternity as the sign of the apocalyptic inbreaking of God's reign; instead, like every other historical moment, Jesus of Nazareth himself only has ultimate meaning in relation to the non-historical event of the resurrection (which is the 'reversal' and 'dissolution' of all historicity, the 'reversal' and 'dissolution' of Jesus' particular historicity as much as ours). And it is here, in this eschatological reversal and dissolution of historicity, that we come to recognize Jesus Christ as 'Lord'. This, according to Barth, is the meaning of Christ's 'lordship', the purport of his 'victory': 'The particularity of the years A.D. 1–30 is dissolved by this divine definition, because it makes every epoch a potential field of revelation and disclosure.'[40]

But with this we come to the crux of the matter for the purposes of developing an apocalyptic historicism. The Barth of *Der Römerbrief* is yet unable to root God's apocalyptic action in the complexities of Jesus of Nazareth's historicity, precisely *because* he has prima facie accepted (and rejected) the terms of 'history' and of 'historicism' as set by the modern historicists. As such, he is forced into a metaphysical construal of the eschaton by which 'Christ' is stripped down to the dialectical bare bones of 'cross and resurrection'.[41] Barth has yet to arrive at a coherent Christological articulation that can take up the logic of apocalyptic within itself and thereby properly communicate the reality of the Kingdom of God and of Christ's lordship in a way that is genuinely transformative of history, and

39 Barth, ER, pp. 202–3.
40 Barth, ER, p. 29.
41 See McDowell, *Hope in Barth's Eschatology*, p. 88.

that positively relates us, *in our historicity*, to the inbreaking of God's Kingdom in Jesus of Nazareth.

But this brings us to the very nerve centre of Barth's theology in the *Church Dogmatics*: namely, its Christological concentration, in which is located his more positive exposition of 'history'.

Towards an Apocalyptic Christology

For the Barth of *Der Römerbrief* the logic of 'apocalyptic' too easily becomes a mere metaphysical cipher for what is ultimate and transcendent. As a result, 'Christian apocalyptic' is unable fully to escape the transcendental idealism that Benjamin's Messianic critique of historicism is meant to overcome. *Der Römerbrief* articulates a kind of 'cessation of happening' that is still not yet an entry into the 'fullness' of 'Messianic time', and the kind of concretely lived historicality that Benjamin thinks such a fullness entails. Looking back on *Der Römerbrief*, and particularly his exegesis of Romans 13, in 1940, Barth recognized this failure. In taking this passage as speaking of the eschaton, he had 'actually meant to speak of God and not of a general idea of limit and crisis'. However, he says: 'In spite of every precaution I interpreted it as if it referred only to the moment which confronts all moments in time as the eternal "transcendental meaning" of all moments in time'; the eternal thus became a 'metaphysico-ethical qualification of our moments in time'.[42]

In the *Church Dogmatics*, however, Barth was able to refocus apocalyptic thinking in such a manner as to draw attention to the lived historicality of God's apocalyptic action. The key turning point for Barth is his interpretation of history under the range of 'incarnational Christology' in *Church Dogmatics* IV, as read especially in light of his treatment of creation history in *Church Dogmatics* III. Indeed, as George Hunsinger has shown, it is through the discovery of Chalcedonian Christology

---

42 Barth, CD II/1, p. 635.

that Barth comes to read the history of Jesus of Nazareth as the dramatic *narrative* of the history enacted between God and humanity. And it is as Barth concentrates on the *event* or *history* of Jesus Christ that he discovers the tools necessary to orient all of history towards the eternal being-in-act of God as displayed in the 'two natures' of Christ's person.[43] What Barth feels he has gained by the later volumes of *Church Dogmatics*, via a more robustly Chalcedonian Christology, is the means by which to articulate Christ's *history* as the enactment the 'inner being and essence of God'[44] and thus to explicate the event of God's triune being as an 'eternal decision' *for* the enactment of this history in time. And he explicates this event in such a way as to render this decision according to a certain 'histori-cization' of God's relation to the world in Christ – an inverted Barthian version to be sure, but a 'historicization' nonetheless. 'This is the new form we have given to Christology,' declares Barth,[45] which now allows him to speak of God's action in the world as a 'dramatic' history and not as the mere unfolding of an 'obscure metaphysics'.[46]

What is important for our purposes here is the way in which this Christological 'historicization' is that of a still-discernible apocalyptic 'logic'.[47] We can demonstrate how this is so by way of three key points. In making these points, my primary aim will be to demonstrate how profound is the importance of the concrete historicity of Jesus for the later Barth in safeguarding

---

43 G. Hunsinger, 'Karl Barth's Christology: Its Basic Chalcedon-ian Character', in *The Cambridge Companion to Karl Barth*, ed. John Webster (Cambridge: Cambridge University Press, 2000), pp. 127–42.

44 Barth, CD IV/1, pp. 52–3.

45 Barth, CD IV/1, p. 107.

46 Barth CD IV/3.1, p. 136.

47 On the apocalyptic dimensions of the *Church Dogmatics*, and particularly of CD IV, as in many ways being in continuity with the cen-tral apocalyptic insights of *Der Römerbrief*, I am especially indebted to Harink, *Paul among the Postliberals*, pp. 45–56; cf. J. Mangina, *Karl Barth: Theologian of Christian Witness* (Louisville: Westminster John Knox Press, 2004), pp. 124–9.

the correct understanding of God's apocalyptic action. At the same time, I shall seek to show how profound is the importance of the concrete particularities of our own human histories for recognizing the cosmic-historical significance of God's apocalyptic action in Jesus, as well as for encountering Jesus as 'Lord'.

First, we have in Barth's later Christology the affirmation that a particular, concrete flesh-and-blood history, that of the first-century Jew Jesus of Nazareth,[48] is the *singular enactment* of God's free eternal action, event, and life. With 'the concrete and unique story of Christ',[49] we really have to do with the *actus purus et singularis* by which God's own eternal life – God's Kingdom – occurs as a 'definite happening' in the midst of world history. Furthermore, as the apocalyptic unveiling of God's eternal life (the 'Kingdom of God'), Jesus Christ is not simply the culmination of world-historical 'development', but is a decisive event of its *interruption from without*. This can be seen by the way in which Barth insists upon presenting Jesus Christ as a 'new and special' event in relation to this creation history, an event which cannot in any way be derived or deduced from this 'history' as its 'product' or immanent *telos*.[50] Neither do we any longer only know of God's Kingdom as a 'limit' term which we have come up against, a 'beyond' which we acknowledge from the inside of our world because we have come up to the edge of it and recognized it to be too small. Rather, we know of God's Kingdom because in the flesh and blood of Jesus of Nazareth 'God has reached and spoken into [our world] from beyond'.[51] The Word of God, which still happens as 'the invasion and irruption of the transcendent', now happens as an 'effective realization' of God's Kingdom in history.[52]

---

48 Barth, CD IV/1, p. 166.
49 Barth, CD IV/1, p. 75.
50 Barth, CD IV/1, pp. 50–1.
51 These are the words of John Howard Yoder, but they capture well what Barth is getting at. See Yoder, EE, p. 126.
52 Barth, CD I/2, pp. 801–2.

Second, Barth reads the interruptive event of Jesus' history in terms of a bringing to an end of the 'old', fallen history in its inherent sinfulness and the bringing in of the 'new' as the *transformation* and *establishment* of history in its genuinely positive relation to God's Kingdom. This is an important but oft-misunderstood effect of Barth's 'juridical' reading of the story of Jesus throughout *Church Dogmatics* IV/1, in its narrative movement from cross to resurrection. Importantly, Barth reads the cross as the *judgment* of God upon human history, which then leads him to read the resurrection as the *verdict* of the Father by which human history is re-established in its positive relation to God's eternal actuality. On this reading, Barth can speak of the cross as the 'end' of fallen history as its own autonomous sphere: 'Human history was actually terminated at this point.' At the same time, however, this 'end of history' is revealed through the resurrection to be a *new creation*, as the decision of God by which the 'eternal life' of human beings 'had already become an event'.[53] This is the new creation of which reconciliation speaks: 'that [God] does not allow His history to be His and ours ours, but causes them to take place as a common history'.[54] The apocalyptic event by which God judges autonomous historical action is thus itself the very event by which God establishes genuine human action as a matter of historical 'correspondence' to the eternal being-in-act of God revealed in Jesus Christ.

The key move that Barth has effected here is that of making history a predicate of Jesus Christ himself, rather than allowing Jesus Christ to become or to remain a predicate of 'world history' as objectively and neutrally conceived by modern historicism.[55] That is to say, Jesus Christ's 'person' is not conceivable simply as a determinate product of history's immanental

---

53 Barth, CD IV/1, p. 734.

54 Barth, CD IV/1, p. 7.

55 Thus echoing the theological maxim of *CD* I/1, that, given the character of the Word of God as divine *act*, history is the predicate of revelation, not revelation the predicate of history. See Barth, CD I/1, pp. 143–62.

developmental processes. Instead, the meaning, or truth, of history is predicated upon, and established by, the very way in which God is *in* history in the person of Jesus Christ. Now, history is what it is just insofar as *God acts*, and acts *apocalyptically*, precisely as revealed in the concrete, particular history of Jesus of Nazareth. As such, Jesus Christ is the one 'primal history': a human being is only truly and genuinely granted a history in relation to this history; 'in or with the history enacted in the existence of the man Jesus, a human being really does have a history'.[56] Thus, in *Church Dogmatics* IV/3.1, we find Barth insisting that the history of Jesus Christ is 'not merely *a* history of the usual historical or mythical type, but history in the supreme sense, history in which we have a share whether we realize it or not, history in which our own history takes place'.[57]

It is on these terms that Barth makes the decisive shift to a *cosmic*-historical understanding of Christ's lordship. Jesus is truly 'Lord' of the cosmos, and the Kingdom of God is made effectively present in his historical person, precisely 'as the happening which determines all history and which embraces all other histories'.[58] As such, 'the history of this One is world history':[59] 'there is no one,' Barth insists, whose history is not 'taken up' and 'assumed into fellowship with God' through him.[60]

Third, as the apocalyptic action of God, Jesus is not only confirmed as Lord by capitulating the whole of history in its cosmic relation to God's Kingdom. True as this is, what is important is that he does this in such a way that every single *particular* of human history as it happens 'here and now' is most truly to be understood as itself an event of the cosmic reconciliatory act of the singular history of Jesus of Nazareth as it occurred 'there and then'.[61] The *operatio* of Christ's particular

---

56 Barth, CD III/2, p. 161.
57 Barth, CD IV/3.1, p. 183.
58 Barth, CD IV/3.1, p. 42.
59 Barth, CD IV/2, p. 269.
60 Barth, CD IV/2, pp. 270–1.
61 See Barth, CD IV/3.1, p. 182.

history is such that 'His history takes place in every age'.[62] Yet
Jesus' history only 'operates' in this way as what it is in the
uniqueness of its historicity, as a history 'which actually happened among men like other events and was experienced and
later attested by them'.[63] As such, Christ can only be 'Lord'
of history insofar as our own histories are transformed by
this event in such a way that, precisely in their own happening 'among men like other events', they are taken up into and
made to display the truth of God's apocalyptic action in their
very contingency and particularity. In other words, Jesus' particular history as it occurred 'there and then' 'takes place in
every age', and so *in us and in our histories*, precisely insofar
as our own histories as they occur here and now are made to
take place in him.[64] Only in this way can God's ongoing apocalyptic action in Christ continue to be thought of as *cosmic* and
also *historical*.

The key point being made here is that the historicity of Jesus
Christ as God's apocalyptic act is so unique, so particular, that
there simply cannot be any presupposed 'world-historical' rule
by which to describe it or to explain it. Rather, in *disrupting*
history and *establishing it anew*, this particular act occurs in
such a way that the manifold contingencies of human history
are themselves established in the truth of their particularity
only as they are brought into a lived, concrete relation with the
ongoing presence of *this* event. At the same time, this means
that God's ongoing presence in Christ, properly conceived, is
not a mechanistic operation to be read off from a single isolated occurrence. This presence is instead the happening of an
apocalyptic *operatio* that is mysteriously yet truly coincident
with the ongoing contingency of particular historical events.

To conclude this section, then: Barth has attempted to effect
a shift from an apocalyptic-*metaphysical* perspective in *Der
Römerbrief* to an apocalyptic-*historical* perspective in the

---

62 Barth, CD IV/2, p. 107.
63 Barth, CD I/2, p. 143.
64 Barth, CD IV/2, p. 270.

Church Dogmatics. This shift in apocalyptic has to do with the way in which Barth concentrates on the *event* or *history* of Jesus Christ, which precisely as *this* human history renders the being and act of God present and effective for *all* of history. As Barth wrote in 1956, in an essay meant very much to clarify the issue of 'continuity' in his entire oeuvre: 'Since God in his deity is human,' theology now 'must occupy itself neither with God in Himself nor with man in himself but with the man-encountering God and the God-encountering man and with their dialogue and history'.[65] And this, of course, represents the genius of Barth's mature Christology and its importance both for the modern 'crisis of historicism' generally and for the constructive aim of this study in particular: the apocalyptic action of God occurs and is encountered in and as *history*, and yet for all that it is no less the action *of God*, the one, free, decisive 'self-intervention of God'[66] by which God inaugurates God's Kingdom and establishes Jesus Christ as the Lord of all times. This, finally, is what qualifies Barth's doctrine of reconciliation as the development (in outline) of an 'apocalyptic Christology'.

History in the Shadow of the Risen Christ: A Twofold Abstraction

The previous section sought to exploit certain of those developments for the purpose of establishing in a preliminary way the rudiments of an 'apocalyptic Christology'. At this point, however, I want to raise the crucial question concerning the materially historicist outworking of this formal 'apocalyptic Christology'. Given that God's reign has broken into history in the particular life history of Jesus of Nazareth, just how is it that we are to *read* this life history, such that it does not abstract from or overrule the contingencies and particularities of

---

65 K. Barth, 'The Humanity of God', tr. John Newton Thomas, in *The Humanity of God* (Richmond: John Knox Press, 1960), pp. 37–65, p. 55.

66 Barth, CD IV/1, p. 55.

ongoing history, but rather gives way to their reality and truth qua contingent and particular?

In this section I want to begin exploring this question by shifting my analysis once again to the critical register, in analysing the way in which Barth's actualist metaphysics 'ontologizes' history as determined by his understanding of Christ's resurrection. For Barth, it is in the resurrection of Jesus that we have the act of God displayed as 'the coming of the kingdom, the fulfillment of the lordship of God in earth'.[67] So it is with the resurrection that, for the purposes of this study, we come to the all-important issue. For here Barth addresses head-on the problem which we have put forward as the motive force for any genuine politics of Christian mission today: namely, the problem of how Jesus Christ is effectively Lord, not in relation to some autonomous religious sphere, but as the reality, meaning, truth of the world and of history, in a way that is at once both cosmic and yet particularly historical. And here, I shall argue, is where Barth fails us. For in stressing the resurrection in the manner that he does, Barth does not properly address, but rather *by-passes*, the problem of modern historicism when it comes to conceiving of Christ's lordship and of the nature of the presence of the Kingdom.

This by-passing of the problem of historicity is actually a negative side effect of Barth's actualist ontology and of the way in which he allows this ontology to determine his Christology and his account of Christ's relation to history at certain critical points. Barth's 'actualism', particularly as it frames his understanding of the resurrection, makes of God's action in Christ an event of history precisely as it maps that history onto a privileged ontological framework, which is part and parcel of a privileged metaphysics of eternity. As a result, Barth identifies Jesus with God's being-in-act in such a way as to effect a twofold abstraction from the *contingent* reality of Jesus' historicity and of ours. Let me explain what I mean here, for my whole criticism reduces to this one point, even if other points can and should be made.

---

67 Barth, CD IV/2, p. 204.

In his magisterial study of Barth's architectonic, George Hunsinger foregrounds the 'motif of actualism' as basic to Barth's whole theology.[68] Hunsinger does this by stressing the sense in which Barth's actualism is a kind of ontological claim which requires thinking of God's being 'primarily in terms of events and relationships rather than monadic or self-contained substances'.[69] Actualism is a way of thinking the transcendence and freedom of God as itself an *event*, one which affirms the ultimacy of temporal categories in giving primacy to God's eternal being-in-act.[70] Therefore, as God's being is itself always a being-in-act, an event which has its own 'temporal' quality, our relation to God necessarily occurs as a temporal *event*, a relation constituted by an ongoing history of correspondence to God's own being-in-act.[71] So Barth's actualism is in fact a kind of strategy for resolving the time-eternity tension, and the problem of 'history', by positing 'duration' as inwardly the principle of God's eternity, and by positing 'time' as the 'formal principle' of God's 'free activity outwards'.[72]

The point here is that we misunderstand the function of Barth's actualism in his thought if we fail to see that it is a strategy for affirming the *historical* nature of God's action as also a means of revealing all of temporal history, and the 'freedom' with which God relates to it, to be externally 'determined' by the inward 'duration' that is God's eternity; 'time' itself becomes a 'formal principle' of God's eternal being-in-act. And the suspicion here is that, inversely, the so-called 'events' of history, as temporal occurrences, are themselves conceived as related to God by way of a 'formal'-ontological construct, rather than by way of their being bound up in the limits and relativities of history.

There is clearly a (Hegel-inspired) idealist residue here, and

---

68 George Hunsinger, *How to Read Karl Barth: The Shape of His Theology* (Oxford: Oxford University Press, 1991), pp. 30–2, 67–70.

69 Hunsinger, *How to Read*, p. 30.

70 See Barth, CD II/1, pp. 609–10.

71 Hunsinger, *How to Read*, pp. 67–8.

72 Barth, CD II/1, p. 609.

we can see this in the way in which Barth's actualism leads him to articulate his theology of history in a conceptually 'dualistic' manner. On the one hand, there is that 'primal' history or *Urgeschichte* by which God's triune being is 'historical even in its eternity'.[73] God's eternal being-in-act is history in its *supra*-temporal dimension, the 'simultaneity of beginning, middle and end' – of past, present, and future – and thus 'pure duration'.[74] On the other hand, there is 'secondary' history, or human world history, which represents history in its 'temporal' dimension; it is 'the one-way sequence and therefore succession and division of past, present, and future; of once, now, and then; of the beginning, middle and end; of origin, movement and goal'.[75] 'History' in its two dimensions occurs as the coincidence or 'correspondence' of humanity's 'time' with God's 'eternity', such that each moment of human temporality in its contingency and passing can be seen for what it truly is, namely, as determined in its being by the 'simultaneity' of God's own eternal history.

It is hard to imagine what this might mean within Barth's actualist framework, if not that each moment of time has been abstracted from its 'contingency' and 'flux' and rendered 'historical' by way of its 'simultaneity' with what is eternally given. The suspicion I am raising here is that the complexities, tragic discontinuities, and broken 'pathways' of fragile human history are eschewed and evaded with respect to what occurs and has been actualized as 'eternal history'. It seems as if Barth's ontology of action has to do here with a kind of 'transtemporalization',[76] according to which the truth of human history lies fundamentally in the *knowledge* of our own eternally actualized situation before God.

These suspicions about Barth's actualism are borne out and

---

73 Barth, CD III/1, p. 66.
74 Barth, CD II/1, p. 608.
75 Barth, CD III/1, pp. 67–8.
76 See D. Ford, *Barth and God's Story: Narrative and the Theological Method of Karl Barth in the Church Dogmatics* (Frankfurt: Verlag Peter Lang, 1981), p. 166.

brought into relief by the way in which Barth treats the person of Jesus Christ as determining history in relation to God's eternity. When Barth moves to consider the person of Jesus of Nazareth as that one in whom human history concretely corresponds to the *Urgeschichte* within God, it is above all to the forty days of the resurrection appearances that Barth turns.[77] What is problematic, from my perspective, is the way in which this *urgeschichtlich* characterization of the resurrection has the effect of claiming an ontological 'completeness' for Jesus of Nazareth's identity which abstracts from its inherent historical contingency and unresolved narrative limitations, in such a way as to treat Jesus' history as a mere 'representation' in time of an already 'achieved', or 'actualized', eternal metaphysical reality.

Let me expound this with respect to Barth's mature Christology. For all Barth's attention to the concrete and particular 'history' of Jesus in the later volumes of the *Church Dogmatics*, when it comes to elaborating the 'identity' of Jesus as manifest in the forty days of Jesus' resurrection appearances, one witnesses a clear shift in focus away from what happens in, to, and for Jesus in his own human historicity (his 'narrative' identity) to the question of Jesus' 'direct origin in God's eternal election, decision and act' (his 'ontological' identity).[78] What this means is that, when it comes to delineating Christ's identity as determinative of history, Barth privileges the *ontological* characterization of Christ's person as determined according to the metaphysically actualized 'unity' of the *naturam humanum* with God as a 'completed work'.[79] In the resurrection, the truth of the doctrine of the two natures – namely, that in Jesus Christ 'the divine acquires a determination to the human, and the human a determination to the divine'[80] – is revealed as the

---

77 Barth, CD IV/1, p. 301; Barth, CD IV/3.1, pp. 40, 42; cf. Barth, CD III/2, p. 449.

78 See Barth, CD IV/3.1, p. 227. See Paul McGlasson, *Jesus and Judas: Biblical Exegesis in Barth* (Atlanta: Scholars Press, 1991), pp. 49–64.

79 Barth, CD IV/2, pp. 140–1.

80 Barth, CD IV/2, p. 70.

completion in time of God's own *Urgeschichte*. 'He was on earth as God was in heaven'[81] – and this means, simply, that God's being-in-act has been enacted in time, in the movement from Bethlehem to Golgotha – as in a way *identical* with what 'is' from all eternity.

This is not to say that Barth does not devote significant time and space in *Church Dogmatics* IV to Christ's 'narrative' identity as a real human, temporal, and historical happening and that what happens in the years AD 1–30 is not somehow integral to 'who' Jesus is. But it is telling that Barth insists that such history can now only be recounted as it is refracted through the resurrection as the revelation of this history's correspondence to what has already been achieved in God's eternity.[82] Barth's extended narrations of Jesus' movement from Bethlehem to Golgotha thus return again and again to what can be said concerning that which is always-already *ontologically* the case for Barth, namely, the 'eternalizing' of this movement as a completed 'history'. Such 'eternalizing' is determined in advance by Barth's actualist ontology and fits perfectly with what Barth means by his earlier definition of revelation as the *repetitio aeternitatis in aeternitate*, a 'temporal' recapitulation of what God *eternally* 'is' 'in eternity'.[83] By insisting, then, that in the resurrection Jesus is known *as* the revelation of God, Barth ensures what we have come to suspect, namely, that the history of Jesus of Nazareth can only make known what is antecedently actualized from all eternity.[84]

The problem here, as I see it, is that Barth's handling of the resurrection abstracts from the contingencies, complexities, and particularities of Jesus of Nazareth's historicity as constitutive of his *human*-historical 'identity'. This is apparent, for

---

81 Barth, CD IV/2, p. 184.

82 See D. Farrow, *Ascension and Ecclesia: On the Significance of the Doctrine of Ascension* (Grand Rapids: Eerdmans, 1999), p. 234.

83 See Barth, CD I/1, pp. 348–83.

84 On this point, see especially Jacques de Senarclen, 'La concentration christologique', in *Antwort: Karl Burt zum siebzigsten Geburtstag* (Zurich: Zollikon, 1956), pp. 190–207.

example, as Colin Gunton has shown, in the way in which the *enhypostasia* determines Barth's narration of Christ's humanity throughout, such that certain episodes in Jesus' story which depict his free *human* activity are overshadowed by an emphasis upon the 'humanity *of God*'.[85] This can be seen especially in §64 of *Church Dogmatics* IV/2, 'The Exaltation of the Son of Man', where Barth's most thoroughgoing retelling of Jesus' life-story coincides with his most rigorous defence of the Chalcedonian definition and the hypostatic union. On the surface, this reads as if Barth is attempting to describe the relations of the two natures in the most historicist manner possible, according to the working out in time of this particular life in this particular historical, political, economic, and religious context. Yet conspicuous by its almost complete absence is any reference at all to the tragic complexities and discontinuities of this life, such as Jesus' temptation in the desert, his agony at Gethsemane, and the freedom with which he goes to Jerusalem, all of which shape his identity as distinctively *human* and *limited* by that humanity. The tendency throughout this entire section, rather, is for Barth to reduce Jesus' human life to a series of episodes that illuminate (or 'represent') the eternal co-enactment of the two natures of God and humanity, the 'common actualization of the divine and human essence', the 'ontological connection' between God and human beings.[86] In his recounting of Jesus' history, then, Barth seems to deploy narrative as simply a tool for 'describing' a given (even if

---

85   See C. Gunton, *Christ and Creation* (Carlisle: Paternoster Press, 1992), pp. 45–69 (emphasis added). Cf. T. F. Torrance's suspicion of a lingering 'docetism' in Barth's account of the risen and ascended Christ, in which he suggests that for Barth the ascended Jesus 'seemed to be swallowed up in the transcendent Light and Spirit of God, so that the humanity of the risen Jesus appeared to be displaced by what he called the 'humanity of God' in his turning toward us'. T. F. Torrance, *Karl Barth: Biblical and Evangelical Theologian* (Edinburgh: T. & T. Clark, 1990), p. 134. Henri Bouillard accuses Barth of a '*monoactualisme*' here, the actualist equivalent of monophysitism. H. Bouillard, *Karl Barth*, vol. 2 (Paris: Aubier, Editions Montaigne, 1957), p. 130.

86   Barth, CD IV/2, pp. 113, 280–2.

'achieved') ontological reality, and Chalcedon functions as a kind of 'strategic' hermeneutical device which allows for the narrative to be so read.[87]

The point in all of this remains simply that a preconceived ontological fact (the union of divinity and humanity) determined according to an assumed actualist metaphysics, and *not* the concrete working out of the complex specificities and particularities of this human historicity, is what determines the narration of Jesus' 'identity' as divine for Barth. The 'character' which such narration displays thus turns out to be that of a general *naturam humanum* transcendentally related to the a priori freedom (being-in-act) of God, such that this character is conceivable in abstraction from this *singular* human being's involvement in the limits and relativities of histories. Thus, the ontologically achieved relation of humanity to divinity in the person of Jesus Christ now appears transcendentally to 'characterize' all of human life in any given historical context, no matter where.[88] The real problem that arises in all of this, then, is that in failing to account fully for the contingencies and complexities of Jesus' human historicity in the rendering of his identity as God, Barth is unable to portray Christ's living *presence* to humanity in a way that does not on some level abstract from the *ongoing* contingencies and complexities of 'history' itself.

Let me illustrate this point by describing how this ontological 'closure' of Jesus' identity effects not only a loss of attention to the particularities and contingencies of Jesus' history but also a loss of attention to our own. It needs to be stressed here before all else that Barth's use of the concept of eternity in relation to the resurrection serves the purpose of presenting Jesus' 'completed' history as 'universal' and so as de facto 'inclusive' of all history as such. In this way, as Rowan Williams has noted, Barth's accounting of Jesus' history is most clearly in line with the Hegelian concern to objectify Christ as representative of the

87 Cf. Hunsinger, 'Karl Barth's Christology', pp. 128, 140n. 4.
88 Ford, *Barth and God's Story*, p. 169.

'concrete universal'.[89] Barth's treatment of Jesus' history thus reveals a certain obsession with the perennial idealist concern to establish 'history' as the mediating link between the particular and universal, with the added dimension that *Christ himself* becomes that 'link' – 'Christ' is now 'identifiable' precisely as the 'one and universal' history. For Barth, then, to read the cross – Jesus' movement from Bethlehem to Golgotha – in light of the resurrection is to read the history of Jesus Christ from the outset in terms of the universal *presence* of Christ to all history. The primary impetus for tying Jesus' history so closely to the eternally actualized *Urgeschichte* of God is to render Christ's universal 'contemporaneity' to all times and all places. It is Christ's 'universal presence' that is in fact the pre-eminent sign of Jesus' completed ontological 'identity' – so much so that Barth risks making our own relation to Jesus' ontological identity a mere function of his noetic presence to us.

However (and herein lies the crux of the matter), whereas Barth finds it necessary, in order for Christ to be made present to all of history in his particularity, to think Jesus' historicity as corresponding to an always-already actualized eternal reality, so it is also that our history is made contemporary with Christ's as our own particularity is conceived in terms of 'an actuality which is already behind us'.[90] This is why Barth must insist so relentlessly upon the 'completed' nature of Jesus' history on the 'side' of AD 1–30, such that Jesus' history after the resurrection is by no means to be 'augmented by new qualities or further developments'.[91] Barth's actualist ontology demands it, if in fact our situatedness within Jesus' history is going to remain bound up with Jesus Christ's own particular relation to God. But all this means that, within this same actualist framework, while the resurrection brings closure to Jesus' history, so also does it bring with it the very foreclosure of all history qua 'history', in its *geschichtlich* dimensions – we

89 See R. Williams, 'Barth on the Triune God', in *Karl Barth: Studies of his Theological Method*, pp. 147–93, p. 188.
90 Barth, CD IV/2, p. 46.
91 Barth, CD IV/2, p. 132.

are left with bare 'facts' (*Historische*). Indeed, world history now runs on as the working out of what is already actualized in Jesus Christ, in a manner analogous to Jesus' own working out of what is already actualized in the divine *Urgeschichte*. 'The last time is the time of the world and human history and all men to which a term is already set in the death of Jesus and which can only run to this appointed end.'[92]

Here we have to do with Barth's puzzling suggestion that the time of the resurrection is the time of the *parousia*, which for Barth means that the time of God's Kingdom has been made contemporaneous with all human beings in their own times as the time of 'his manifestation of effective presence in the world'.[93] What has occurred here is that with the doctrine of resurrection Barth has reintroduced the notion of Christ's eternal presence (*parousia*) as a way of relating us in our histories to a kind of transcendent ideal – the eternity of God. Thus, when Barth turns in *Church Dogmatics* IV/3 to consider 'The Vocation of Man', that event by which the particular human being is revealed to be in concrete relation with Jesus Christ in her own time, Barth speaks in terms of the human being's coming to awareness of her 'origin in eternal life' and of her history as 'controlled and determined' by the history of Jesus Christ and itself rooted in 'God's eternal election of grace'.[94] Certainly, with regard to this 'eternal election', we must say 'history' goes on, but in its *historicity* – in its contingencies and complexities – human history itself now takes on a kind of epiphenomenal character in relation to the always-already realized *Urgeschichte* of God's being-in-act. It is, at any rate, a mere 'postscript'.[95]

So to sum up: by reading history through the lens of the forty days of Christ's resurrection appearances, as determined by his actualist ontology, Barth has effected a twofold metaphysical abstraction with respect to Jesus' history and to ours.

92 Barth, CD IV/3.1, p. 295.
93 Barth, CD IV/3.1, p. 293. Cf. Barth, CD IV/1, p. 316.
94 Barth, CD IV/3.2, p. 500.
95 Barth, CD IV/3.2, pp. 736–7.

First, Barth frames the question of Christ's 'identity' in such a manner that it is ontologically determined in abstraction from the contingencies and complexities of Jesus' historicity. Second, Barth develops this ontological identity for the purpose of elaborating the nature of Christ's 'universal presence' and 'eternalizes' the question of this presence in such a way as to generalize about ongoing history's direction and flow by making it a function of Christ's *parousia*, conceived in terms of a kind of an already-achieved 'end'. Barth thus conceives of Christ's ontological identity in such a way as to abstract from the contingencies and complexities of ongoing history as themselves constitutive of our relationship to Jesus and to God, as well as to reinscribe a certain teleo-eschatological (and 'pan-historical') goal as the means by which 'Jesus' is finally determinative of history's movement and direction. In the end, Barth's actualism submits his 'apocalyptic Christology' to that which, as we noted in the previous section, it was meant to overcome, namely, the unfolding of a certain 'obscure metaphysics'.

* * *

We began this chapter by arguing that certain metaphysical presuppositions prevented the early Barth of *Der Römerbrief* from deploying apocalyptic as a matter of reading history as oriented positively to God's Kingdom on the basis of Christ's dawning reign *within* and *amidst* history's contingencies and particularities. Now here, in the end, we find that the later Barth cannot fully carry out an 'apocalyptic' *historicization* of Christ's own history and of ours, inasmuch as certain prior ontologico-metaphysical commitments leave him unable to consider the inbreaking of God's reign in Christ in its concrete *historicity*. And so apocalyptic categories are deployed in a tropological manner, for the sake of 'emplotting' history according to a privileged actualist framework.

Therefore, while we must admit, finally, that in his loyalty to an actualist Christology, Barth has indeed struck a great blow to a certain kind of methodological historicism that regards the telos of history according to the inductive working out of immanental developments, we must also admit that, in doing so, he has bruised his own theological heel. One could say that Barth's problem lies precisely at the point of his greatest strength. The *identity* of Jesus' particular history with God's eternal being-in-act has been stressed so strongly that Jesus-history has been generalized to the point of ontological abstraction. The more Barth focuses upon the resurrection as revelatory of Christ's history and ours, the more Barth relies upon the idealist residue that this actualist ontology provides. As such, Barth tends to elevate Christ as Lord above the messy complexities of history, making his lordship over history and the presence of God's Kingdom the result of a transhistorical and still pre-temporal transaction within the eternal Godhead. In thus making his end-run around the question of historicity in the name of dogmatic and ontological faithfulness, Barth comes to think of the Kingdom of God and of Christ's presence as 'Lord' in no less a transcendental (and ideological) manner than that of modern historicism, with its subjective 'psychologizing' of Christ and his Kingdom.

And as such, the proclamation of Christ's lordship in the world has very little to do with the hard core of real history, the tragic contradictions and intricate complexities of history's broken pathways, but has much to do with the totalizing and unifying of certain privileged horizons of meaning. If, in contrast, we are to think of Barth's apocalyptic Christology as providing a genuinely cosmic-historical conception of Christ's lordship, it will be necessary to expound such lordship otherwise than as an 'ontologically achieved' *given*, which achievement Jesus' presence in and to history now 'represents' as 'finished' or 'fixed'. Rather, it will be necessary to conceive such lordship more dynamically as that which is to be lived and enacted within the manifest complexities and contingencies of history, because of the way in which it has been received (and given) as *gift* in the specific historicity of this single human being, Jesus of Nazareth.

Conclusion

So where then does all this leave us with respect to the question of 'Christ, history, and apocalyptic'? Certainly, with Barth I claim to have found in Jesus Christ the interruption and 'end' of 'history' as a mere process of immanental development. And with Barth I have argued that with this interruption we really have to do with the inauguration of God's eschatological Kingdom, an apocalyptic inbreaking which resituates history in terms of the 'already' and the 'not yet' of this Kingdom's simultaneously immanent and transcendent reality. And yet I have maintained that we cannot rest content to locate the truth of these claims in some sort of alternative, idealist metaphysics of history (vis-à-vis that of Troeltsch) that is oriented toward a Christ conceived in terms of his abstract 'character' as God's being-in-act. To an extent, Troeltsch is exactly right: the truth of Christ's apocalyptic relation to history is not to be found in Jesus just because we claim that he is the Logos by which God created the world or that through the incarnation he took on sinful flesh or that his resurrection has made him Lord of the cosmos by means of his ongoing presence in history. As essential as these basic convictions are, in themselves they are just empty concepts which function for humanity as (ideological) sources of transcendent meaning.

Rather, the truth of Christ's apocalyptic relation to history is the concrete life of the peasant Jew from Nazareth on the basis of whose very *historicity* we come to confess Jesus as God's Son and Lord. If then, in contrast to the later Barth, I refuse to conceive of Jesus' history (and of the particularities of the events of AD 1–30) merely in terms of its general ontological significance, it is because I want to argue all the more thoroughly this point that Jesus in his very historicity is Lord, that the resurrection, ascension, and *parousia* have really to do with the *ongoing* and living enactment of Jesus' historicity within the complexities and contingencies of history, and that in his very historicity Jesus *gives himself* to being involved in very different circumstances associated with the realities of history as such. As such, this would be a way of saying that Christ is made to be Lord precisely *in* the flux and contingency of history, and that it is *through* such flux and contingency that we are made to be 'contemporaneous' with him, as we in our historicities are brought into conformity with the truth of Jesus' own 'apocalyptic historicity'.

And here we come to the upshot of this chapter and to the importance of Barth for the genealogy I am tracing and for this book as a whole. The centre of this chapter has been an analysis of the conceptual development and theoretical 'historical' outworking of Barth's own 'apocalyptic Christology'. And yet, as surely as Barth's apocalyptic Christology provides an indispensable framework for conceiving Christ's relation to history in apocalyptic terms, it points up the need to work out that relationship even more narrowly in terms of concrete *historicity*. In other words, if Barth's conceptualization of a lived, apocalyptic historicality (his own peculiar version of Benjamin's 'Messianic time') is going to give way to the concreteness of an altogether different kind of subversive political *action* – then we will need to push beyond Barth's 'actualism' and towards an even more 'historicist' account of the nature of God's apocalyptic reign in Christ. That is to say, Barth's apocalyptic Christology will need even more explicitly to become, in its material outworking, an apocalyptic *historicism*.

I shall be seeking to expound (with the help of John Howard Yoder) such an apocalyptic historicism in Chapter 5 below, as the basis for articulating the kind of concrete, apocalyptic politics of mission this book is calling for. Before doing so, however, it will be necessary to grapple with the ecclesiological and political implications of Barth's actualist Christology and with one thinker's attempt to supplement Barth's apocalyptic vision in a more robustly 'ecclesiological' and 'political' manner. And so we turn to the work of Stanley Hauerwas.

4

Stanley Hauerwas: Apocalyptic, Narrative Ecclesiology, and 'The Limits of Anti-Constantinianism'

The present chapter will focus upon the supplementation of Barth's apocalyptic Christology by what has come to be known in contemporary theology as 'narrative ecclesiology', particularly as developed in the work of Stanley Hauerwas. My analysis will focus upon the way in which Hauerwas's ecclesiology deploys the logic of apocalyptic for the sake of developing a conception of the church as an alternative *polis* in opposition to modern political liberalism and its Constantinian assumptions. My primary argument will be that, in shifting the doctrinal locus of apocalyptic from Christology to ecclesiology, Hauerwas articulates a 'community-dependent' understanding of Christ's person that is reductive of Jesus' historicity or 'independence' as a singular event of God's apocalyptic action. Having made this argument, I shall suggest that this shift is determined from the outset by Hauerwas's anti-liberal agenda and that his concern to secure a certain fixed narrative and linguistic 'identity' for the church forces him into a structurally imperialistic and functionally 'ideological' articulation of the church's political and missionary existence in the world. This will set the backdrop for assessing the distinctiveness of John Howard Yoder's own more historicist, though no less ecclesial and political, supplementation of Barthian apocalyptic in the final two chapters.

With and beyond Barth against Liberalism

Though Hauerwas's many descriptions of 'liberalism' and 'liberal political theory' are rather complex and nuanced throughout his work, he does provide a helpful orienting definition in the Introduction to *Against the Nations*, his most sustained book-length consideration of the 'liberal society':

> In the most general terms I understand liberalism to be that impulse deriving from the Enlightenment project to free all people from the chains of their historical particularity in the name of freedom. As an epistemological position liberalism is the attempt to defend a foundationalism in order to free reason from being determined by any particularistic tradition. Politically liberalism makes the individual the supreme unit of society, thus making the political task the securing of cooperation between arbitrary units of desire. While there is no strict logical entailment between these forms of liberalism I think it can be said they often are interrelated.[1]

While a full analysis of political liberalism is beyond the scope of this book, this passage allows us to isolate three interrelated points at which Hauerwas wishes to speak 'against liberalism'. First, Hauerwas is concerned to indict liberalism as a *political theory*. Liberalism can operate politically only by abstracting from particular communities, traditions, and narratives and appealing to extrinsic, universalized, and rationalized conceptions of what it means to be human. Yet precisely thereby liberalism is forced to attribute to the state and civil society a hegemony they are not meant to have.[2] Liberalism concedes to the state an imperialistic and totalitarian power: as the state is the objective arbiter of universality, so the state alone is the given condition of power according to which 'politics' might be conceived.

Second, liberalism is bound up with a faulty view of *history*.

---

1 Hauerwas, AN, p. 18.
2 Hauerwas, AN, pp. 61–106.

Because liberalism understands the meaning of history as determined for human individuals at a level of 'universal' progress abstracted from the narrative particularity of a given embodied community, the human agent is forced to 'act' historically at this level of abstraction, on the basis of a will freed from any necessary recourse to the language and practices of that particular community.[3]

Third, liberalism speciously appeals to an a priori religious universal dimension which can yet be theorized and described in distinction from its socio-political import.[4] Hauerwas attributes this especially to a gnostic sensibility, which he traces to a docetic understanding of the person of Jesus in theological liberalism. The key point at which Hauerwas thus critiques thinkers such as Troeltsch and the brothers Niebuhr is in their insistence that the message of Jesus and early Christianity was purely religious and lacking any socio-political ethic in itself. Since liberal theology conceives of Christianity (and especially the relation of history to Jesus Christ) essentially in terms of a religious dimension which can be rendered in abstraction from any distinctive social ethic, Hauerwas believes that the Christian community or church becomes in such an environment merely an institution which serves as an ideological resource for given social and economic powers.[5]

We might sum up these three points of critique by indicating that Hauerwas's main hostility to political liberalism is fundamentally related to what he understands as *theological liberalism's unwillingness to read history through Christology*. For such an unwillingness disallows any understanding of the church as a sustained socio-political option in its own right, which through the practices of 'discipleship' provides a place to stand vis-à-vis the 'Constantinian' economic, state, and military powers that dominate history. It is at *this* point that Hauerwas ultimately wants to speak 'with and beyond'

---

3 Hauerwas, WW, pp. 32–47, 62–81; cf. Hauerwas, CC, pp. 111–28.

4 See Hauerwas, BH, pp. 55–69.

5 See Hauerwas, WW, pp. 48–61.

Barth against liberalism. For what is important about Barth's work, for Hauerwas, is not only that he provides an account of history as Christologically disciplined (which is the point at which Hauerwas wants to speak *with* Barth), but that he does so in such a way as to indicate the necessity of the recovery of the church's life as its own distinctive socio-political option (which is the point at which Hauerwas finds it necessary to go *beyond* Barth).

Hauerwas makes essentially two points with respect to Barth here. First, to speak of Christ's lordship over all of temporal life as Barth does means that no account of Christ's relationship to history can be intelligible without a robust account of the church's embodied witness to that lordship. And second, to attend to this necessity is to become aware of the fact that Barth's ecclesiology is not sufficient to display the robust socio-political implications of Christ's lordship in opposition to the politics of modern liberalism. Let me take up each of these points in turn.

The first point is important insofar as it provides a point of departure for considering Hauerwas's more significant criticisms of Barth's ecclesiology. In his Gifford lectures, Hauerwas offers a significantly nuanced but largely favourable treatment of the centrality of the concept of *witness* to Barth's theology as a whole and particularly to his Christology and his understanding of the church.[6] At the outset of this treatment, Hauerwas provides a wonderful genealogical account of Barth's emergence from and rejection of Protestant liberalism, in which he demonstrates, among other things, how Barth learned to wrest history from the hands of the modern historicists by coming to read the history of Jesus Christ's life, death, and resurrection in such a way that all of time and history could be said to have its origin and content in the particular history of God's relation with humanity that is there displayed.[7] Furthermore, as Hauerwas reads Barth, the 'truth' of Christ's lordship for

6 Hauerwas, WGU, pp. 141–204.
7 Hauerwas, WGU, pp. 164n. 50, 178–9.

history is thus not some universal that can be systematically 'considered' and abstractly 'described'.[8] Rather, it can only be performatively 'proclaimed', demonstrated in its 'telling'[9] – that is, it must be *witnessed to* in history.

The ecclesiological upshot of this is that the church is *constituted* by this very proclamation. In the important §72 of *Church Dogmatics* IV/3, Barth accounts for the main task of the church in terms of such (missionary) 'witness', which he notes as 'the sum of what the Christian community has to render'.[10] The point of departure for determining this witness is 'the new reality of world history' that is the decisive and final judgment and act of God rendered manifest in the cross and resurrection of Jesus Christ.[11] In this sense, a missionary ecclesiology of witness is the natural correlate of a robust apocalyptic Christology. What this means is that on the basis of the apocalyptic refiguration of all of history in Christ, the church is given an existence which is rooted in nothing other than the free action of God.[12] As such, the church is liberated from the need to secure and maintain its existence in history through correspondence to and compromise with the given 'powers' of this world and is free to proclaim the reality of the Kingdom of God, to witness to the lordship of God established in the world in Jesus Christ.[13] For Barth, the church just *is* as it is constituted by God in its witness to God's Kingdom as defined by Christ's lordship over history.

By nature of the fact, however, it follows for Hauerwas that the obverse must be true: Christ's lordship, and the account of history that is disciplined thereby, is not only unintelligible and unknowable but also *untrue* apart from the church's existence as the community of witness in the world. It is here that Hauerwas makes his second, critical point with regards to

---

8 Barth, CD II/2, p. 188. Cited in Hauerwas, WGU, p. 180.
9 Hauerwas, WGU, pp. 180–1.
10 Barth, CD IV/3.2, p. 843.
11 Barth, CD IV/3.2, p. 712.
12 See Barth, CD II/1, p. 20.
13 Barth, CD IV/2, pp. 655–6.

Barth's ecclesiology. For while Barth's apocalyptically Christo-centric point of departure reestablishes witness as the basis of the church's existence in the world, it yet 'remains an open question whether or not Barth's ecclesiology is sufficient to sustain the witness he thought was intrinsic to Christian-ity'.[14] The problem is that of the church's own participation in and determination of the truth of Christ's apocalyptic reality. As Hauerwas puts it: 'Barth, of course, does not deny that the church is constituted by the proclamation of the gospel. What he cannot acknowledge is that the community called the church is constitutive of gospel proclamation.'[15] Given Barth's well-known comment that 'the world would not necessarily be lost if there were no Church',[16] Hauerwas concludes that it is 'by no means clear what difference the church makes for how we understand the way the world is and, given the way the world is, how we must live'.[17]

It is important to understand the *socio-political* import of this critique. For Hauerwas, Barth defines the church in such a way that it 'is' (in its essence) and is comprehensible apart from its human-historical visibility. As such, Barth loses the *historical concreteness* of the church as a political community the empirical shape of which matters decisively for its witness to Christ. The political significance of the visible church is of ancillary significance to its primary task of witness. The point here is that what distinguishes the church as the event of witness grounded solely in the being-in-act of God no longer clear-ly distinguishes the church as a counter-social and counter-political reality. If the empirical socio-political existence of the church – as a visible cultural-linguistic configuration of practices, doctrines, and beliefs – is not really *constitutive* of its witness, then it is not clear that this witness can be lived, and lived well, vis-à-vis the political, economic, and cultur-al forces that make up modern liberalism. In other words, if

---

14 Hauerwas, WGU, p. 39.
15 Hauerwas, WGU, p. 145.
16 Barth, CD IV/3.2, p. 826.
17 Hauerwas, WGU, p. 193.

what makes the church's witness distinctive is not its ownmost counter-political existence, then the church as a political reality in fact cannot help but be determined by these liberal forces.

Interestingly, Hauerwas traces these concerns back to a concern with Barth's actualism as determinative of the Christian life and witness. In an early essay,[18] Hauerwas expresses the suspicion that Barth's concern to reassert the freedom and prevenience of God's gracious action issues in a command ethics that segregates God's Word in Christ from the church and that inadvertently privileges the individual human consciousness over the political community as the site of Christian ethical reflection. Barth's theology of the Word, grounded as it is in his actualism, engenders a kind of idealistic theology in which engagement with the transcendent Word theoretically occurs in abstraction from the practices of the Church.[19] The irony here is that Barth's apocalyptic understanding of the Kingdom of God as Christ's lordship over history subverts the anthropocentric historicism of liberalism in such a way as to make his ethics and politics susceptible to that 'individualistic interpretation that his theological program is meant to counter'.[20] Within the conception of witness that Barth develops, Jesus Christ appears as Lord at a transcendental, Kantian level rather than at a robustly communal and political one. This meant that Barth's command ethics retained the docetic tendency of liberalism to 'verticalize' one's relationship to Christ on the basis of God's free action, the temporality of which action cannot in any way be confused with that power and agency we experience as humans in the world.[21]

---

18 Hauerwas, DFF, pp. 58–79.

19 See J. Thomson, *The Ecclesiology of Stanley Hauerwas: A Christian Theology of Liberation* (Aldershot: Ashgate, 2003), pp. 98–101.

20 Hauerwas, DFF, p. 79. Cf. the assessment of Stephen Sykes that Barth's actualism ironically represents the apotheosis of liberal subjectivism and interiority in ethics. S. Sykes, *The Identity of Christianity: Theologians and the Essence of Christianity from Schleiermacher to Barth* (Philadelphia: Fortress Press, 1984), p. 193.

21 Hauerwas, DFF, p. 60. See also Hauerwas, CCL, pp. 177–8.

William Werpehowski has noted that Hauerwas explicates this failure in terms of Barth's inability to express the ethical and political self 'as shaped through history'.[22] This is because the conception of Christ's lordship as rooted in God's pure being-in-act leaves Barth unable to explicate the meaning and truth of Christ's lordship as a political reality that is to be worked out in the contingencies of concrete historical life.[23] Here we see the importance of Hauerwas's critique of Barth's ecclesiology in relation to my critique of Barth's actualism and of his actualist Christology in the previous chapter. That is, Barth's apocalyptic anti-historicism succumbs ultimately to an idealism of historical abstraction in relation not only to Christology but also to ecclesiology. Just as Barth's apocalyptic Christology does an end-run around the problems of modern historicism, so his ecclesiology of witness does an end-run around the political ideology of modern liberalism. These two failures are inextricably bound up with one another. For if Christ is Lord and God's Kingdom is present to history at a fundamentally transhistorical and metaphysical level, then the 'witness' of the church is left to be determined in a way that is other than 'historical'. And so Barth's failure to counter the hegemony of political liberalism is of a piece with his inability to provide a genuine counter-historicism in response to the modern 'crisis of historicism'.

Alternatively, Hauerwas thinks that the condition for overcoming this failure is found in attention to the embodied Christian community and the assertion of its distinctive narrative and historical identity, by means of which the truth of Jesus as the Christ and Lord of history is not only proclaimed but also *constituted* and *enacted* as such. It is at this point that Hauerwas decisively goes *beyond* Barth in developing his own constructive position. Yet Hauerwas only desires to go beyond Barth by remaining *with* Barth on the question of apocalyptic,

---

22 W. Werpehowski, 'Command and History in the Ethics of Karl Barth', *Journal of Religious Ethics* 9 (Fall 1981), pp. 298–320, p. 300.

23 Hauerwas, CCL, pp. 169–77.

and by carrying forward Barth's attempt to deploy the 'logic' of apocalyptic as a means of conceiving Christ's relationship to history.

Christ, History, and Apocalyptic in Hauerwas's Narrative Ecclesiology

If Christian witness is genuinely to counter the metaphysically idealist assumptions of modern liberal historicism and the Constantinian assumptions of liberal politics, then the church must visibly exist in history as its own cultural-linguistic reality whose language and practices are sufficient to form persons into a counter-historical and counter-political identity. It is on the basis of this conviction regarding the necessity of the church's existence as such that Hauerwas is led to develop that for which he is perhaps best known: his 'narrative ecclesiology'. My concern in this section will be to analyse the way in which for Hauerwas the logic of apocalyptic functions primarily as a means of recovering a narrative perspective on Christ's person, and of foregrounding the church as the *subject* and *agent* of that narrative in history.

Hauerwas has devoted relatively little space to developing in any explicit or overt way his own apocalypticism. The clearest indication of the centrality of apocalyptic to his work comes in fact from his affirmation of the apocalyptic character of others' work, most notably that of Yoder and William Stringfellow. Two essays in particular, however, are important for helping us to understand the way in which the logic of apocalyptic functions within the framework of Hauerwas's work as a whole: 'The Reality of the Kingdom: An Ecclesial Space For Peace'[24] and 'Creation as Apocalyptic'.[25] Briefly treating each of these essays in turn will help us to understand Hauerwas's appropriation of apocalyptic in continuity with, and yet at an angle to, that of Barth laid out above.

---

24 Hauerwas, AN, pp. 107–31.
25 Hauerwas, DFF, pp. 107–15.

The first essay, 'The Reality of the Kingdom', constitutes a critique of the Protestant liberal (and modern historicist) notion of the Kingdom of God, in which the Kingdom is reduced to a transcendental, teleological-historical ideal.[26] By contrast, Hauerwas advocates an apocalyptic-eschatological perspective on 'Jesus as the form and content of the kingdom' as a way of orienting the discussion (in good Barthian fashion) around the question of how it is that *God* acts decisively in history to make the Kingdom present. For Hauerwas, God's apocalyptic activity as such is known 'by looking at the life and death of Jesus Christ' as it assumes an importance for history in continuity with God's action in relation to the people of Israel and the church.[27] That is, the importance and meaning of God's apocalyptic action for history lies in the manner in which Jesus' death and resurrection is constitutive of a people whose lives are formed by the 'irruption into history' of God's Kingdom as a distinct political reality.[28] It is precisely as a distinctive 'community formed by Jesus' story' that the 'Kingdom's inbreaking' is realized in history as the reality of God's action which makes impossible any universalization of the kingdom as an 'ideal' which might underwrite humanity's own most deeply held conceptions of socio-political 'progress'.[29]

The second essay, 'Creation as Apocalyptic', deploys apocalyptic as 'a way of reminding us of the intrinsically political character of salvation'.[30] Here Hauerwas is especially concerned with understanding the nature of the church as 'the necessary correlative of an apocalyptic narration of existence'.[31] What is interesting about this essay is that, while apocalyptic is still considered mainly as a 'mode of taking seriously Christ's Lordship over the public, the social, the political',[32] Hauerwas's em-

---

26 Hauerwas, AN, pp. 113, 110.
27 Hauerwas, AN, pp. 114–15.
28 Hauerwas, AN, pp. 115–16.
29 Hauerwas, AN, pp. 119, 110.
30 Hauerwas, DFF, p. 109.
31 Hauerwas, DFF, pp. 110, 109, 112.
32 Hauerwas, DFF, p. 109.

phasis falls much less upon the irruption of God's Kingdom in the particular history that is the life, death, and resurrection of Jesus of Nazareth. Rather, the focus is more clearly upon the visible Christian community as that community which alone can 'give evidence of existence of God's Kingdom in the world'.[33] The truth of apocalyptic is thus aligned more firmly with an understanding of the church as an 'alternative community', whose task is that of cultivating a 'life of resistance'.[34] Finally, this 'way of apocalyptic resistance' is identified concretely as a matter of the church's counter-political reality to the 'nonapocalyptic vision of reality that dominates American public life',[35] namely, Protestant liberal Constantinianism.

From these two essays, one can readily detect an account of apocalyptic in continuity with my critique of Troeltsch's reduction of the Kingdom to an ethico-metaphysical ideal in Chapter 2 above and also in continuity with the key impetus underlying the apocalyptic logic of Barth's entire oeuvre, namely, the priority of God's action in history. Given this continuity, however, what is interesting about the logic of apocalyptic as deployed by Hauerwas is the marked shift in emphasis in his writings away from an understanding of history as determined by the singular action of God focused in the exceptional particularity of Jesus' historicity and toward an understanding of history as determined by the action of God focused in the substantive narrative presence of the church in the world. There is a double-bind here in which Hauerwas seems to be caught. On the one hand, the apocalyptic perspective on history is identifiable only by way of the inbreaking of God's action in a singular human life with its own unique, contingent, and interruptive historicity. On the other hand, the privileged locus for the display of that action is a given 'historical' tradition. Hauerwas's way out of this double-bind is his 'narrative ecclesiology', by which he seeks to ally the *particularity* of Jesus' story with the

33 Hauerwas, DFF, p. 112.
34 Hauerwas, DFF, pp. 113–14.
35 Hauerwas, DFF, p. 114.

universal scope of God's action as displayed in the world-wide and diachronic church.[36]

My suspicion here, however, is that the apocalyptic perspective on Christ's relation to history is for Hauerwas overdetermined by the 'comprehensiveness' of the ecclesial narrative framework and underdetermined by what John Howard Yoder calls the ongoing 'independence' of Jesus in history.[37] The upshot of this overdetermination/underdetermination is that Hauerwas gives normative priority to a particular narrative *in* history in a manner that illegitimately privileges that narrative's own meta-perspective *on* history. Such privileging leads Hauerwas to presume a system of socio-linguistic Christian 'practice' which can neither adequately account for the reality of Jesus' ongoing historicity (the continuing and determinative 'independence' of his identity and activity as *this* singular human being in history), nor provide for a non-reductive recounting of secular (non-Christian) history. In the remainder of this section, I shall substantiate these suspicions by way of critical evaluation of two key aspects of Hauerwas's narrative ecclesiology:

1 the church as the continual narrative and historical embodiment of the story of God as identified by the name 'Jesus'; and
2 the 'truthfulness' of the Christian narrative as dependent upon the church's interpretive 'integration' and 'incorporation' of all other narratives or histories.

36 Hauerwas, CC, p. 51. See also Hauerwas, TPK, pp. 72–95.

37 We shall explore in more detail Yoder's own constructive usage of this term in the next chapter. For now, it is enough to note that what I mean by the 'independence' of Jesus' identity and activity vis-à-vis what we shall see is Hauerwas's 'community-dependent' understanding of this identity and activity is something akin to what Barth understands by the 'freedom' of God's act in relation to the human action, and especially what Rowan Williams calls 'the freedom of Jesus to act' in history apart from the Christian 'church' as such. R. Williams, *On Christian Theology* (Oxford: Blackwell, 2000), p. 192.

The first aspect has to do with the way in which Hauerwas seeks to integrate his assessment of the person and work
of Jesus Christ with its ecclesial resultant. In an early essay
entitled 'Jesus: The Story of the Church', Hauerwas stresses
the 'narrative dimension of Christology' as a way of prohibit-
ing the 'separation of Christology from ecclesiology, that is,
Jesus from the church'.[38] The truthfulness of Christ's person
and work 'is known by the kind of community his story should
form'; Jesus just *is* 'the story that forms the church'.[39] The basic
point Hauerwas is making here is one that will be emphasized
throughout his writings: the political witness of Christian discipleship that is the church is an indispensable condition for
confessing the truth of Jesus Christ. In order for Jesus to be
recognized as Lord 'over all creation and history', the 'Kingdom' (and thus Christ's *person*) must be visible as a distinct
political reality that is not simply 'accidental' to Jesus' life,
'but the necessary outcome of his life and of his mission'.[40] The
apocalyptic *work* of Jesus determines the Kingdom by creating a new socio-political reality defined by conformity to the
way of the cross that is the life of this singular human being.[41]
Only in accordance with this new socio-political reality can
we discern what it means for 'Jesus to be worthy of our worship', that is, to know this *person* to be 'Lord'.[42]

It should be noted straightaway that there is really nothing
to object to here. In fact, insofar as the main thesis of this book
is that an apocalyptic understanding of Christ's person and
work norms our reading of history in a way that is constitutive
of Christianity's irreducibly political existence and mission, I
would not fundamentally disagree with Hauerwas's concern
to recover an indispensable *ecclesial* dimension of Christology.
Neither would I disagree in principle with Hauerwas's claim
that 'the social ethical task of the church . . . is to be the kind

---

38 Hauerwas, CC, p. 37.
39 Hauerwas, CC, pp. 37, 51–2.
40 Hauerwas, CC, pp. 44–9.
41 Hauerwas, CC, pp. 46–9.
42 Hauerwas, CC, p. 37.

of community that tells and tells rightly the story of Jesus'.[43] Insofar as Scripture renders the particular identity of Jesus as it emerges from within the contingent and historical *narratively*, the question of *who* Jesus is remains bound up with the telling of this particular story. Furthermore, insofar as Scripture testifies to the Spirit-inspired existence of the church as a sign of Christ's unique presence in and with the ongoing contingencies and complexities of history itself, this particular narrative is and should remain determinative of ecclesial existence in the world. In other words, because of *who* Jesus Christ is as witnessed to in *the biblical narrative*, Hauerwas is correct to suggest 'telling this story rightly' is a matter of real ecclesial and socio-political importance.

What is problematic, however, from my perspective, is the way in which Hauerwas comes later to insist upon privileging the church itself as *subject* and *agent* of the Christ-story, such that it is the church's own narrative history that constitutes the 'storied' identity of Jesus. Hauerwas's tendency here is to stress the primacy of the church for the rendering of the narrative relationship of the history of Jesus to the world, to such an extent that the ecclesial narrative itself is treated as almost a mere metanarrative that transcends and subsumes the histories of both Jesus *and* the world.

Let me explain what I mean by this. In a later essay, 'The Church as God's New Language',[44] Hauerwas goes some way toward clarifying his earlier pregnant suggestion that 'Jesus' names 'the story that forms the Church'.[45] In the earlier essay, Hauerwas seems content with the claim that the 'narrative character of the Gospels' renders Jesus' identity as the Kingdom of God irreducibly political, in such a way that the narration of this identity necessarily involves the question of how the church is 'formed' in the world. Hauerwas thus indicates the inseparability of Christology from ecclesiology, while still

---

43 Hauerwas, CC, p. 52.
44 Hauerwas, CET, pp. 47–65.
45 Hauerwas, CC, pp. 51–2.

maintaining the priority of the former over the latter (and of the history of Jesus of Nazareth vis-à-vis that of the church) with respect to identifying the Kingdom.[46] With the later essay, however, Hauerwas seems to be moving progressively towards *identifying* Jesus' 'story' with the ongoing lived narrative that is the church; that is, in its telling of it, the church *is* itself 'the story being told' – 'the teller and the tale are one'.[47] Hauerwas's intention here is to move the emphasis in 'narrative theology' away from the biblical 'text' and toward the concrete ecclesial 'people' as the bearers of the narrative.[48] That is, Hauerwas's concern is to argue that the cultural-linguistic practices which make up the ecclesial community are from the beginning as integral to the narrative manifestation of God, that is, to revelation, as are the unique and unrepeatable sequence of Jesus' actions as rendered by the Gospel stories themselves. Yet in making this argument, Hauerwas betrays his preference for a certain kind of transcendental narrativity which privileges a 'story' whose referent is not simply that of the man Jesus confessed as God and Lord, but rather a single, though dynamic, cultural-linguistic 'practice' that constitutes an alternative, habitable 'history'.

This preference is borne out by Hauerwas's affirmation of John Milbank's 'metanarrative' perspective upon the relationship of Jesus to the church. In an even more recent essay,[49] Hauerwas fully endorses Milbank's 'ecclesiocentric' construal of the 'narrative manifestation of God', by which 'the Church stands in a narrative relationship to Jesus and the Gospels,

---

46 Hauerwas, CC, pp. 37, 40–4.

47 Hauerwas, CET, p. 54.

48 Hauerwas, CET, p. 59. 'The Church as God's New Language' was originally an essay written for a Festschrift on Frei. In it, Hauerwas is most critical of Frei for his tendency to treat of the biblical text's 'paradigmatic' reference to Christ without treating of the way in which the text functions 'syntagmatically' to refer to the people that is the church. I am borrowing the terms syntagmatic/paradigmatic from John Milbank's critique of George Lindbeck. See Milbank, *Theology and Social Theory*, pp. 382–8.

49 Hauerwas, WW, pp. 188–98.

within a story that subsumes both'.[50] As such, the Christian metanarrative 'is *not* just a story of Jesus, it is the continuing story of the Church'.[51] The problem that this move presents, however, is that it gives ontological primacy to the 'alternative history' that is the church in the world and makes of this alternative history an 'ontological necessity' for the narrative display of God's story, as well as of Jesus' 'identity'.[52] For not only has ecclesiology itself come to have priority over Christology in the display of Jesus' identity and of the truth of his story, but the church itself has also come to be the very 'goal' in the telling of Jesus' story, the 'end' of the narrative.[53] What this means is that a particular community in history – a particular set of cultural-linguistic practices – is made to bear the full ontological weight of the meaning of what God has done to establish the Kingdom in our midst. The focus of the narrative thus comes to centre less upon the question of *who* Jesus of Nazareth is, and more upon that of 'the kind of community his story should form'.[54] As a consequence of this, Hauerwas comes essentially to *identify* the 'meaning' or the 'truth' of Jesus' story with this alternative narrative history embodied in the Christian community's distinct social practices.

This is confirmed by the way in which Hauerwas renders the question of faithfulness to Christ as principally a matter of one's habituation into a given community's inherited languages, practices, and institutions. It is through our formation in the church and its practices that we are trained to see the world as redeemed in Christ.[55] This is not necessarily problematic, except as Hauerwas suggests that the ecclesial community itself, as defined by a very distinct set of socio-cultural practices, supplies the very *ontological* and *linguistic* conditions of

---

50 Milbank, *Theology and Social Theory*, p. 387. Cited in Hauerwas, WW, pp. 192–3.

51 Milbank, *Theology and Social Theory*, p. 387.

52 See Hauerwas, CET, pp. 60–1.

53 Hauerwas, CET, pp. 54–62.

54 Hauerwas, VV, p. 37.

55 Hauerwas, VV, p. 67; see Hauerwas, AC, pp. 93–111.

possibility for the story of Jesus to be told and lived, encountered and followed, in history. The upshot of this is that, when
it comes to conceiving of the church's 'witness', the focus is for
Hauerwas almost solely upon the practices and virtues that
constitute the church as a 'habitable world' and sustain it as
a community with its own 'alternative history'.[56] As a result,
the narrative 'identity' with which Hauerwas seems most concerned is *not* that of the unique and unrepeatable event of who
God is in Jesus Christ as he confronts us, through the Spirit, in
our own particular times and places, but that of the church itself – the place, the memory, the practices by which one comes
to find one's own life as 'characterized' by the alternative vision
of reality appropriate to the church's 'language'.

So it seems as if Hauerwas's concern to integrate the history
of the church into Jesus' story runs the risk of subordinating
Jesus of Nazareth himself to a more 'metanarrative reality',
namely, the alternative *polis* of the church, according to whose
historical existence alone Jesus is made 'present' and 'effective'
in history. But this can only mean that, to some very real extent, *who* Jesus Christ truly is is itself a function of and dependent upon the community's ability to make God believable by
making its vision of the world 'habitable' through its distinct
socio-political practices.

This leads us to the second key aspect of Hauerwas's narrative ecclesiology, which is the idea that the Christian story
is 'true' in accordance with the church's 'interpretive power'
or ability to resituate all of history with respect to itself, to
're-narrate' history in the telling of its story.[57] 'Through the
church . . . the world is given a history.'[58] This is a common
refrain in Hauerwas's writings, the overall thrust of which
seems to be that the truth of the Christian narrative lies with

---

56 See Hauerwas, WGU, p. 214. Nicholas Healy elaborates this
point with great acuity and insight in 'Practices and the New Ecclesiology: Misplaced Concreteness?', *International Journal of Systematic
Theology* 5.3 (November 2003), pp. 299–303.

57 See Hauerwas, CC, pp. 89–110.

58 Hauerwas, CC, p. 91.

the fact that through it the world is provided with a set of practices and a language by which one might be integrated into a communal discourse sufficient to sustain her identity as a creature of God in the face of the presumed 'necessities' of a relativistic and tragic existence.[59] For Hauerwas to insist, then, that 'the church is an ontological necessity if we are to know rightly that our world is capable of narrative construal', or that 'without the church the world would have no history',[60] is to insist upon the practices of this given cultural-linguistic community as 'necessary for us to locate the final causes shaping our history as God's ongoing work of creation'.[61] Without such practices, 'the world would be without a history sufficient to understand itself as God's creation'.[62] The world *is*, its own particularities and contingencies 'exist' and have a 'history', as they are able to be received and integrated ('accepted' and 'incorporated')[63] into the machinations and operations of those 'Christian' practices which guarantee their perdurance as narrated occurrences of God's ongoing act of creation.

What is significant here, from the perspective of an apocalyptic Christology, is the way in which for Hauerwas the metaphysical and ontological decisiveness of Jesus for the world turns upon a description of the church's history as that which 'ultimately interprets and locates all other histories'.[64]

Take, for example, Hauerwas's understanding of Christ's 'lordship' as itself a function of the church's linguistic-narrative construct. As Hauerwas puts it in the aptly titled essay, 'The Church's One Foundation is Jesus Christ Her Lord or In a World Without Foundations All We Have is the Church', Christ is truly 'Lord' precisely to the extent that the whole world is 'given a history' and 'storied' by way of the universalizable social reality made possible through the church's habits

---

59 Hauerwas, CC, pp. 101–8.
60 Hauerwas, CET, p. 61.
61 Hauerwas, WW, p. 192.
62 Hauerwas, CET, p. 160.
63 See Hauerwas, PF, pp. 91–5.
64 Hauerwas, WW, p. 192.

and practices.[65] Crucially, Hauerwas only makes such claims for the universality of the church insofar as he insists that we human beings 'share the same Lord', whose name is marked by that very particular history that is Jesus of Nazareth,[66] whose 'presence is not confined to the Church',[67] and whose story 'trains us to see one another as God's people'.[68] But as we have seen, Hauerwas conceives of Jesus' relation to the church in such a way that who Jesus is *outside* of the church can really only ever be a kind of hermeneutical function of the internal linguistic and narrative construct that is the church's habits, practices, and institutions. Thus, Hauerwas says, 'it is in the church that we learn to recognize Christ's presence outside of the church'.[69] Again, like many of Hauerwas's formulations, there seems to be little to object to in this statement, on the face of it. And yet, what this would seem to mean for Hauerwas is that precisely insofar as Christ has now been *identified* within the ecclesial story, he is now identifiable outside the church as in accordance with the church's task of 'overaccepting' and 'reincorporating' the givens of the world with relation to the comprehensiveness of its own metanarrative ontological vision.[70] Thus, when I say that Christ's identity as Lord is itself a 'hermeneutical function' of the church, I am suggesting that for Hauerwas Christ is 'outside' the church in a way that is reducible to the Christian community's consistent interpretation of its own 'internal' story. And insofar as this ecclesial metanarrative functions *metaphysically* for Hauerwas, as a way of telling us *who* we *are* in the world, as also *what* the truth of the world *is*,[71] to say that we as human beings 'share the same

---

65 Hauerwas, IGC, pp. 33, 38.

66 Hauerwas, CC, p. 106.

67 Hauerwas, TPK, p. 97.

68 Hauerwas, CC, p. 51.

69 Hauerwas, TPK, p. 97.

70 The themes of 'overaccepting' and 'reincorporating' are those of Samuel Wells. On Hauerwas's affirmation of these themes as consonant with his and Milbank's concern to 'out-narrate' and 'resituate' the givens of world history, see Hauerwas, PF, pp. 91–7.

71 Hauerwas, PF, pp. 144, 146.

Lord' is to say that the church's storied 'habits' and 'practices' are themselves constitutive of a 'rule' – a 'theocracy'[72] – to which we as humans always-already belong.

I realize that these are tendentious claims and that I have articulated them with an edge that some more sympathetic readers of Hauerwas might find discomforting.[73] But I think this 'edge' is of vital importance to the central question driving this book: namely, the nature of the 'truth' of Christ's lordship for history. For if I am right about all this, the church's 'loyalty' to Christ-as-Lord has now become fully a matter of its own 'self-regard',[74] through its attention to those habits and practices by which it retains 'continuity' and 'integrity' as a community in history.[75] And the world is to be treated as subject to Christ's reign insofar as its given realities can be 'translated', 'out-narrated', and 'resituated' so as to 'fit' the cultural-linguistic trajectory of this particular community. The point is that the particular human being Jesus is conceivable as truly Lord only to the extent that the church is conceivable as a distinct historical community that is *universally realizable* via its ability to 're-narrate' the world in accordance with its own practised belief system.[76] The church is 'faithful' to Christ's 'lordship' as

---

72 Hauerwas has readily consented, in his most recent writings, that his ecclesial politics constitutes a 'theocracy' and that the church's way of living is a different way of 'trying' to 'rule'. See S. Hauerwas and R. Coles, *Christianity, Democracy, and the Radical Ordinary: Conversations between a Radical Democrat and a Christian* (Eugene, OR: Cascade Books, 2008), p. 22n. 5. Of course, given the putative 'comprehensiveness' of the Christian metanarrative, such a 'trying to rule' would itself seem to involve the church in seeking 'total rule'.

73 For a very helpful reading of apocalyptic in Hauerwas's work which is more sympathetic than my own, and to which I am much indebted, see Harink, *Paul among the Postliberals*, pp. 67–103.

74 Hauerwas, VV, p. 216.

75 Hauerwas, CCL, p. 226.

76 This way of putting things highlights the extent to which Hauerwas's narrative ecclesiological construal of Christ's relation to history more or less corresponds to the methodological presuppositions of 'intratextuality', particularly as formulated by George Lindbeck and Bruce Marshall, in *The Nature of Doctrine* and *Trinity and Truth*, re-

through such practised beliefs it situates 'the world's "givens" within a more determinative, peaceable, and hence more encompassing narrative'.[77] And so the 'orthodox' confession of Christ's lordship is but a means, as Hauerwas has put it recently, of 'keeping the story of Jesus straight'.[78] But insofar as that story is now *identifiable* with church itself, to confess 'Jesus is Lord' in the name of the 'straight story' will tend inevitably to make of this confession (and of 'orthodoxy' itself) an instrument of the church's own narrative (and institutional) self-preservation and expansion.[79]

With this observation we reach the crux of the problem with Hauerwas's particular attempt to extend Barth's apocalyptic rendering of the Christ-narrative into the realm of ecclesiology, namely, its 'community-dependent' way of relating Jesus to history. Significantly, the point I am here making is similar to that made by John Howard Yoder, in which he criticizes Hauerwas for obscuring 'the objective reality of salvation history':

One reason Hauerwas does not do text-based Bible study is that he is overawed by the notion of community-dependency and underawed by the objective reality of salvation history.

---

spectively. For Hauerwas's indebtedness to Lindbeck on this point, see Hauerwas, AN, pp. 1–9. For his indebtedness to Marshall, see idem, WGU, pp. 207–15. See also S. Wells, *Transforming Fate into Destiny: The Theological Ethics of Stanley Hauerwas* (Carlisle, UK: Paternoster Press, 1998), pp. 55–7 and passim. For a fine critical treatment of Lindbeck's notion of 'intratextuality' as the criterion for 'truth', with some reference to Marshall's work, see P. DeHart, *The Trial of the Witnesses: The Rise and Decline of Postliberal Theology* (Oxford: Blackwell, 2006), pp. 80–9, 171–84.

77 Hauerwas, PF, p. 92.

78 Hauerwas and Coles, *Christianity, Democracy, and the Radical Ordinary*, p. 30.

79 For a critique of Hauerwas's concern to sustain 'orthodoxy', with relation to the nature of Christ's 'lordship' in both Hauerwas and Yoder, see Peter Dula and Alex Sider, 'Radical Democracy, Radical Ecclesiology', *Cross Currents* 55.4 (2006), pp. 482–504.

Also underawed by the study of real (unsaved) history. He would rather read novels.[80]

As I read Yoder here, his criticism is that by shifting the narrative emphasis away from the Gospel 'text' as that which renders Jesus Christ the irreducible 'object' of the Church's witness to God's action in history and towards the ecclesial 'people' as both the narrating and narrated 'subject' of God's 'story', Hauerwas has risked elevating the language and culture of the Christian community to a meta-historical level which 'orders' the historicity of Jesus of Nazareth, as well as that of every other event, and which is somehow 'sufficient to explain them'.[81] In

---

80 J. Yoder, 'Absolute Philosophical Relativism is an Oxymoron' (unpublished 1993 supplement to the essay, 'Meaning after Babble: With Jeffrey Stout beyond Relativism', *Journal of Religious Ethics* 24 [Spring 1996], pp. 125–39).

81 Yoder may or may not have had Hauerwas in mind when he wrote the following: 'One will welcome the creative imagination of structuralists who protect narration from reduction to "truths" and "concepts"; yet an equal vigilance is needed to defend the particularity of Abraham and Samuel, Jeremiah and Jesus from reduction to mere specimens of a new kind of universals, namely narrative forms, lying deeper than the ordinary events and sufficient to explain them' (Yoder, PK, 36). We have seen that while Yoder is not averse to appealing to the category of 'narrative' as a matter of scriptural hermeneutics with regards to identifying the particularity of Jesus in relation to the church and the world, clearly he refuses to accord narrative the kind of 'meta' status which would afford one a presumed universal perspective on history. As this section has tried to show, even despite his protestations to the contrary, Hauerwas risks falling into this error. For example, though Hauerwas has insisted that his concern all along has been with the *particular* narrative that is the 'story of Jesus', he nevertheless reads the 'gospel' as displaying a 'narrative form', which 'form' he associates (following Milbank) with the Christian narrative as a metaphysical 'mode of comprehension' of 'all that is'. So Hauerwas's continuing emphasis upon the Christian narrative yet turns on a fundamental ontologico-metaphysical concern with 'the way things are', which, for all he says about this narrative being the 'story of Jesus', still runs the risk of making the identity and historicity of Jesus that which he wishes to avoid, namely, 'but a manifestation of a "deeper reality"'. Hauerwas, PF, pp. 135–49.

other words, Hauerwas's narrative construal of the ecclesial community harbours a pretension to universality, which is inimical to the 'vulnerability of the particular' that Yoder believes the church has committed itself to in its own 'evangelical Christology'.[82] Yoder's point is this: the distinctive identity of the human being Jesus of Nazareth, in the particularities and contingencies of whose life is embodied the action of God by which the Kingdom breaks into history and according to whose life the contingencies and particularities of all of history are positively related to the coming of that Kingdom, is entirely dependent upon and conditioned by a certain set of discourse-practices as developed in direct relation to the duration and sustenance of a particular historical community's virtues, habits, and institutions. As a result, Christology is subordinated to ecclesiology, and the apocalyptic 'truth' of Christ's person and work is made to be dependent upon the 'effectiveness' and 'perdurance' of a certain narrative trajectory towards a clearly discerned meta-perspective on history, a perspective which is, as we have seen, at odds with the very logic of apocalyptic itself.

So it appears as if Hauerwas's narrative-ecclesiological development of Barthian apocalyptic leads all-too-easily to a concern for the Christian community's own 'internal identity'[83] as providing a metanarrative (and metaphysically universal) perspective upon all of history. To be fair, it is not at all clear that

---

82 Yoder, PK, pp. 44, 61.

83 The phrase is used by George Hunsinger and William Placher in an introduction to an essay by Hans Frei to describe Hauerwas's position in relation to other 'postliberals' such as Frei and George Lindbeck. See H. Frei, *Theology and Narrative: Selected Essays*, ed. G. Hunsinger and W. Placher (New York: Oxford University Press, 1993), pp. 213–14. Hauerwas cites this passage and claims it as a 'misunderstanding' of his position, in Hauerwas, IGC, pp. 20–1. I am not sure whether Hauerwas succeeds in demonstrating how this is so. Nevertheless, I hope this section has shown that as consonant with the logic of Hauerwas's narrative ecclesiology as a whole, and in direct congruence with other statements and positions that Hauerwas has made and laid out elsewhere in his oeuvre, Hunsinger's and Placher's characterization is more or less apt.

this is Hauerwas's real and final intention. And yet we must insist that without some more thoroughgoing account of the objective, 'independent' identity of Jesus of Nazareth as determinative of history outside of and beyond the received tradition of the church, it will be almost impossible *not* to think of the church in terms of a supposed or claimed possession of that universal recapitulation of all of history which the world itself secretly seeks. If, however, we are rather to think of the church as constituted by way of an ongoing encounter with the 'apocalyptic' independence and singularity of Jesus Christ amidst the contingencies and particularities of history, we will need to eschew the 'community-dependent' understanding of apocalyptic which is intrinsic to Hauerwas's narrative ecclesiology. Our ability to avoid the errors of community-dependence while retaining a concern for the politics of Jesus and the importance of apocalyptic for Christian political and missionary action will turn on how the 'singularity' and 'independence' of Jesus' 'apocalyptic historicity' are conceived in Chapter 5. But first, I need to 'complete' my critique of Hauerwas by showing how his narrative-ecclesiological concern for the church's communal-historical identity is bound up with a (still too-ideological) anti-Constantinian political position, one which is finally reductive of the church's missionary task.

Anti-Constantinianism, Political Ideology, and Mission

As Rusty Reno describes it, 'Constantinianism' for Hauerwas (a protean term in his writings, to be sure) boils down essentially to a matter of the 'spiritualization' of Christianity.[84]

Constantinianism names any 'attempt to make Christianity intelligible without that set of habits called the church'.[85] 'Thus,' Reno explains, 'a "Constantinian" is anyone who

---

84 R. Reno, 'Stanley Hauerwas', in *The Blackwell Companion to Political Theology*, ed. P. Scott and W. Cavanaugh (Oxford: Blackwell, 2004), pp. 310–12.
85 Hauerwas, STIT, p. 159.

would make the church invisible and weightless. Assumptions and practices are "Constantinian" if they disembody rather than solidify Christian identity.'[86] This spiritualization of the church creates a political power vacuum, which is left to be filled only by the state: the state itself comes to define and determine the bounds and meaning of those aspects of our lives most central to the shaping of our socio-political identity, while 'Christianity' carries out a concern for the human 'soul' in a way that more or less buttresses the ideological legitimation of secular state power.

So Hauerwas essentially agrees with Yoder's basic understanding of Constantinianism as outlined in Chapter 1 above. Yet Hauerwas's assessment is unique in that he seems consistently to have interpreted the Constantinian problem more narrowly in terms of the 'church-state' question as defined by 'modern political liberalism'.

The irony, however, is that this way of conceiving the church means that Hauerwas's ecclesiological politics remains caught within certain 'ideological' modes of thinking. It remains bound, on the one hand, within a negative interpretation of state sovereignty as ideologically determined. The upshot of this is that the church's political task is literally defined as a matter of the church's *survival*,[87] to the extent that such survival guarantees the existence of the kinds of 'disciplined communities that are necessary to keep the state limited'.[88] But this raises the critical question as to whether Hauerwas too narrowly conceives of the church's 'political' legitimation as that of a counter-*polis* as *over-against* the liberal state.

The force of this question can be demonstrated by noting a certain parallel to the German political theorist Carl Schmitt's

---

86 Reno, 'Stanley Hauerwas', p. 310.

87 Hauerwas, IGC, pp. 42, 234–5n. 30. See D. Harink, 'For or Against the Nations: Yoder and Hauerwas, What's the Difference?', *Toronto Journal of Theology* 17.1 (2001), pp. 169–74.

88 S. Hauerwas, 'Faith in the Republic: A Frances Lewis Law Centre Conversation', *Washington and Lee Review* 45 (1988), pp. 467–84, p. 471.

'antiliberal' conception of 'the political'. One of Hauerwas's fundamental problems with liberalism (*pace* Schmitt) is the way in which it presumes the ideological claim of certain 'state' apparatuses – capitalist economics, democracy, civil society – to arbitrate the supposedly neutral space of 'politics'. And yet, in speaking of the church in terms of *counter*-political communities that exist (in part, at least) 'to keep the state limited', is not Hauerwas himself seemingly assuming his own (rather Schmittian) ideological conception of 'the political' as a contested 'space', wherein politics is impossible apart from the theoretical and practical engendering of 'friends' and 'enemies'?[89] Is Hauerwas not echoing Schmitt's view that 'the high points of politics' are those moments in which 'the enemy is, in concrete clarity, recognized as the enemy',[90] when he writes: 'Christianity is unintelligible without enemies. Indeed, the whole point of Christianity is to produce the right kind of enemies'?[91]

My concern here is not to argue that Hauerwas is a 'Schmittian' political theorist, but to borrow Schmitt's categories and phrasing to suggest that, in insisting that the church be conceived as a counter-*polis* that engenders its political identity in opposition to state liberalism, Hauerwas has allowed his assumptions as to what the enemy *must* be to generate and condition what 'we' as friends of the church must be, politically. My argument is not that Hauerwas is wrong about the 'ideological' function of state liberalism but rather that, in conceiving the church-as-*polis* as over-against the state as such, Hauerwas has put himself in a position such that the 'church' can only be defined as a kind of political 'identity' that requires its own mode of ideological legitimation if it is to 'survive'. Hauerwas appears thus to risk repeating the error of his own *bête noire*, Protestant liberalism, by conceiving the

---

89 This is suggested by the title of one of Hauerwas's sermons, 'No Enemy, No Christianity: Preaching between "Worlds"', in Hauerwas, STIT, pp. 191–200.

90 Carl Schmitt, *The Concept of the Political*, tr. G. Schwab (Chicago: University of Chicago Press, 2007), p. 67.

91 Hauerwas, STIT, p. 196.

church's political existence in the world as conditioned in part by its positioning vis-à-vis the secular ideological forces of imperialistic nationalism and cultural liberalism.

One can see how this is the case by noting the way in which Hauerwas considers himself duty-bound by his anti-liberal, metanarrative ecclesiology to conceive of the church as its own 'imperialistic polity'.[92]

Here again Hauerwas's mode of reasoning appears structurally analogous to that of Schmitt in his book *Roman Catholicism and Political Form*. There, Schmitt argues that the Church's claim to political authority rests upon the manifestation of its 'power of representation', by which it manifests a certain 'political universalism'.[93] The Church 'is' for Schmitt the 'realization of an idea' of the universal *civitas humana*, and it is this idea itself which requires the Church's survival in the mode of a given 'political form'.[94] It is in this sense that the political form of the Church not only presupposes but *is* the outworking of what Schmitt sociologically describes elsewhere as a kind of 'radical ideology'.[95]

The parallels with Schmitt arise with the way in which Hauerwas conceives of the church primarily as a distinctive society with a particular historical trajectory that is yet *representative and distributive of an effectively universal reality*. Hauerwas thus turns out to advocate a modified form of 'Christendom', in which there is embodied within the Christian 'community and way of life' a distinct 'society in which all of life is integrated under the Lordship of Christ'.[96] As we have seen,

---

92 Hauerwas, IGC, p. 22; Hauerwas, AC, p. 169n. 23.

93 C. Schmitt, *Roman Catholicism and Political Form*, tr. G. Ulmen (London: Greenwood Press, 1996), pp. 18–19, 5.

94 Schmitt, *Roman Catholicism*, pp. 5, 19, 25.

95 C. Schmitt, *Political Theology: Four Chapters on the Concept of Sovereignty*, tr. G. Schwab (Chicago: University of Chicago Press, 2005), pp. 42–6.

96 The language is that of Gerald Schlabach, cited approvingly by Hauerwas as indicative of his position, in Hauerwas, BH, p. 44. Particularly telling here is the way in which Hauerwas speaks directly of his 'lingering longing for Christendom' as describing perhaps the major

however, Christ can only be conceived as Lord for Hauerwas to the extent that the church's social existence can be seen as constituting a single cultural-linguistic story into which all the 'givens' of history can be integrated and subsumed. The point here is subtle, but consequently all the more important to grasp: the church's distinctiveness in history *is* the representative universal basis for the lordship of Christ, just to the extent that Jesus is 'made' to be Lord through the 'political form' of faithful Christian practice across history. Hauerwas's final word to liberalism is thus: *extra ecclesiam nulla salus* – the meaning of which statement we must deem from within Hauerwas's anti-Constantinian framework as no less ideological and imperialistic than the 'individualistic' mantra of state liberalism. That is to say, the *extra ecclesiam nulla salus*, when politicized in this way, bears within it the *idea* of a higher type of political universalism, which the practices, disciplines, and organizational structures of the church serve as 'instruments' of its embodiment.

There is much more that could be said about this ideological-instrumental bind within which Hauerwas's theorization of the church-as-*polis* remains caught. But of particular importance here is the way in which it is determinative of Hauerwas's understanding of Christian mission. For example, Hauerwas characterizes 'mission' and 'witness' as two of the essential 'survival skills' for a church living under the conditions of secular liberalism.[97] 'Mission' is essentially the means by which

---

point of departure between himself and John Howard Yoder. Hauerwas, BH, p. 227n. 39. As he put it in his remarks to the 1999 meeting of the Society of Christian Ethics: 'I am much more Catholic, more Constantinian, than John' (quoted in Harink, *Paul among the Post-liberals*, p. 102n. 59). Indeed, given what Hauerwas has said recently about his concern for a 'theocracy' according to which Christians 'try to rule', such claims are bound to amount to some kind of apologia for what John Howard Yoder insists must be abandoned, namely, 'a Christian total society'. See Yoder, FTN, p. 107. Elsewhere, Yoder articulates this 'establishment of a total society' as the fundamental way in which 'mission' is 'compromised'. Yoder, RP, pp. 75, 89.

97 Hauerwas, WW, p. 217.

the church maintains and extends its identity as that cultural-linguistic community in terms of which all history can be narrated. Furthermore, it is precisely in terms of this ongoing narrative identity that the church is able to speak of and to proclaim the gospel as that which '"engulfs" the world'.[98] That is to say, the church's narrative relation to the world and history is 'missiological' precisely as it tells and lives its story in an integrative, world-absorbing way. Thus, the church is most missionary, 'most relevant to society', when it is intentionally 'self-regarding'.[99] Through such 'self-regard', the church 'serves the world' by maintaining its integrity and character as the continuance of Jesus' 'story' across history and into the present, for precisely thereby it gives 'the world the means to see itself truthfully', namely, to 'understand' itself as determined by what God is doing in and through the narrative identity of this particular cultural-linguistic community.[100]

With this, Hauerwas has effectively rendered the church itself as the very *object* of mission, such that it makes the 'truth' of the world itself (as with the 'truth' of Jesus) 'community dependent'. As such, the primary objective of Christian mission ceases to be thought of as the ongoing 'conversion' to the singular lordship of Christ as embedded within the evernew particularities and contingencies of history, and rather becomes thought of as 'conversion' *into* a particular narrative community,[101] as the meaning and reality of Christ's lordship over history is now recognized as embedded within this particular community's culture, language, and practices.

Perhaps most problematic of all is that mission is here no longer conceived as that which 'makes' the church (a refrain that Barth never tires of repeating throughout *Church Dogmatics*

---

98 Hauerwas, CET, pp. 64–5n. 17. Cf. Hauerwas's early definition of a 'truthful' narrative as one which can receive and integrate the 'other' into its own story without threat or fear of loss of identity. Hauerwas, CC, pp. 129–52.

99 Hauerwas, VV, p. 216.

100 Hauerwas, TPK, pp. 101–2.

101 Hauerwas, WW, p. 189.

IV/3 and that I shall foreground in Chapter 6 below), in such a way that the church is seen to be *constituted* as *sent* to proclaim the mystery of Jesus Christ as living and as Lord and as *gathered* by the evernew discovery of that life and lordship in the strangest of times and places. Rather, if mission is in any way 'constitutive of Christianity', as Hauerwas has recently suggested, it is such as a mode of the church's own 'discovery' of itself, of that which it had not previously recognized as part of its 'story'.[102] But in this way, 'mission' is subordinated to 'narrative' and is constitutive of the church not so much at the level of *action* as of *interpretation* – as a matter of 'keeping the story of Jesus straight', as it were. And here again, ideology raises its ugly head: 'mission' appears to be merely an instrument for displaying Christianity as its own 'habitable world', capable of 'integrating' and 'absorbing' all of history. In mission, by way of its own internal 'narrative', the church itself retains the initiative in determining what will be 'discovered' beyond its borders.

Hence we see the way in which Hauerwas's political anti-liberalism forces him into an account of Christian mission that is methodologically 'imperialist': the church's mission just *is* to maintain its distinctiveness from the state as a *polis* that is 'encompassing' and 'universal' in a way that the latter could only ever pretend to be.[103] We have already indicated this as a *Christological* failure. What I should like to do in closing this chapter is to bring the discussion back around to apocalyptic, by showing how this Christological failure is bound up with an *eschatological* failure. For it is in constructing his ecclesiology according to a kind of 'realized eschatology' that Hauerwas is unable to sustain a properly *apocalyptic orientation* to the singular human being Jesus of Nazareth as the real motive force of Christian mission in history.

There are two points to consider here. First, there is Jon

---

102 Hauerwas and Coles, *Christianity, Democracy, and the Radical Ordinary*, p. 332.
103 See Harink, 'For or Against the Nations', p. 174.

Thomson's suggestion that Hauerwas's ecclesial politics structurally represents a form of 'presentative millenarianism'.[104] By this it is meant that Hauerwas regards the existence of the church in history as representing the real possibility 'of living as a Christian society freely reflecting the international embrace of God's reign'.[105] As such, Hauerwas depicts the church as *the* eschatological reality par excellence, not only here below, but also as the very *end* of history, as the very purpose and meaning of Christ's *parousia*. Take, for example, the way in which Hauerwas more or less identifies certain 'Christian' practices with those 'final causes shaping our history as God's ongoing work of creation'.[106] Such a concern with 'final causes' betrays a certain *non-apocalyptic* interpretation of the eschaton as a kind of *telos* to the narrative, a mere 'end' to the creation story.[107] But also, within such a narrative-teleological approach to the final presence (*parousia*) of the Kingdom, the emphasis is placed squarely upon the second coming as the fulfilment or perfection of certain *historical practices* inaugurated by Jesus and carried on in the church.[108] The coming of the Kingdom of God is conceivable just to the extent that the church's 'activities, procedures, and policies' are understood to be not simply 'signs' or 'parables' of the Kingdom but themselves to be '*transparent* to God's eschatological reign'.[109]

Thus, Hauerwas at points very clearly identifies the apocalyptic inbreaking itself with the appearance of the *church* in time as the recapitulation of Jesus' story and as 'the continuation of

104 Thomson, *Ecclesiology of Stanley Hauerwas*, p. 206.
105 Thomson, *Ecclesiology of Stanley Hauerwas*, p. 206.
106 Hauerwas, WW, p. 192.
107 Samuel Wells nicely illustrates how Hauerwas is here very much influenced by Alasdair MacIntyre's understanding of human life as the quest for a determinate 'goal' or 'telos'. Samuel Wells, 'Stanley Hauerwas' Theological Ethics in Eschatological Perspective', *Scottish Journal of Theology* 53.4 (2000), pp. 433–7.
108 Hauerwas, AN, p. 116.
109 Hauerwas, IGC, p. 30; emphasis added.

the history of creation';[110] it is not now the particular interruption of history that is the life, death, and resurrection of Jesus of Nazareth, but the existence of the 'alternative history' (or historical social logic) that is the Christian *polis*, which is for Hauerwas the definitive apocalyptic reality and so determinative of the time of the *parousia*. Thus, even though Hauerwas will readily admit that there is still a *future* to be had for this ecclesial society, his failure to articulate any real disjunction between this future and the *parousia* of the singular human being Jesus Christ means that this future must really be conceived teleologically as *always-already present* in the church's political life here and now.[111]

The second point follows upon the first, and that is that Hauerwas compromises the eschatological tension between the 'two ages' that is characteristic of apocalyptic by reifying this tension in terms of a church-state dualism. As a result, while Hauerwas rightfully makes use of the two ages tension as a way of rendering the church's distinctiveness in relation to the 'world', he exploits this tension in such a manner as to reduce the question of the church-world distinction to a question of two conflicting 'historical' narratives – that of 'Christianity' versus 'liberalism'. The church lives and embodies the new aeon inasmuch as it exists *against* the modern liberal nation state, and precisely as such does it limit, and resist assimilation to, the powers of the old aeon. But this just highlights all the more the problematic nature of Hauerwas's shift from Christology to ecclesiology as the proper locus for understanding apocalyptic. For here Hauerwas has moved considerably away from the New Testament understanding of the 'two ages' as determined by the two advents of Christ and of the *ecclesia* as existing provisionally 'between the times' of Christ's life on earth and of his coming in glory. Instead, living 'between the

---

110 See, e.g., the way in which this identification is made most clearly in Hauerwas, CET, p. 51.

111 This is a point made by John Milbank with regards to Hauerwas's ecclesiology, though of course to positive effect. J. Milbank, 'Critical Study', *Modern Theology* 4.2 (1988), pp. 211–16, pp. 214–15.

times' has come itself to be thought of as 'living in between' Church and World as between the 'new' and the 'old' polities of 'Christianity' and 'liberalism', respectively.

   These last two points demonstrate well the central role that a certain misplacement of apocalyptic emphasis plays in Hauerwas's attempt to develop a more robustly 'political' ecclesiology, as well as in the ideologically informed account of mission that his particular ecclesiology carries with it. But, most importantly, these last two points highlight the importance of returning the focus of apocalyptic to a consideration of the distinctive historicity of Jesus of Nazareth, and to an interpretation of the church-world relation and the two ages tension which is more conditioned by the already-not yet 'interval' between who the human being Jesus of Nazareth was on earth as God and who he will be in his final coming as Lord of history. Barth's apocalyptic Christology should have served as a brake upon Hauerwas's chiliastic ecclesiology. Instead, Hauerwas has allowed his anti-Constantinianism (and his critique of Barth) so to determine his ecclesiology as to force him into giving apocalyptic a communal-historical locus, and into an ideological portrayal of this community's distinct political identity as itself the motive force and object of Christian mission.

Conclusion

What I have sought to argue in this chapter is that Hauerwas's anti-liberalism involves 'the church' in a strategic project of self-constancy and self-possession that is still formally determined by the 'logic of effectiveness' according to which liberal political ideology and indeed the 'Constantinian' project itself goes forward. Indeed, 'narrative ecclesiology' itself turns out to be the basis for determining that 'identity' by which the church itself might construct its own 'effective history' (to use Gadamer's phrase).[112] Thus, Hauerwas's attempt ecclesiologically to 'narrate' God's apocalyptic action in history leads him

---

   112 See esp. Hauerwas, CC, pp. 89–110.

to repeat, from within his own 'postliberal' perspective, some of the same kinds of theological mistakes that I suggested were at the heart of Troeltsch's own 'Constantinianism', in Chapter 2 above. Most notably, Hauerwas's anti-liberalism involves the church in its own *teleological*-eschatological concern to 'organize' and to 'order' the given contingencies and complexities of human historicity, precisely for the sake of 'keeping [its] story straight' in history,[113] a concern that brings with it its own metaphysical pretensions to 'universality'. Perhaps, then, in the end, the real source of the opposition between the 'postliberal narrative' historicism of Hauerwas and the 'modern liberal' historicism of someone like Troeltsch is that, ideologically, they are born twins.

If, then, it is still possible to articulate a genuinely apocalyptic construal of Christ's relationship to history that bears within it an understanding of the church as existing in a manner that is as irreducibly 'missionary' as it is 'political' and that yet traces a path between and beyond the Scylla of the 'Constantinian temptation' and the Charybdis of 'anti-Constantinianism', we shall need to carry forward the Barthian project of an 'apocalyptic Christology' in a different manner altogether, while still retaining the ecclesial and political emphases of Hauerwas. The way forward, I want to suggest, will be one which restores the singular, apocalyptic historicity of Jesus of Nazareth as constitutive of the Christian politics of mission and which is thus able to conceive of the church's politics in terms of a more subtle and more complex 'missionary' engagement with the irreducibly contingent, finite, relative, and pluralistic events of this world's history. This will necessarily entail, at the same time, a more rigorous engagement with the historicist concerns of Troeltsch. This way of proceeding is one that I think is taken up most fruitfully in the work of John Howard Yoder, which I shall seek constructively to develop in the final two chapters.

---

113 See the comments of Romand Coles, in Coles and Hauerwas, *Christianity, Democracy, and the Radical Ordinary*, pp. 329–30.

5

John Howard Yoder: The Singularity of Jesus and the Apocalypticization of History

The last two chapters have resituated the questions of history, politics, and mission within an alternative 'apocalyptic' framework in conversation with the work of Karl Barth and Stanley Hauerwas. I have sought to trace the arguments by which one might justify the claim that the life story of Jesus of Nazareth turns out to be the rich and complex content of God's Kingdom breaking into and transforming the manifold contingencies of this created world. But the radicalism both of Barth's apocalyptic Christology and of Hauerwas's narrative ecclesiology revealed certain new challenges beyond those of modern theological historicism. For the horizons opened up by the actualist ontology of the former and the metanarrative communal-dependency of the latter finally proved reductive, in their own ways, of the ever-shifting relativities and complexities of historical reality, as well as of the contingent particularity of Jesus' own historicity. This left us unable, with Barth, to think 'politics' otherwise than in the mode of liberalism and, with Hauerwas, to think 'mission' otherwise than as the church's assertion of its own antiliberal political 'identity'.

However, I find the underlying intention of Barth and Hauerwas to situate the question of history Christologically and apocalyptically, for the sake of thinking 'ecclesia' politically, to be exactly right. And so in this and in the final chapter, I should like to take up, and constructively to follow through with, yet another thinker's attempt to do just that: John Howard Yoder.

Genealogically, in this chapter I shall reconsider Yoder's relationship to Hauerwas, for the sake of repositioning his work with respect to Barth and Troeltsch. My analysis of Yoder will be devoted to a two-pronged exposition of the logic of Jesus' 'apocalyptic historicity' as a dual logic of 'singularity' and of 'excess'. This dual logic amounts to an 'apocalypticization of history' that is irreducibly political.

With and beyond Hauerwas (and Back to Barth and Troeltsch)

To begin with, we need briefly to take up the question of Yoder's own relation to Hauerwas's project, so as to clarify the sense in which we will be seeking to read Yoder on his own terms, as well as demonstrate why such a reading requires us to read Yoder anew vis-à-vis Troeltsch and Barth.

For some time now, it has been the working assumption of many that the ecclesiological project of Hauerwas can more or less be faithfully rendered as a taking up and extension of the ethico-political exposition of the history of Jesus and the church as supplied by John Howard Yoder. Hauerwas himself is mostly to blame for this assumption, insofar as he has continued throughout his career not only to express admiration for Yoder's life and work but also to give almost unqualified approval to many dimensions of Yoder's own project.[1] The cumulative effect, it seems, is that Yoder has come to be read less and less on his own terms and more and more through the lens of Hauerwas's writings, the latter all too easily being taken as a programmatic (and more polemically potent) development of ideas culled from and nurtured through the tutelage of his one-time Notre Dame colleague.

---

1 See, e.g., S. Hauerwas and C. Huebner, 'History, Theory, and Anabaptism: A Conversation on Theology after John Howard Yoder', in *Wisdom of the Cross*, pp. 391–408; Hauerwas, 'Foreword' to C. Carter, *The Politics of the Cross: The Theology and Social Ethics of John Howard Yoder* (Grand Rapids: Brazos Press, 2001).

Now, it certainly is the case that Hauerwas and Yoder were and remain 'allies' in the task of constructing a non-Constantinian politics rooted in the story of Jesus and made visible in the life of the church, and I do not want to challenge this alliance as such. What I do want to suggest is that we need to reconsider the nature of this alliance and view it from a new angle altogether – namely, from the perspective of that which is unique about Yoder's own project vis-à-vis that of Hauerwas. So the first task of this chapter will be to re-examine a key point of *convergence* between Yoder and Hauerwas – their shared point of departure from within Barth's apocalyptic Christology – as itself the most important point of *divergence* between the two. I shall suggest that this point of divergence, which has to do with the nature and understanding of Jesus' 'historicity' from within an apocalyptic perspective, requires us to inquire into the viability of affirming, beyond the presumed incompatibilities, Barth's apocalyptic Christology while also accounting for a kind of radical plurality and contingency as advocated by a historicist such as Troeltsch.

It is important to be reminded of what it was from the beginning that drew Hauerwas to Yoder's theology and of what I find to be *right* about Hauerwas's reading of Yoder. From the outset, Hauerwas encountered Yoder's theology as a way of constructively liberating American Christian theology from the distorting categories of Troeltsch inherited by the brothers Niebuhr,[2] especially as concerns the depoliticizing of 'Jesus' in the name of 'history'.[3] Moreover, as argued in Chapter 2, Yoder helps us to see that this de-politicization of Jesus is thoroughly underwritten by a 'Constantinian' ideology that makes the church itself 'morally necessary but politically irrelevant',[4] continually subject to the auspices of some other established or conventional governing power.

For Hauerwas, Yoder cuts across Christianity's ideological

---

2 See Hauerwas, VV, pp. 197–221.
3 Hauerwas, BH, p. 131.
4 Hauerwas, BH, p. 134.

accommodation to 'society' with his account of 'the politics of Jesus'. More specifically, Yoder understands the apocalyptic action of God in Christ as constituting an altogether *new* political possibility in the world, as the emergence of a new *event in history* – the concrete life history of Jesus of Nazareth. Furthermore, this apocalyptic understanding of the history of Jesus Christ *as* political is what allows for us genuinely to conceive of the church itself as the visible sign and presence of a new political possibility, an altogether different kind of 'politics'. Here especially Yoder speaks 'with' Hauerwas, for it is Yoder himself who provides the impetus for Hauerwas to speak 'with and beyond' Barth on the question of apocalyptic and politics: the concrete political 'gathering' that is the *ecclesia* is not ancillary to, nor is it a declension from, the apocalyptic irruption of God in Christ, but is rather immanent to its very logic.

With regard to Hauerwas's alliance with Yoder, then: so far, so good. Jesus' apocalyptic interruption *of* history must itself be the instauration of a visible movement *within* history which witnesses to and embodies Jesus' own penetration and subversion of the various forms of established 'worldly' and 'historical' logic. And yet it is precisely at this point that we witness a marked *divergence* between Hauerwas and Yoder. For it is here that Hauerwas insists upon integrating the history of Jesus into the ongoing narrative existence of the church, thereby shifting the centre of gravity of Christian 'apocalyptic' from Jesus to the church, and from Christology to ecclesiology, in such a way as to make of apocalyptic itself the basis of yet another theoretical, universalizing perspective on 'history', namely, that of the church's intra-textual 'counter-narrative', which yet remains too 'Constantinian' in its logic. In short, by rushing so quickly to articulate the 'politics of Jesus' as also the 'politics of the church', Hauerwas is left with an account of the ecclesial community that unintentionally abstracts from the historicity of Jesus and of all of the contingencies and complexities of historical reality, which Yoder's apocalypticism is meant especially to affirm.

What I am suggesting is that if Hauerwas had lingered just a little longer with the nuances of Yoder's apocalyptic perspective on Jesus, he might have recognized a way beyond what he perceived as Barth's ecclesio-political failures that would have been yet more consistent with the trajectory of Barth's own apocalyptic Christology. This is because, for Yoder, apocalyptic is fundamentally a means to thinking history, politics, and the church on the basis of the 'objective reality' of Jesus' singular historicity, or what he calls Jesus' 'independence'. In its most basic sense, to speak of Jesus' 'independence' is to say that Jesus lives, concretely and in history, a life-story that is entirely free from and irreducible to any pre-given 'historical' coordinates, any general or 'meta' principle that might serve to range the complexities and contingencies of his history within any universalizable scope or logic. At the same time, Jesus' independence demarcates also the way in which his apocalyptic historicity happens concomitantly as the *intensification* and *transformation* of the historically contingent as such.

It is important to appreciate the angle at which this places Yoder with respect to Hauerwas. Whereas for Hauerwas apocalyptic becomes essentially an ecclesiological strategy for establishing the church-as-*polis* vis-à-vis the modern liberal nation state, for Yoder apocalyptic remains principally a tactical process of negotiating the ordinary (secular) contingencies and particularities of the everyday world and seeking from within them to articulate the truth of the gospel, the divine inbreaking of God's Kingdom which is the very historicity of Jesus of Nazareth. This is not to say that the church is not itself a political upshot of this process, embedded within and inseparable from this history; but it is to say that in the working of the church conceived from within this apocalyptic perspective the centrality of Jesus' own historicity – his 'independence' – everywhere retains its primacy.

What I want to stress here is that this particular point of divergence between Yoder and Hauerwas is at the same time what qualifies Yoder's apocalypticism as remaining yet more faithful to the intentions of Barth's own 'apocalyptic Christology', namely, a deep commitment to a richly textured account of God's action in Christ amidst the contingencies and complexities of history. But even here Yoder also diverges from Barth just as quickly as he converges with him. For Yoder will not allow his Christology and his account of Jesus' historicity to give way to an account of history that is based upon such a hierarchical construal of the relation of eternity to time as Barth's metaphysical actualism.

Against this, Yoder argues that, if we are truly to understand Jesus Christ as 'a political person', we need not only to think of the incarnation as simply a matter of stressing that God became a particular human being at a particular time in history but also to think in a more thoroughgoing fashion in 'historicist' terms about Jesus' (and God's) very own human historicity.[5] Yoder's point here is clear: a genuinely apocalyptic perspective on Jesus forbids any Christology that bids or allows for a retreat from the complexities of real, concrete history. In Christ, God's Kingdom has paradoxically broken into history as a Kingdom that is *coming* and that is *present* as breaking everanew into the contingencies and particularities of history, from out of which contingencies and particularities alone the decision to remain faithful to that coming emerges. In short, political faithfulness to Christ and his Kingdom lies ahead of us, as it breaks *into* history itself, and not behind us, in some reified 'particular' that has been rendered historically abstract by way of its reductively 'vertical' relation to eternity.

In other words, any genuinely 'apocalyptic Christology' must entail and be filled out as *its own distinct historicism*. And thus, just as we find in Yoder's apocalypticism a half-turn back to Barth, so also do we find a nod in the direction of Troeltsch. Indeed, Yoder's refusal to prescind at any point from the uniqueness and independence of Jesus is bound up with his insistence, *pace* Troeltsch, that 'reality always was

---

5 See Yoder, DPR, pp. 53–4.

pluralistic and relativistic, that is, historical'.[6] At the same time, however, this is not to force a 'choice' of history over dogmatics (as Troeltsch had presumed), but rather to insist that the dogmatic basis of the Christian faith – the confession that 'Jesus Christ is Lord' – is a statement concerning the most radically contingent and most thoroughgoing *historical* reality of all, namely, the event of the crucifixion and resurrection of the man Jesus of Nazareth.[7]

The important point to make with regard to Yoder in this case is that for him the very uniqueness of any event or reality in relation to its interconnection with other events in history is bound up with who Jesus Christ is as Lord of the cosmos; such uniqueness and relativity cannot themselves be communicated and lived apart from the particular historic, cosmic, and indeed apocalyptic reality that is Jesus of Nazareth. In other words, this singular apocalyptic perspective upon Jesus of Nazareth is that which alone allows us to confront the particularities, complexities, and contingencies of history for what they are, without either abstracting from them to some kind of idealist 'total perspective' or fixing them within an immanental web of historical causality. Thus, vis-à-vis the 'universal' theological historicism of Troeltsch we shall need to articulate and set the 'Jesus-is-Lord' historicism of Yoder.[8]

Herein, then, lies our task: to consider the way in which a properly 'apocalyptic Christology' at once addresses the challenge and subverts the assumptions of modern historicism itself (as from the inside, perhaps). Only then will Jesus' political mission emerge as a genuine challenge to a world and a polity guided continually by the hegemony of modern historicism – as the event of a kingdom that displays the 'truth' of history's contingencies and complexities *via* a certain interruption and

---

6 Yoder, PK, p. 59.

7 See Yoder, PJ, p. 103.

8 See H. Huebner, 'Learning Made Strange: Can a University Be Christian?', in *God, Truth, and Witness: Engaging Stanley Hauerwas*, ed. L. G. Jones, R. Hütter, and C. R. V. Ewell (Grand Rapids: Brazos Press, 2005), pp. 280–308, p. 295.

transcendence of the universalizing *historical* and *political* story that modern theological historicism presupposes and presumes to tell.[9]

The Politics of Jesus and 'Apocalyptic Historicity' (1): Jesus' Moral Independence and the Logic of Singularity

In this and the next section, I want to articulate an alternative 'apocalyptic historicity' as supplying the 'scaffolding' or 'framework' for a more genuinely political understanding of the church-as-mission. Keeping as close as possible to the text of *The Politics of Jesus*, I shall seek to do two things:

1 primarily in conversation with Troeltsch, I shall attempt to correlate God's interruption of history in Jesus Christ with a historicist 'logic' of *singularity* that is irreducible to or in excess of any presumed notion of historical or political 'universality'; and
2 in conversation with Barth, I shall try to demonstrate that there is *within* Jesus' singularity an internal 'logic' of divine *excess* by which Jesus' own apocalyptic historicity – through which alone he emerges as *Logos* and 'Lord' of the cosmos – is inseparable from the 'more' that God is doing in relation to that which emerges contingently within and across history.

In making these two points, I shall be seeking to isolate a historicist apocalyptic logic in order then to begin discerning how this logic is at work in determining the life of the church in the world as an altogether different mode of political engagement and action.

Let me begin by recalling what is at stake in Christian

---

9 Cf. A. Weaver, 'Missionary Christology: John Howard Yoder and the Creeds', *The Mennonite Quarterly Review* 74.3 (July 2000), pp. 423–39, p. 438. Cf. also Rasmusson, 'Historicizing the Historicist: Ernst Troeltsch and Recent Mennonite Theology', in *Wisdom of the Cross*, pp. 213–48.

apocalyptic as a particular theological perspective on history vis-à-vis the dominant perspective of modern theological historicism. For Yoder, apocalyptic is fundamentally an 'idiom' or 'style' of living and thinking history as eschatologically oriented.[10] In Chapter 2, I stressed the way in which modern theological historicism conceives of history as teleo-eschatologically oriented, in such a way that the 'Kingdom of God' functions as the absolute, transcendent (transhistorical) reality *beyond* history, which yet marks the limits *of* history and provides the universal goal towards which the individualities of history are nevertheless progressing via their own particular intrahistorical development. On the one hand, then, against this teleo-eschatological perspective, 'apocalyptic' for Yoder names the particular operation of God's 'transcendence' and of God's 'Kingdom' *within* history, on the basis of its having *broken into* history *from beyond*. This is the apocalyptic imagination that Yoder finds to be at the heart of the Judeo-Christian prophetic tradition and literature. In a passage that we should be careful to read as directly challenging the presuppositions of modern theological historicism, Yoder writes:

The seers differ . . . in that they proclaim the 'known world' to be too small not because they have from the inside come to the edge of it, but because God has reached and spoken into it from beyond. In our age 'transcendence' is sometimes a code word for the fact that, from within our own system, we know ourselves to be finite, thereby creating by extrapolation the notion of 'beyond' even though there be nothing (nothing we can know) 'out there'. Prophetic transcendence comes from the other end; the 'beyond' came first. Divine command, divine agency, divine will are prior to, not derived from, extrapolated from our finitude.[11]

---

10 Yoder, EE; Yoder, AE. On the notion of an apocalyptic 'style', see D. Toole, *Waiting for Godot in Sarajevo: Theological Reflections on Nihilism, Tragedy, and Apocalypse* (Boulder, CO: Westview Press, 1998), pp. 206–10.

11 Yoder, EE, p. 126.

As a way of characterizing the relation of God's Kingdom to history, then, 'apocalyptic' is but an alternative way of portraying history's eschatological orientation, and of portraying the finite and contingent realities of the world as operative of divine 'transcendence', now conceived as the priority of God's free and interruptive action in Christ.

At the same time, this alternative apocalyptic-eschatological perspective on history requires a certain cosmic-historical conception of Jesus Christ, which stands in contrast to the psychological-historical portrayal of Christ offered by Troeltsch. Yoder makes this point succinctly with respect to the question of Christ's 'rule' or 'lordship': 'The challenge to which the proclamation of Christ's rule . . . speaks a word of grace is not a problem within the self but a split within the cosmos.'[12] That is to say, the apocalyptic perspective cuts across the psychological dualisms – between 'spirit' and 'nature', the 'individual soul' and 'material history', etc. – that the universal-historicist perspective necessarily trades upon by insisting that the life history marked by Jesus' '"cross and resurrection" designates not only a few days' events in first-century Jerusalem but also the shape of the cosmos'.[13]

The important point I wish to stress here, in relation to Troeltsch, is that for Yoder, from within an apocalyptic-eschatological perspective, the cosmic and historical dimensions of Christ's person retain their relevance only and always at the level of Jesus of Nazareth's own irreducible *historicity*. The cosmic and historical relevance of God's apocalyptic action in Christ is not finally articulable at some prior or more general level – whether that be metaphysical, psychological, ontological, or in the form of metanarrative – of which the contingent human historicity of Jesus of Nazareth is merely a particular illustration, expression, cipher, or point of departure. Rather, such relevancy is alone articulable through the *politically historicist* retelling of the life story of that one whom the

---

12 Yoder, PJ, p. 161.
13 Yoder, PJ, p. 160. Cf. Yoder, FTN, p. 87.

Sanhedrin hounded and the Romans killed and of whom the Christians witness as having been raised on the third day.

It is here that the first key aspect of Jesus' apocalyptic historicity emerges clearly into view: that of a *singular* event in history which is solely conceivable apart from, and so as irreducible to or in excess of, any presumed notion of historical or political 'universality'. As such, we can only really begin to understand the apocalyptically historicist logic of Jesus' singularity by indicating the precise sense in which for Yoder Jesus' 'identity' is that of one living 'morally independent' of the 'powers and principalities', which themselves function in history according to a universalized and immanentized 'logic of causality'.[14]

In the chapter of *Politics* entitled 'Christ and Power',[15] Yoder deploys the Pauline language regarding 'the principalities and powers' in an attempt to show that the powers functioned for Paul in a manner 'structurally analogous' to the way in which certain customs, institutions, and ideologies function for modern social and political science; 'the Powers', Yoder says, are not unlike what contemporary social science is wont to call 'structures'.[16] The 'Powers' for Paul, like our modern sociopolitical 'structures', function in such a way as to presuppose their own universal coherence and self-maintenance: 'the concept "structure" functions to point to the patterns or regularities that transcend or precede or condition the individual phenomena we can immediately perceive'.[17] In other words, the powers function according to the priority of certain pre-individual and 'universal' modes of social organization and operation, which are de facto sovereign with respect to the particular and the contingent.

---

14 My understanding of the way in which the powers function politically for Yoder has been significantly enriched by conversations with Dan Barber. See also D. Barber, 'The Particularity of Jesus and the Time of the Kingdom: Philosophy and Theology in Yoder', *Modern Theology* 23.1 (January 2007), pp. 63–89.

15 Yoder, PJ, pp. 134–61.

16 Yoder, PJ, p. 142.

17 Yoder, PJ, p. 138.

Thus, the concrete socio-political function of 'the Powers' is what might be called 'ideological'; that is, the powers function to provide the given structural 'handle' by which one can 'get a hold on' the course of history and move it in the 'right direction'.[18] What ultimately determines this 'right direction' is that one privileged socio-political 'thread of meaning which is more important than individual persons, their lives and well-being, because it in itself determines wherein their well-being consists . . . We pull this one strategic thread in order to save the whole fabric.'[19] In short, what the powers presume is that the particulars of history are themselves to be related to some more universal reality or goal, which relation involves its own immanently determined nexus of causality, the proper negotiation of which is determinative of the powers' political 'dominion' or 'sovereignty'.

Now, it should be stressed that Yoder does not pretend to offer up this reading of Paul's 'exousiology' as a matter of strict exegesis, nor is he seeking to suggest that such language is for Paul straightforwardly 'socio-political', in the sense that term has for us today. His intention rather is to show how this powers language (and especially the apocalyptic-eschatological cosmology of Paul within which such language operates), might shed some light upon the (perennially universalist) presuppositions of modern political and historical thought, as well as bring into sharper focus the specific challenge that a retrieval of the 'idiom of apostolic apocalyptic' poses to such thought. For what the apocalyptic idiom or style does, first of all, is refuse to appeal to the system-immanent accounts of instrumentality and technique according to which the powers have conditioned us to relate to our world.[20] The apocalyptic hope is hope for a world and for a history that is not immanentized. It is rather a hope which believes with the good news of the gospel that God has reached out and spoken into the world

---

18 Yoder, PJ, p. 228.
19 Yoder, PJ, p. 229.
20 Yoder, PJ, pp. 228–33. Cf. especially Yoder, EE, pp. 120–3.

and history, in such a way as to display the way the world and history really work in the life, death, and resurrection of Jesus Christ.[21] To think apocalyptically according to God's inter-ruptive action in Christ is to live within the world and history *differently*, to live within a cosmos whose edges have been de-cisively 'reopened',[22] and to live history as itself a kind of 'open future',[23] which future is itself 'timed' by the *historic* inbreak-ing of God's coming Kingdom in Jesus. It is living within this alternative world and history which defines our freedom from the dominion of the powers, from the presumed universal-historical logic of 'power and causation' according to which the rulers of this world find it necessary to operate.[24]

What must be stressed here, however, is that we are able to think and to live the world and history in this way solely on the basis of the singular life history that is Jesus of Nazareth – the stark historicity of *this* one's life, death, and resurrection. For it is in this historicity that Jesus is 'independent' of the Powers in such a way as directly to *challenge* them and to prove *victori-ous over* them. Jesus was a 'threat to [the powers'] dominion' because 'he existed in their midst so morally independent of their pretensions'.[25]

Christ *challenges* the pretensions of the powers by living in history a life that is irreducible to the powers at both an opera-tive and constitutive level. In order to demonstrate how this is so, Yoder focuses upon the way in which the biblical narrative presents the complexes of historical event and circumstance which led to Jesus' death on the cross as the attempt of the powers to preserve their sovereignty against a life history that refuses categorization within their own logics of causal effect-iveness and ideological relevance. To live as Jesus does in the world – in faithfulness to the *agape* of God, even to the point of loving one's enemies and freely accepting death at their

---

21 See Yoder, PJ, p. 126; Yoder, AE, 49.
22 Yoder, PJ, p. 52.
23 Yoder, EE, p. 126.
24 Yoder, EE, pp. 120–3.
25 Yoder, PJ, 145.

hands; to practise a suffering-servant love for those whose very subjugation the sovereignty of the powers is dependent upon (the sick, the imprisoned, the poor, the marginalized); to refuse violence amidst a world pervaded and determined by antagonism – is precisely to 'give up every handle on history', to refuse the compulsion to effectiveness and the urge to 'manage' one's world. Thus Jesus challenges the sovereignty of the powers 'concretely and historically, by living a genuinely free and human existence. This life brought him, as any genuinely human existence will bring anyone, to the cross. In his death the Powers – in this case the most worthy, weighty representatives of Jewish religion and Roman politics – acted in collusion.'[26] Indeed, these particular powers even contort their own presumed moral and political paradigms in order to preserve their sovereignty against this 'genuinely free and human' life and existence:

> [Jesus] permitted the Jews to profane a holy day (refuting thereby their own moral pretensions) and permitted the Romans to deny their vaunted respect for the law as they proceeded illegally against him. This they did in order to avoid the threat to their dominion represented by the very fact that he existed in their midst so morally independent of their pretensions.[27]

So the very fact that the powers in this case will break with what has previously been posited as normative and paradigmatic in order to extend and maintain their sovereignty is an indication that the powers recognize in Jesus a concrete life that their previously operative logic is unable fully to determine.

It is extremely important that we grasp this point, for in killing Jesus in the attempt to preserve their own sovereign determination while at the same time breaking with their own operative logic, the powers (unwittingly) testify to the

---

26 Yoder, PJ, pp. 144–5.
27 Yoder, PJ, p. 145.

displacement of their basic constitutive function. That is to say, the powers' very attempt to carry out their universal causal-determinative function with respect to Jesus' life and death is itself conditioned by the fact that they recognize in Jesus' singular historicity the (divine) possibility of a contrary logic, namely, that of the cross and resurrection.

This alternative 'logic' turns out to be the concrete obedience of a singular human being to the inbreaking of God's Kingdom into the world as the way of suffering love.[28] The point here is that not only is Jesus' life and death in the world not *positively* determined by the logic of the powers and principalities of this world, but neither is it *negatively* determined by this logic, as something which is to be stubbornly resisted. Thus, tracing the rhythms of the Christ hymn in Philippians 2.6–11, Yoder presents Jesus' going to the cross and his free acceptance of death at the hands of the Powers as an acceptance borne first (and *only, singularly*) out of obedience to his mission from the Father, which binds him as a sacrifice of love to and for his fellow men and women. In turn, the resurrection reveals Jesus' acceptance of 'impotence' and 'powerlessness', as well as his renunciation of the 'effective sovereignty and assured survival' by which the powers presume to 'govern history',[29] to be neither an instance of nihilistic political *ressentiment* nor an alternative 'strategy' for securing the future, but rather a sign that the Kingdom of God, as well as the glorification by which Jesus is to be recognized as Christ and Lord are *gifts* to be received freely from the Father, in the posture of love alone. Thus, Jesus' cross and resurrection do indeed mark for us God's apocalyptic action to invade a cosmos politically enslaved to the powers and the principalities, as well as to interrupt and to challenge the powers' governing universalist presumptions. But they do this only as God's action is conceived as at one with the singular historicity which is Jesus Christ, which historicity is independent of the universalist

---

28 See Yoder, PJ, pp. 237–41.
29 Yoder, PJ, pp. 234, 237–9.

pretensions of the principalities and powers inasmuch as it is at once (and paradoxically) *conditioned by* and *constitutive of* that transcendent reality which is *beyond* the powers as *prior* to them – the reign of God's *agape*.

Only here can we truly begin to understand in what sense 'the cross is victory', in what sense Jesus' 'independence' represents not simply a political *challenge to* the Powers but a *triumph over* them. Borrowing an extensive quotation from Hendrikus Berkhof, Yoder describes this triumph by way of reference to Colossians 2.13–15:

> On the cross [Jesus] 'disarmed' the Powers, 'made a public example of them and thereby triumphed over them' . . . It is precisely in the crucifixion that the true nature of the Powers has come to light. Previously they were accepted as the most basic and ultimate realities, as the gods of the world. Never had it been perceived, nor could it have been perceived, that this belief was founded on deception . . . Now they are unmasked as false gods by their encounter with Very God; they are made a public spectacle. Thus Christ has 'triumphed over them'. The unmasking is actually already their defeat . . . The concrete evidence of this triumph is that at the cross Christ has 'disarmed' the Powers. The weapon from which they heretofore derived their strength is struck out of their hands. This weapon was the power of illusion, their ability to convince us that they were the divine regents of the world, ultimate certainty and ultimate direction, ultimate happiness and the ultimate duty for small, dependent humanity. Since Christ we know that this is illusion.[30]

What I want to isolate here is the way in which Yoder depicts Jesus' political challenge to and defeat of the powers as an ancillary function of his 'moral independence', as itself a kind of logical operation of singularity as embodied in the historicity of Jesus' cross and resurrection. In the concreteness of the 'self-giving, nonresistant' love by which the human being Jesus goes

---

30 Yoder, PJ, pp. 146–7.

freely to his death on the cross, there is an operation at work
– the *agape* logic of God's Kingdom – that no given political
theory or formula will be sufficient to categorize, encapsulate,
or explain: 'Here we have for the first time to do with someone
who is not the slave of any power, of any law or custom, community or institution, value or theory.'[31] What Yoder means to
say here, it seems, is simply that Jesus' identity (which is indeed
an 'ethic', a 'way of life') cannot be captured by any of the
universalist 'human' categories by which we seek to 'control',
'manipulate', 'cause', 'effect', and 'sustain' life and death. For
Jesus' sole purpose is to 'love in the way of the cross and in the
power of the resurrection'.[32] To say then that in the cross of
Christ 'effectiveness and success were sacrificed for the sake of
love', and that in the resurrection 'this sacrifice was turned by
God into a victory which vindicated to the utmost the apparent
impotence of love',[33] is to say that in the face of the undiscrimin-
ating and unconditional, yet singular, nature of this love, the
pretensions to universality by which we presume to discrimin-
ate and condition – to control – history and life in this world
are just that: namely, illusory presumptions and pretensions.

Within this apocalyptic-eschatological framework, then, the
logics of singularity and of Jesus' independence operate in such
a way that any teleo-eschatological conception of history that
universalizes and transcendentalizes the Kingdom of God with
respect to the particularities and contingencies of history collapses. That is, Jesus is operative (that is, he *acts*) *in* history
in such a manner as singularly to disrupt and transcend the
universalizing function of all causal immanental systems and
their corresponding teleo-eschatological frameworks. Such a
way of operating 'identifies' Jesus as the paradigmatic act of
what Jean-Yves Lacoste calls 'a grace beyond the universal',[34]

31 Yoder, PJ, p. 145.
32 Yoder, OR, p. 58.
33 Yoder, OR, pp. 56–7.
34 J.-Y. Lacoste, *Experience and the Absolute: Disputed Questions
on the Humanity of Man*, tr. M. Raftery-Skehan (New York: Ford-
ham, 2004), p. 65.

where the 'beyond' retains the sense of the *priority* of the free and contingent coming of the reign of God.[35] Jesus (as the crucified one) is so absolutely abandoned to this coming as to be indistinguishable from it (as the resurrected and ascended one) – and he is this as precisely an interruption of our 'world', of our 'history', and of the 'meaning' which we presume to make for ourselves. Jesus thereby inaugurates an apocalyptic challenge to teleology in the name of the eschatological reign of God. And he does this insofar as his historicist particularity singularly identifies this apocalypse.

The radical upshot of all this is that 'history' and 'politics' now have no autonomy or integrity, no inner 'telos' vis-à-vis the Kingdom of God as such. One can no longer speak of 'history' and of the 'Kingdom' and of 'politics' without articulating the singularly historicist nature of Jesus' independent and alternative operation of love.

The Politics of Jesus and 'Apocalyptic Historicity' (2): Incarnation, Contingency, and the Logic of Excess[36]

If the moral independence of Jesus (by which alone the Kingdom of God is instantiated and identified) operates in such an *apocalyptically singular* manner, how then are we also to think of this singularity as *cosmic* and *historical*, without thereby abstracting from the contingencies and complexities of that very 'history' which God's Kingdom in Christ invades and interrupts? The force of this question is only heightened when we recall that, for Yoder, Jesus, precisely by way of his moral independence and this logic of his historicist singular-

---

35 See Yoder, RP, 104.

36 On this notion of 'excess' in Yoder's writing, I am indebted first of all to R. Coles, 'The Wild Patience of John Howard Yoder: "Outsiders" and the "Otherness" of the Church', *Modern Theology* 18.3 (July 2002), pp. 305–31, p. 325; but also to Barber, 'Particularity of Jesus', *passim*. The interpretation of this 'excess' (which is Yoder's language) as that of God's ongoing apocalyptic action in history, however, is entirely my own.

ity, 'incorporate[s] a *greater* righteousness than that of the Pharisees, and a vision of an order of social human relations *more* universal than the Pax Romana'.[37] There is no doubt that this 'more' arises from the sense in which Jesus' moral independence is 'a social, political, *structural* fact'; and yet it is this precisely as 'a declaration about the nature of the cosmos and the significance of history'.[38] Yoder's point is that what Paul's account of Christ's triumph over the powers teaches us is that the way to think history and politics in a manner genuinely free from the presumed universalizing and ideological mechanisms of control is to think the singularity of Christ's cross and resurrection as the key to all of history. Yet the challenge is to do this in such a way that Christ's singular historicity is not itself falsely universalized, in a manner that a priori and metaphysically severs the resurrected crucified one from ongoing history, with all the contingency and complexity it involves.

In this section, I want to interpret the 'historicist' nature of this 'more' that is internal to Jesus' 'moral independence' from the powers and principalities, by interrogating Yoder's understanding of the Incarnation as a further (dogmatic) specification of Jesus' historicist singularity. It is ultimately by way of a certain trinitarian 'logic of excess' that Jesus' singularity – his cross and resurrection – entails for Yoder an *apocalyptic* conditioning of the 'cosmic' and 'historical'. What I shall be tracking is the sense in which Jesus' singular identity is so embedded within and bound up with the historicist particularities surrounding his cross and resurrection that his historicity cannot be the apocalyptic inbreaking of God's Kingdom into history except as this apocalyptic inbreaking is itself conceived of as at one with the 'more' that God is doing amidst the contingencies of ongoing history (contingencies with which the living Jesus – as the resurrected crucified one – is yet still bound up, by way of this 'more', through the power of the Spirit).[39] In the course

---

37 Yoder, PJ, p. 145 (emphases added).

38 Yoder, PJ, p. 157. Cf. Yoder, FTN, p. 87.

39 It is extremely important to note here that Yoder everywhere and unequivocally identifies this 'more', this divine 'excess', as 'the life-

of my analysis, it will hopefully become clear that Jesus' apocalyptic singularity is not only rendered *Christologically* unintelligible apart from its operativity (qua apocalyptic) within
the ongoing contingencies of history, but that his singularity
operates with respect to this 'more' in such a way as apocalyptically to *intensify* and *transform* the contingencies of history
in relation to the coming reign of God.

Perhaps the best way to get clear on this point is to read
Yoder's stress upon Jesus' 'moral independence' and the logic
of singularity entailed therein as an attempt to develop with
much more robustness the 'historicist' trajectories of Barth's
apocalyptic Christology. In fact, we could say that Yoder
develops his account of Jesus' apocalyptic historicity precisely
by loosing key aspects of Barth's later, narrative Christology
from the residual metaphysical formulations according to
which Barth still related 'Jesus' to 'history'. The rapproche-
ment between Yoder and Barth that is most significant for us
occurs at the point in which Yoder seeks to take up and extend
the later Barth's emphasis upon the human historicity of Jesus
of Nazareth as God. Yoder's concern, *pace* Barth, is especially with 'demonstrating how profound is the importance of the
concrete historicity of Jesus as man and servant, to safeguard
the correct understanding of incarnation'.[40] For here Yoder
glimpses the possibility of narratively describing 'the Jesus
of the gospels in his full humanity and lifestyle', in a manner that yet resists the temptation to found the shape of this
narrative on the basis of an isolated Christological formula,[41]
and so succeeds in breaking free, as Barth intended all along
with his actualist perspective on Christ, from a vision of history as the mere unfolding of an 'obscure metaphysics'.[42]

Let me demonstrate how this is the case. Throughout his

---

giving power of the Spirit', by which power alone Jesus' person and
work are identifiably at one with the coming of God's kingdom. See,
e.g., Yoder, OR, pp. 49, 51.

40 Yoder, KBPW, pp. 141, 152.
41 Yoder, KBPW, p. 141.
42 See Barth, CD IV/3.1, p. 136.

oeuvre, Yoder struggles to articulate an understanding of the Incarnation in terms of the human-historical or lived character of Jesus' identity with God. In doing so, Yoder aims to eschew a too easily assumed 'metaphysical' or 'logological' sense of the Incarnation, which would make of the idea that Jesus is 'the Word become flesh' a mere representation to us of some metaphysically conceptualized relation of the Logos to God, according to which conceptualization we might then proceed ontologically to 'locate' or 'emplot' history within a mediated hierarchy of eternity and time.[43] Against this, Yoder argues for what he calls the 'historical' or 'Jesulogical' sense of the Incarnation:

> When the Jewish writer of the Fourth Gospel sang 'the word became flesh and tabernacled among us' . . . he meant to describe the setting for the entire earthly work of the man Jesus, fully human, vulnerable, to whom that other John pointed as the 'Lamb who takes away the world's sin'. 'Incarnation' then means that *in* the concrete historical reality of the life and death and rising of Jesus, the otherwise invisible God has been made known normatively.[44]

What I take Yoder to mean here is that we can only speak of Jesus as God – but not only that, of the eternal Logos itself – from within the density and angularity of his constituent life-story. Yoder remarks, for example, that the statement at Jesus' baptism, 'Thou art my Son', is 'not the definition or accreditation of a metaphysically defined status of Sonship; it is the summons to a task. Jesus is commissioned to be, in history, in Palestine, the messianic son and servant, the bearer of the goodwill and the promise of God.'[45] The words of Rowan

---

43 J. Yoder, 'Historiography as a Ministry to Renewal', *Brethren Life and Thought* 42 (2004), pp. 216–28, p. 216.

44 Yoder, 'Historiography', pp. 216–17. Cf. J. Yoder, 'On Not Being Ashamed of the Gospel: Particularity, Pluralism, and Validation', *Faith and Philosophy* 9.3 (July 1992), pp. 285–300, p. 294.

45 Yoder, PJ, p. 24. Cf. Yoder, RP, p. 185: 'The concept of Incarnation, God's assuming human nature, has often made us direct our

Williams help to sum up Yoder's point here: 'There is no sense in thinking that we can talk about the Incarnation without talking of the whole course of Jesus' life, the whole historical identity of Jesus' – with all the ambiguity, uncontrollability, and contingency that such an identity entails.[46]

So for Yoder, we clearly do not rightly conceive of the historicity of Jesus of Nazareth if we persist in thinking of Jesus' unity with God as some kind of already realized, unshakeable, 'eternal' given.[47] Instead, who Jesus is emerges for us ultimately in the resurrection and ascension of *this* crucified one, as the history of the one who was hounded by *this* body of religious ideologues, as the one who is put to death by *this* Roman government – that is, he is the risen Christ as inseparably bound up with the social and political concerns that are at work in the world wherever he appears most concretely as *this* human being, with all of the specificity and contingency that entails.[48]

---

thought to metaphysics; asking how it can be that the human nature and the divine nature can be present together in one person. Whether this substantial miracle be joyously affirmed . . . or found unthinkable . . . it seems agreed by all that metaphysics is the question. But when, in the New Testament, we find the affirmation of the unity of Jesus with the Father, this is not discussed in terms of substance but of will and deed. It is visible in Jesus's perfect *obedience* to the *will* of the Father.' It should be noted here that it is clear from the contexts in which this passage and the one from the text proper above appear that Yoder is not advocating a form of 'adoptionist' Christology, as if Jesus were somehow not *eternally* 'Son of God'. Rather, what Yoder is suggesting is that if it is in fact *Jesus* that is eternally the Son of God, then the nature of his 'eternal Sonship' as such is not to be determined or affirmed in isolation, but is rather inextricably bound up with 'the conferring of a mission in history'. In other words, for Yoder, the language of 'history' and of 'historicity' is no less true a way of talking about and conceiving eternity's relation to time than is the language of 'substance' and 'metaphysics'. See Yoder, PJ, pp. 24–5. Cf. Yoder, PT, pp. 124–5, 139–40, 275–6.

46 Rowan Williams, *On Christian Theology*, p. 82; see p. 159.

47 Yoder, PT, pp. 86–7.

48 Yoder, PJ, p. 234.

Yet as we saw in the previous section, Jesus emerges thus as the one who lives this specificity and concreteness in a way that absolutely refuses the temptation to gain control of *these* social and political circumstances, as the one who 'unhandles' these human realities (and so unhandles 'history'),[49] such that, in Jesus' singular historicity, history itself is paradoxically 'held open' by, and to, the free and unpredictable coming of God. In other words, what the cross reveals is that Christ is involved in the contingencies of history as one whose identity and action is inassimilable to any immanent 'historical' arrangement of these contingent 'givens'. Rather, Jesus lives in and through the contingencies of history as that one whose life of perfect love is entirely coincident with (because entirely given over to) the *more* and *new* that God gives to history as God reaches into history from *beyond*.[50] And precisely here, in this human life, as it comes into view as a life lived in and through the contingencies everywhere surrounding his journey to the cross, Jesus, *as this human being*, is singularly and unsubstitutively identified as 'God' and 'Lord'. For here on the cross hangs one whose entire identity is dependent upon the irruption into history of an event which no immanent concatenation of historical contingencies is able to determine or produce: Jesus' resurrection to new life in the power of the Spirit.

There is surely much that could and must be said here to try and justify this exposition, not the least of which has to do with the extent to which all this resonates with the various elements of a classical Chalcedonian 'high Christology'.[51] But

---

49 Yoder, PJ, p. 233.

50 Yoder, OR, pp. 46–9.

51 We can only note here that, from the very beginning and throughout his oeuvre, and in *Politics* explicitly, Yoder seeks very much to confirm 'what the church has always said about Jesus as Word of the Father, as true God and true Human', yet in such a manner as to take the implications of this doctrine more seriously, 'as relevant to our social problems, than ever before' – especially the entwined problematics of 'politics' and 'history'. Yoder, PJ, p. 102. For discussion and analysis of the 'creedal orthodoxy' of Yoder's socio-political Christology, see Carter, *Politics of the Cross*, pp. 93–136; Weaver, 'Missionary Christology'.

our immediate focus here has especially to do with the force of Yoder's apocalyptic Christology with respect to the question of 'historical contingency'. Specifically, it is my contention that we are here presented with one way of beginning to develop the kind of 'radicalized and transformed' notion of the contingent that Donald MacKinnon has suggested is required by any properly 'high' Christology.[52] For what God does, for Yoder, in becoming Incarnate, is break through our standard definitions of human historicity and give this historicity a new, normative definition in the historicity of Jesus.[53] Jesus, 'by living a genuinely free and human existence',[54] at once *relativizes* and *intensifies* the question of historical contingency. To put this more pointedly, the radical character of Christ's apocalyptic historicity is not that it re-projects the questions of contingency and particularity onto an altogether different 'universal-historical' horizon, per se, but rather that it recapitulates the question of 'history' within an apocalyptic-eschatological framework, thereby inaugurating a mode of historical contingency that resists the possibility of being fully captured by any given 'universal-historical' logic whatsoever. This is not to abstract from, or to eschew continuing involvement in, the ongoing contingencies of history, but rather to insist that Christ's apocalyptic historicity (and so a genuine 'apocalyptic Christology' as such) has as its counterpart a new vision of history, which entails a new contingency rooted firmly in the apocalypse of the crucified and risen Christ.

---

52 See D. MacKinnon, *Borderlands of Theology and Other Essays*, ed. G. W. Roberts and D. E. Smucker (London: Lutterworth, 1968), p. 81.

53 Yoder, PJ, p. 99. I have intentionally reworded this sentence in a paraphrase of Yoder, as a way of pointing up the seriousness with which Yoder takes the modern problematic of 'history'. Where I use the language of 'historicity' Yoder uses the language of 'humanity'. Yoder insists in our day that we must understand 'humanity' in terms of 'history' and 'historicity', not merely in terms of 'natures' and 'essences', and therefore that a certain kind of historicism is necessary for developing anew and aright our understanding of the work of Christ. See Yoder, PT, pp. 306–7.

54 Yoder, PJ, pp. 144–5.

We might best trace out the contours of this new vision of history and historicity by looking more closely at those points at which Yoder loosens key aspects of Barth's understanding of Jesus' relation to history from its roots in the metaphysics of actualism. Yoder is entirely following Barth when he insists that to stress the concrete historicity of the incarnate Logos is to stress even more the sense in which the Logos incarnate passed through the cross and, ultimately, the resurrection. In following Barth here, however, Yoder permits us to make several crucial moves which Barth's own actualism seemingly prohibits. For one, Yoder is in full agreement with Barth that with the resurrection and ascension we are presented with the definitive and final revelation of Jesus as the 'Lord' of history. But what the resurrection does, for Yoder, is establish Jesus as Lord in his apocalyptic historicity, as it is 'finished' in its culmination *on the cross*. As a result, rather than merely representing to us the ontological 'completeness' of Jesus of Nazareth's identity (as it does for Barth), the resurrection rather drives us back into the cross, and even into the life of Jesus of Nazareth's own cruciform journeying, as the key to the risen Jesus' relationship to history as its sovereign Lord. For Yoder, this move is the one most fully in line with an apocalyptic stance. Commenting upon Revelation 5 (a favorite passage of his), Yoder insists that the sole hermeneutic which drives the Christian vision of history is 'the lamb that was slain': history is for the Christian a *via crucis*; providence works *through* the *via crucis*.[55]

What I would like to emphasize here is the way in which for Yoder the *via crucis* is Christ's victory as precisely a kind of 'historical failure'.[56] By renouncing the claim to control history, Christ puts himself in the most terrifyingly contingent position of all: as one whose life can only now have 'meaning' as an event of God's apocalyptic action from beyond history. And yet, as such, Christ is in the most gloriously free position of all:

---

55 Yoder, PJ, p. 232.
56 Yoder, PJ, p. 236.

free to love as God, with utter self-abandon, without concern for historical 'effectiveness' or 'responsibility', and free to live according to the 'more' that God is always doing *in* history as *beyond* what 'the historical' as such makes possible.

It is in this light that Yoder works over our assumed understandings of the nature and meaning of Christ's 'lordship'. Christ is Lord as that one whose life is purely that of God's own 'self-giving way of love',[57] by way of his entering into a 'suffering servanthood' through which alone he loses 'control' and renounces 'the claim to govern history'.[58] Reading Philippians 2.5–11, Yoder suggests that to say that Christ is Lord of history is to take such servanthood and renunciation themselves to be 'the leitmotif' of an apocalyptic perspective on 'cosmic history', as also of God's providence.[59] In this way, Yoder is following through with even more rigour Barth's emphasis in *Church Dogmatics* IV/2 upon 'Jesus Christ, the Servant as Lord' without thereby needing first to elaborate, as Barth feels he must in IV/1, the sense in which the servant is already, 'pre-existently', Lord. This is an important point: Jesus is not servant *because* he is previously Lord, but Jesus is Lord precisely *in and through such service*.[60]

The nature of Christ's lordship thus emerges as coincident with the logic of *excess* according to which Jesus' singular historicity is operative. We can see this in the way in which for Yoder Jesus is finally Lord and King insofar as he is first of all the perfect *priest*.[61] Jesus *gives himself*: his 'unhanding' of history on the cross concretely coincides with the unhanding of his own life to the 'more' that God is doing amidst the particularities and contingencies of history. But the more that God is doing is precisely to root the contingencies of ongoing history in the radical contingency of the cross, so that such contingencies might themselves be unhanded and transformed in their

---

57 Yoder, RP, p. 218.
58 Yoder, PJ, pp. 233–4.
59 Yoder, KBPW, p. 152.
60 Yoder, KBPW, p. 152.
61 Yoder, PT, pp. 118–20.

givenness to the evernew life in history that is the excess of the Spirit, by whose power humanity participates in God's perfect *agape* as the sign of God's coming reign. It is not just that Jesus gives himself, but as *this man* giving himself as God to God, he gives his very own 'identity', his own life, to be made real and effective within the *naturam humanum* which he became: 'The self that he gives is the self that became like us'[62] – historical, because radically and irreducibly contingent. To say then that Jesus emerges as Lord 'only after the cross',[63] while maintaining also that history itself is a *via crucis*, is to say in some sense that Christ's lordship is yet still – and eternally 'is' – a gift to be received from the future, as his own life is yet still to be given – and made present – to us in our very own cruciformity in history with the Lamb who was slain.

By conceiving the nature of Christ's lordship in this way, Yoder articulates the importance of ongoing history as a real and meaningful 'hiatus' between the resurrection/ascension and parousia of Christ.[64] And this is another key move which Yoder makes vis-à-vis Barth: the ascension, Pentecost, and the expected parousia are thought of as real 'historic' events whose meanings are determined by and bound up with the apocalyptic historicity displayed in the resurrected crucified Jesus of Nazareth, and not as mere 'episodic' moments within a larger event called 'Resurrection'. The Christian idea of the Second Coming obliges us also to take seriously the 'historic' reality of the return of Christ,[65] as also the fact that we know neither the day nor the hour of this return, as a matter of significance for *how* Christ is present – singularly and contingently – to us in the ongoing realities of history.

The key here is to understand that within the logic of Christ's historicity, this reaffirmation of the 'delay' of the parousia and of the 'hiatus' created by Christ's resurrection and ascension has the effect not of an (all-too-modern) 'historicizing' of the

---

62 Yoder, PT, p. 119.
63 Yoder, KBPW, p. 153.
64 See especially Yoder, PT, pp. 240–80.
65 See Yoder, PT, p. 276.

apocalypse, but rather of a thoroughgoing *apocalypticization* of history. What matters is not the 'end of history' or of 'the historical' as such; what matters is the manner in which, by way of these discrete events, and so by way of this very 'hiatus' itself, God is at work to orient us towards a promised future that roots us all the more firmly in the concrete historicity of Jesus of Nazareth and opens us all the more radically to the 'excess' of God's agapeic action amidst the *here and now* of our own contingent localities.

The real upshot of this is that we have here the basis for a positive reassessment of the canonical New Testament understanding of the eschatological 'already-not yet' tension as it functions most constitutively within an apocalyptic vision of history. For now, the resurrection is an event that not only throws us backwards onto the cross as the key to the truth of history but also points us forward in such a way as to drive us deeper into the contingencies and pluralities of ongoing history in order to find there our own mode of participation in the apocalyptic historicity of the resurrected crucified one, through the 'more' that the Spirit is doing in relation to those contingent realities. This understanding of the already-not yet tension is important especially for the way in which it allows us to take up and to conceive differently two fundamentally 'Barthian' insights, which lie behind Barth's vision of Christian witness and which will be important for understanding aspects of my own proposal for an apocalyptic politics of mission in the next chapter:

1 the 'finality' of Jesus and the 'unsurpassiblity' of his life history as the future of the world; and
2 the 'historicity' of the Spirit's work with respect to Christ's ongoing presence in history.

With respect to the first of these, we can glimpse in Yoder's understanding of Christ's cross and resurrection a definitive consummation of history without seeing this history as predetermined. On the one hand, in Christ the Kingdom has certainly *come*, has truly been inaugurated by a singular irruption into history; and it has come with a promise of fulfilment, namely, that this one who was crucified for us will return 'in the same way as you saw him go into heaven' (Acts 1.11). On the other hand, however, the final nature and content of that coming is not merely the outworking of something that is always-already the case. Indeed, it will be the case that, in the end, all things will be subjected to the Son, at which time he will hand over the Kingdom to the mystery of the Father (1 Cor. 15.24–28). As it is now, however, 'we do not yet see all things subjected to him' (Heb. 2.8). It is important to maintain this eschatological reserve with respect to both who Christ is, as well as who we are finally to be in him: 'Beloved, we are God's children now; what we will be has not yet been revealed. What we do know is this: when he is revealed, we will be like him, for we will see him as he is' (1 John 3.2 [NRSV]).

Reading this concatenation of verses in a Yoderian way, I can here deepen the force and significance of my earlier point that Jesus' identity as the incarnate Son of God is unable to be expounded in terms of a metaphysically preconceived divine 'essence' but can only emerge in the light shed by the resurrection upon a specific set of political events surrounding the crucifixion of a first-century Jewish rebel. So now, concomitantly we are unable to conceive of the final descent of the New Jerusalem except as it emerges as a new light shed upon the eschatological verdict already laid across our ongoing attempts to control history and be sovereign unto ourselves by the cross and resurrection of Jesus Christ. This means that we are unable to live eschatologically except in the light of the contingent shape of our own 'unhandling' of history as we are made to participate in Christ's own cross and resurrection – and thus his singular, apocalyptic historicity – through the Spirit's opening to the excess of God's perfect love with respect to our own specific localities.

Thus, we might say that Jesus' apocalyptic historicity 'holds open' the shape of the world to come, rather than prematurely foreclosing it. And yet this is because it holds open history itself to the 'more' that is God's Kingdom, which has been inaugurated in a no less final and definitive way in this very historicity, the cross and resurrection of Jesus Christ. It is according to this 'open finality'[66] that we might best retrieve and extend that second key aspect of Barth's understanding of Christ's relation to history: the connection of the Spirit with 'historicity'. As has already been indicated, Yoder directly associates the Spirit with the 'more' and the 'new' that God is doing with respect to the givens of 'history' as such. At the same time, however, this excess is nothing less than the life of perfect love – the 'genuinely free and human existence' – that arises as the concrete historicity of Jesus' cross and resurrection, the life which takes 'shape' in direct relation to Jesus' receiving of the Spirit at his baptism, the complete givenness of his person to the movement of that Spirit throughout his life even in and beyond his death on the cross, as well his own bestowing of that Spirit upon the disciples in his return to the Father. So we can say that Jesus' life happens – 'it is finished' – in its concrete historicity on the cross; there is nothing 'more' to be added to him. For here Christ embodies the perfect human openness to God's love and the perfect outgoing of God's love to a lost and dying world. Precisely by way of this 'openness', however, Jesus himself is the 'more' of history into which the Spirit is continually at work to draw us.[67] The Spirit's work is truly that

---

66 The concept and phrasing of an 'open finality' are borrowed from C. Cunningham, *Genealogy of Nihilism: Philosophies of Nothing and the Difference of Theology* (London: Routledge, 2002), see esp. pp. 226–7, 264. There, Cunningham speaks of 'the open finality of the Word as testified to by the work of the Spirit'. Whereas Cunningham speaks of the 'open finality of the Word' as that of 'form', 'essence', or 'being', however, I (following Yoder's lead) want to speak of it in terms of life-history, history, and historicity. In many ways there is a resonance here with the 'historicist' terms according to which Rowan Williams relates 'Word' and 'Spirit' in Williams, *On Christian Theology*, esp. pp. 118–27.

67 By 'more' here, I am thinking of something like the *huper* of Romans 5.8, or especially that of Philippians 2.9, where Christ is said to be given 'the name that is above (*huper*) every other name', which we might also very well translate as 'the name that is "the more of"

of making Christ 'present' to us in our own contingency and particularity (as Barth puts it), but the Spirit does this by interrupting and liberating us from our own 'histories', self-made from among the contingent 'givens' history has bequeathed us, and by making us genuine participants in the excessive mode of divine life that is the singular, apocalyptically *contingent* historicity of Jesus Christ.

Thus it is that the work of the Spirit 'rounds out' the trinitarian shape of the apocalyptic-eschatological vision of history which flows out of attention to the concrete historicity of Jesus of Nazareth.[68] For the Spirit just *is* what gives us and situates us within the apocalyptic inbreaking that is Jesus' unhanding of history to the Kingdom of the Father. And this means that, through the power of the Spirit, this apocalyptic inbreaking and unhanding of history are continually performed amidst the contingencies of our own histories, with which the resurrected crucified Jesus is now forever – eternally – bound up by way of the operation of his lived historicity. As such, in Jesus the Spirit gives us to *receive* the Kingdom everanew in our own particular circumstances.

(or "more than") every other name'. Herein especially lies the importance of focusing the category of 'narrative' firmly upon the historicist specificity of Jesus in telling the 'story of Jesus', and thus of not letting the 'name' or the 'story' become a cipher for something more universal. Only as such can we then speak (as Yoder does) of Jesus' 'story' as being one into which we are 'incorporated' without thereby losing the distinctiveness of the name of Christ or of our own 'names' which, as called by God, identify us as *uniquely who we are* 'in Christ'. For an extended exposition of this 'narrativity of naming', as well as for a fuller account of this alternative reading of *huper* in Philippians 2.9 and other New Testament passages, see N. Kerr, 'The Logic of the Name of Jesus: Derridian Nomination and the Radical Alterity of Theology', *ARC, The Journal of the Faculty of Religious Studies, McGill University* 31 (2003), pp. 60–7.

68 Hence Yoder's concern to demonstrate the importance of the *concrete historicity* of the human being Jesus not only 'to safeguard the correct understanding of incarnation' but also of the 'trinity'. Yoder, KBPW, p. 152. Cf. Yoder's critique of H. R. Niebuhr on this point in idem, HHRN, pp. 58–65.

So, to end this section where we began: Jesus in his singular, apocalyptic historicity is also, in his cross and resurrection, Word and *Logos*, the 'inner logic of things'.[69] But as such, this 'logic' can itself only be rendered rightly by rethinking the idea of the incarnate Word in terms of the concrete outworking of this apocalyptic historicity – of Christ's cross and resurrection.[70] The relation of Jesus to history is precisely that of a *crucified Logos*,[71] the logic of which is the cruciform interruption of history and its radical exposure to the excessive life of the Spirit that is the power of the resurrection as the sign of the coming reign of God – a reign that is now the 'truth' of all of life's radically contingent historicity as the 'truth' of Jesus' own apocalyptically contingent life as God. As such, this crucified *Logos* 'carries a proclamation of identification, incarnation, drawing all who believe into the power of becoming God's children'.[72] Thus Yoder can say: 'The cross is not a detour or a hurdle on the way to the kingdom, nor is it even the way to the kingdom; it is the kingdom come',[73] while also affirming that the cross is the key to all of history. For in the cross, God's interruption of 'history' and the very grace by which we are given to live vulnerably *in* history, by way of the excess of God's agapeic love which comes ever anew from 'beyond', uniquely coincide – in the singular, narratively specific apocalyptic historicity of Jesus of Nazareth.

Conclusion

If my analysis is correct, this logic is that of what I have named the 'apocalypticization of history': the *singularity* of Jesus as

---

69 Yoder, PJ, p. 246.

70 Yoder, PK, p. 51.

71 On this notion of a 'crucified Logos', which he gets from Michel de Certeau, see F. Bauerschmidt, 'The Wounds of Christ', *Journal of Literature and Theology* 5 (1991), pp. 83–100.

72 Yoder, PK, p. 51.

73 Yoder, PJ, p. 51.

John Howard Yoder

the *excessive* historicity – the *more* – of history itself. What a full-fledged 'apocalyptic historicism' gives us, then, is not another 'universal history', but rather the singularly *catholic* historicity of Jesus Christ, to which we in our various contingencies are bound by God's perfect *agape* through the work of the Spirit and by which we are interwoven into the single cosmic fabric that is 'cross and resurrection', and by which we ourselves are inscribed into the action of the 'original revolution' that is God's perfect *agape*.

This kind of Christian 'apocalyptic historicism' thus addresses the modern historicist crisis in a manner that positively surpasses the residual idealism of Barth's apocalyptic Christology as well as the antiliberal and anti-Constantinian functionalism of Hauerwas's apocalyptic ecclesiology. At the same time, this apocalyptic historicity 'holds open' history in a way that is irreducible to the kind of transcendental-historical 'opening to the future' that Derrida and postmodernism assume as the 'given' 'universal structure' of apocalyptic/messianic experience.[74] Rather, history 'breaks open' – is irrupted – according to the *singular* logic of a concrete political *action*, which is operative in history as the *excessiveness of singularity itself.* It is according to this dual logic of 'singularity' and 'excess', I am suggesting, that Christian apocalyptic articulates the kind of action by which alone we make the kind of passage from historicist political ideology to the revolutionary transformation of history that we find Walter Benjamin calling us to in his conception of 'Messianic time'.

What this finally means, however, is that the Christian apocalyptic vision is not finally sustainable or even theorizable apart from our own participation in *God's singular, revolutionary action*, apart from the *living* Christ being made visible in the very political 'unhanding' of history as it occurs in those converted by and to the inbreaking of God's reign into

---

74 J. Derrida, *Specters of Marx: The State of Debt, the Work of Mourning and the New International*, tr. P. Kamuf (London: Routledge, 1994), p. 210.

their own actual and contemporary-contingent histories. In a typically rich passage, Yoder puts it thus:

> The point that apocalyptic makes is not only that people who wear crowns and who claim to foster justice by the swords are not as strong as they think – true as that is: we still sing, 'O where are Kings and Empires now of old that went and came'? It is that people who bear crosses are working with the grain of the universe. One does not come to that belief by reducing social process to mechanical or statistical models, nor by winning some of one's battles for the control of one's own corner of the fallen world. One comes to it by sharing the life of those who sing about the Resurrection of the slain Lamb.[75]

It is by way of *doxology* that we move beyond ideology and come to participate in the lived 'Messianic time' that is the singular political *act* of Jesus. And so it is according to this mode of *doxological action* that I shall seek to follow the political logic of the 'apocalypticization of history' as it occurs in Jesus' historicity on its way to becoming an 'apocalyptic politics of Christian mission'.

---

75 Yoder, AE, p. 58.

6

Towards an Apocalyptic Politics
of Mission

The preceding chapters have endeavoured to offer an account
of Christian apocalyptic that sustains my description and critique of modern theological historicism, while at the same
time articulating an alternative 'apocalyptic historicism' that
offers new ecclesial and political challenges. The question that
remains for us, then, is this: given the definitive display of apocalyptic political action in the singular historicity of Jesus of
Nazareth, how might we speak of this historicity in terms of a
Christian apocalyptic politics? That is, in what way is Christ's
historicity constitutive, as the author of Ephesians suggests,
of an *ecclesial* challenge to the powers and principalities? Or,
to put the question in Yoder's terms: In what sense does the
historicity of Jesus retain, 'in the working of the church as she
encounters the other power and value structures of her history,
the same kind of relevance that the man Jesus had for those he
served until they killed him'?[1]

In this final chapter, then, I intend to ask after the specific
mode of *Christian* and *ecclesial* participation in the apocalyptic politics of Jesus. My claim is simple: our own participation
in the politics of Jesus emerges as a *missionary* politics of liturgical *encounter* with the world. In commending a politics of
mission, I mean to argue that the inbreaking of God's reign
– the apocalyptic politics of Jesus – is made real and available
as a way of *seeing* or an *imaginative act* (doxology) and as a

---

1 Yoder, PJ, p. 158.

mode of *work* (liturgy) that concur as that praxis by which the world (and thereby also the church) is *converted* by and to the subversive excess of God's coming Kingdom.

'To See History Doxologically'

The fundamental impetus for my focus on doxology as constitutive of Christian socio-political action is the claim that doxology uniquely exposes and surpasses the intimate connection between functionalist socio-political reasoning and totalizing, ideological schemes of meaning. Of course, to say this is from the outset to refuse to treat 'doxology' itself as a new universal or to deploy the practices of praise either heuristically or metaphysically as a condition of possibility for all meaning.[2] The decision for doxology as constitutive of Christian political action is thus not primarily moral, or pragmatic, or metaphysical, but *eschatological*.[3] In other words, doxology is a modality of God's apocalyptic action, or better, our own mode of participation in the singular, apocalyptic historicity that is Jesus of Nazareth. Doxology lives and acts by way of a certain 'messianic orientation', as fundamentally a mode of living *from* and *into* the 'new world' that is breaking into the here and now as Christ's ongoing historicity.[4] Doxology thus labours according to the 'vulnerability of the particular',[5] or of what I am

---

2 On the pre-eminence of the doxological, I am indebted to the work of Catherine Pickstock, particularly her brilliant reading of 'liturgy' in *After Writing*. Yet precisely here I am in disagreement with the way in which she tends to 'universalize' doxology as that which grounds all human meaning, a thesis I find to be at odds with her most incisive claim, namely, that genuine liturgy is only ever conceivable as the possibility of an *action*, the decisiveness of an *event*. See C. Pickstock, *After Writing: On the Liturgical Consummation of Philosophy* (Oxford: Blackwell, 1998).

3 Yoder, FTN, pp. 210–11.

4 See Yoder, FTN, pp. 199–218. On the phrase 'messianic orientation', see Yoder, RP, pp. 207–8.

5 Yoder, PK, p. 44.

calling the 'logic of singularity', insofar as it is by doxology that one is made a participant in (is 'timed' by) the messianic life and action that is the singular, apocalyptically contingent historicity of Jesus Christ. As such, I want to argue, doxology frees one *from* the 'historicist' mode of action reflexively constrained by the concerns of 'political effectiveness' and *for* participation in that action by which history is 'unhanded' or 'opened' by and to the radically subversive love of God's reign. In what follows, I present my case through a sequence of five points that relate to and expand upon the previous exposition of Jesus' 'apocalyptic historicity' in Chapter 5.

First, doxology maintains the priority of *the reign of God*; it is rooted in and flows out of the 'higher loyalty of King-dom citizenship'.[6] As Rowan Williams puts it, by definition the Kingdom of God is that free divine *action* in Christ by which *all* persons are 'delivered from the claims to finality of the definitions given them by their social and political con-text'.[7] For doxology binds us to Jesus, who inaugurates the reign of God precisely insofar as his appearance in history is *not* that of 'a competitor for space in this world'.[8] His life is rather the very denial of 'territory' – whether geographical, epistemological, narrative, or metaphysical – as precisely con-stitutive of the coming Kingdom he calls us actively to seek. It is not a given or imagined 'world', 'culture', 'language', 'civili-zation', 'habitus', or even a particular 'character' or set of 'vir-tues' that first defines and describes our 'politics', but rather the always-apocalyptic imminence of the Kingdom.[9] Doxolog-ically, 'that action is right [or, righteous] which fits the shape of the Kingdom to come'.[10]

Second, the doxological act is a particular operation of God's *transcendence*. 'To see history doxologically', as Yoder

---

6 Yoder, PK, p. 181.

7 Williams, *On Christian Theology*, p. 282. Cf. Yoder, PK, p. 54.

8 R. Williams, *Christ on Trial: How the Gospel Unsettles Our Judgment* (Grand Rapids: Eerdmans, 2000), p. 6.

9 Yoder, PK, p. 54.

10 Yoder, RP, p. 136; cf. Yoder, JCSR, p. 74.

puts it, is to 'belong to a frame of reference in which we acknowledge being the graced objects of meaning from beyond ourselves'.[11] The coincidence of the language of the 'beyond' and of 'grace' are key here, for it recalls for us the contours of Yoder's distinctively *apocalyptic* notion of transcendence, which we traced in the previous chapter. As there, so here: the language of the 'beyond' refers above all to the *priority of grace* in the coming of God's Kingdom. Yoder's correlation of the 'beyond' with the *coming* Kingdom inverts our common presumptions regarding a self-transcendent human subject whose movement is one 'from here to there' and refocuses the question eschatologically, as a matter of God's apocalyptic movement 'from there to here'.[12]

> To say that the kingdom is at hand, that the new world is on the way, is first of all to anchor our thoughts in the priority of grace. Before we can set out toward the New World, it must have – and by God's goodness it has – come to us. We can only be on our way because of that prior coming. We do not go out to find or build the kingdom but only to meet it.[13]

To say, then, that the doxological act is an operation of God's transcendence is to say that it is rooted in the free *initium* or 'initiating action' of God: the coming of God in Christ is the *initium* of God's reign, and doxology is a political 'act' just to the extent that it takes this initiating activity of God as its 'rule'.[14]

Yoder's appeal to the category of transcendence is of critical importance considering the contested place of this category in recent debates on the relation between 'theology' and 'the political'.[15] The critical force of 'transcendence' as Yoder

---

11 Yoder, 'Burden and Discipline', p. 34.

12 Yoder, FTN, pp. 210–11.

13 Yoder, RP, p. 104.

14 See B. Wannenwetsch, *Political Worship: Ethics for Christian Citizens*, tr. M. Kohl (Oxford: Oxford University Press, 2004), p. 10.

15 On this issue, see Creston Davis, John Milbank, and Slavoj

conceives it stems precisely from the fact that a consistently 'messianic' appeal to the transcendence of God (which is, politically, an appeal to 'the other Jerusalem' to come) accentuates the manner in which 'a different way of being [politically] keeps breaking in here and now'.[16] This 'way of being represents the promise of another world, which is not somewhere else but which is *to come here*'.[17] Transcendence is thus accentuated, for Yoder, in the interest of a uniquely subversive political action, and this because God's apocalyptic transcendence operates in such a way as to make concrete a world of life and action that the socio-political powers and principalities are themselves unable to imagine. The Kingdom's 'very existence is subversive at the points where the old order is repressive, and creative where the old is without vision. The transcendence of the new consists not in escaping the realm where the old order rules, but in its subverting and transforming that realm.'[18] This is to say that the necessity of divine transcendence for theopolitics lies not in the way it functions metaphysically so as to analogically secure immanence for theology as the 'historical' domain within which a certain political 'power' might then be effectively deployed. Rather, the primacy of transcendence accords with the *initium* of the divine *act*, whose operation is that of a uniquely sovereign act that occurs as apocalyptically *prior* to all merely 'immanental' and 'universal-historical' frames of reference.

This leads me directly to my third point: if the transcendence of God's Kingdom is the free grace of God's *initium*, then the pattern for our vision and action will be doxological as it conforms to the concrete action that is Christ's *incarnation, cross, and resurrection*. When Yoder says that 'the criterion of Christian ethics is not effectiveness but incarnation', he means by this that the basis for our action is not 'a set of abstract and

---

Žižek, eds, *Theology and the Political: The New Debate* (Durham, NC: Duke University Press, 2005).

16 Yoder, PK, p. 94.
17 Yoder, PK, p. 94.
18 Yoder, FTN, p. 84.

impersonal principles' but *a person*.[19] Furthermore, if our action is to be determined doxologically, then what we are to see in the incarnation, death, and resurrection of Jesus is not simply an *object* of praise and adoration (which would make of 'Jesus' – whether in the form of his eternally actualized resurrected 'history' or in the form of his unshakable metanarrative presence – yet another instrument of order and security). Doxology rather sees in Jesus' incarnation, cross, and resurrection and coming again the very concreteness of our own *way* into the Father's Kingdom.[20]

This point is of vital importance, insofar as it is precisely in terms of the incarnational pattern of 'cross and resurrection' that Yoder most clearly insists that we are liberated not only from cause-effect thinking about human history, but also from the burden of emphasizing our own Christian 'obedience' or 'worship' as a mode of political 'effectiveness' or 'survival'. If 'to see history doxologically' means, with the Seer of the Apocalypse, to proclaim that 'the lamb that was slain is worthy to receive power', it is only because Christ's cross and resurrection themselves carry 'a proclamation of identification, incarnation, drawing all who believe into the power of becoming God's children' – 'sons of the Kingdom'.[21] Here again, we see what is at stake in doxology as the preeminent mode of political action: to eschew 'effectiveness' is not to *react* in the mode of *ressentiment* against a political order we have discovered we cannot control; it is rather the result of having *already acted* – on the basis of God's incarnational initiative – according to another order altogether and having found that so to act is precisely to have already been involved in 'losing track of my own effectiveness in the great reservoir of the pressure of love'.[22] In doxology, we need not *refuse* the logic of effectiveness, for in love we act in such a way as always-already to have been left, by the very *doxa* that is the reign of God's *agape*, bereft of effectiveness itself.

---

19 Yoder, FTN, p. 108.
20 Yoder, FTN, p. 111.
21 Yoder, PK, pp. 51, 195.
22 Yoder, RP, p. 206.

Fourth, doxology is a matter of dealing concretely with the political implications of the confession that 'Jesus Christ is Lord'. Doxology is political in that the 'meaning' of Christ's lordship as his *giving* of himself in service and in radical love, through the 'unhanding' of his crucified flesh to the 'more' of history that is his resurrected life, is to be explored and articulated through our own engaged and embodied action. It is precisely by way of such engaged and embodied action – as we ourselves are made to be 'priests' and 'servants' – that 'the path of Christ' itself (Christ's *life*) is 'doxologized'.[23] Doxology, then, is indeed a way of maintaining what Yoder calls 'fidelity to the jealousy of Christ as Lord',[24] but only so far as 'lordship' itself is now understood not only as the fundamentally cruciform ordering of the cosmos towards God's coming Kingdom but also as the work of risk, service, and vulnerability needed to be open and receptive to the ever*newness* by which the grace of God's kingdom breaks forth and is made concrete in the world.

Finally, 'to see history doxologically' is to recognize that it is the Spirit who works in us, and delivers us over to the work of worship; only by the Spirit can we confess that 'Jesus is Lord' (1 Cor. 12.3). Here I am adopting the position attributed to the Cappadocians that if the Son is the one *through* whom the Father works reconciliation with the world, and thus the *way* by which in worship we enter into the Kingdom, the Spirit is the one *in* whom we worship.[25] For the Cappadocians, the point is simple: it is impossible to approach or to acknowledge the glory of the Father and the Son except by the Spirit. Yet, one might add that such acknowledgment occurs only by way of a *pneumatic* irruption of the Kingdom whereby one is made to participate in that *Christic* pattern of life by which 'history' is 'unhanded' to the Father in the mode of incarnation, cross, and resurrection.

---

23 See Yoder, RP, p. 86

24 Yoder, PK, p. 86.

25 See Basil of Caesarea, *On the Holy Spirit*, tr. D. Anderson (New York: St. Vladimir's Seminary Press, 1980), pp. 93–7.

This is to reassert the correlation of the Spirit with 'historicity'. In an important essay, Yoder insists upon a *pneumatological* orientation towards 'the very particular story' of Jesus
of Nazareth as the most critically *historicist* orientation of all,
insofar as it is by the 'excess' of the Spirit that the Word Incarnate apocalyptically subverts any so-called 'perspective' on
'history' that mistakes 'a word for a concept' and thus slides
inevitably into ideology with its attempts to account for contingency and change in such a way as to 'freeze' history within
the very structures by which it claims to be taking responsibility for it.[26] For Yoder, there is no way to disentangle our
confession of Christ's Lordship from the ongoing relative, particular, and complex realities of history, nor is there a way
discursively to 'display' these realities according to Christ's
lordship as conceived in advance. Rather, Christ is Lord only
as we are made by the Spirit's ongoing irruption to participate
in his cruciform 'unhanding' of these realities to the 'more' of
God's coming Kingdom in the here and now. In short, by the
Spirit Christ's singularly *apocalyptic* historicity is embodied
– and this is no doubt a miracle of God's grace[27] – in our own
singularly *doxologic* historicity.

Doxology is apocalyptic. This is the point I have tried to
substantiate in this section. But more than that, I have tried to
articulate the reasons why, according to the logic of apocalyptic, 'our political mood must be doxological'.[28] To turn to doxology is to insist that the quintessence of Christian political
action is to be located at the point where God's activity interrupts all forms of political *givenness* through the enactment of
Jesus' apocalyptic historicity. Bernd Wannenwetsch has made
this point in stating that real political action on behalf of the
Kingdom 'happens where human beings are liberated from
concentration on themselves and from the idolization of what
is politically and economically good, and are freed for the

---

26 Yoder, PK, pp. 124, 200n. 7.
27 Cf. Yoder, OR, p. 121: 'Christian ethics calls for behavior which
is impossible except by the miracle of the Holy Spirit.'
28 Yoder, FTN, p. 227.

praise of God'.[29] But it is important to understand that doxology refuses the idolization and instrumentalization of politics in a manner that is decisively *not* apolitical; in praise we 'are not called out but *sent* into the real (public) world where sacrifice and sovereignty happen'.[30] It is by the grace of such *sending* that we are given over to that action which lives from and is timed by the 'messianic hope' of Christ's apocalyptic historicity. It is this sending especially that is constitutive of 'ecclesia'.

From 'Church-as-*Polis*' to 'Mission Makes the Church'

Before moving on to articulate the kind of *missionary* practice I think doxology calls us to, in this section I want to deepen my critique of the Hauerwasian position, inherited from Yoder and shared by a host of contemporary followers, that the church alternatively *is* a *polis*, with respect to the role that 'doxology' plays within such a position.

Paul Doerksen has argued that one of the key points of convergence between Yoder and Hauerwas lies not simply in their shared concern for the social and political visibility of the church, but the central role that worship and the liturgical practices of the church play in this concern.[31] Yet I am worried about the ways in which this emphasis upon worship gets inflected in the work of Yoder and Hauerwas, as well as in those most influenced by them. My worries have to do with the political *ontologization* of the church, on the one hand, and a concomitant *instrumentalization* of worship, on the other hand. My concerns here reflect those of Romand Coles, in the sense that I am afraid that this ontologization of the church's political worship risks conceiving the church's liturgy as primarily

29 Wannenwetsch, *Political Worship*, p. 63. Cf. Yoder, RP, pp. 109–10, 128–9.

30 Yoder, FTN, p. 36.

31 Paul Doerksen, 'Share the House: Yoder and Hauerwas Among the Nations', in *A Mind Patient and Untamed*, pp. 195–8.

an '*interior volume*, a prior preparatory space (separated from the world) that is the most elemental space-time of the formation of peoplehood'.[32] My worry is not only, with Coles, that this 'risks getting Jesus wrong', but that it mistakes the sense in which worship only 'is' as an apocalyptic pneumatological event. That is, this understanding of the church-as-*polis* 'gets Jesus wrong' just so far as it effects an ecclesiological domestication of the work of the Spirit.

To begin with, consider again the strong ontological claim that the church *is* a *polis*. The problem I want to isolate with this claim is the manner in which it tends to generate the notion that the ecclesial community or 'gathering' is an entity available in its 'historical' actuality as a primordially *given* political 'context', which then acquires its 'public' character from the access it offers the surrounding world to its own 'polis'.

One can see this dynamic at work, for example, in Yoder's twin claims that 'the ultimate meaning of history is to be found in the work of the church' and that 'the meaning of history is carried first of all, on behalf of all others, by the believing community'.[33] When combined with Yoder's assumptions regarding the epistemological and ontological priority of the church as an 'alternative society' qua counter-*polis*,[34] these claims amount to an inversion of what is identified throughout Yoder's work as the 'Constantinian' problematic. The 'meaning' of Christ's lordship is displaced from the operativity of Jesus' 'independence' and onto the operation of the church as a *polis* in history, such that the meaning of history is borne along precisely by the 'social function' of the Christian community, which is now bound to the world precisely as 'a microcosm of the wider society'.[35] Thus Yoder's counter-society perpetuates a residual ecclesiological positivism, inasmuch as it requires

---

32 Hauerwas and Coles, *Christianity, Democracy, and the Radical Ordinary*, pp. 210–11.

33 Yoder, RP, pp. 118, 151.

34 See Yoder, CWS, pp. 17–18.

35 Yoder, RP, p. 92.

the maintenance of a solid, stable 'centre' – a 'social datum'[36] – according to which alone the church is 'visible' vis-à-vis 'the world'.

It is this politically 'concentric' understanding of the church's relation to the 'wider world' that needs especially to be challenged, for three distinct reasons. First, there is the danger of intensifying the Christian community's concern for its own interior *identity* overagainst the world. This danger is especially present where the theme of the church as a counter-*model* to the larger society is emphasized. For in order to remain structurally 'counter' to the world, yet still 'model' itself to the world, the Christian community is forced to engender or to identify the world on its own homologous terms, as a 'cultivated outsider' (to use Wannenwetsch's phrase).[37] More problematically still, this concentricity requires such intense focus upon the 'internal activities' of the church that its engagement with the world cannot help but be conceived in a subsidiary and conjunctive way. As Yoder puts it, each of the five key practices that he identifies as constitutive of the church-as-*polis* 'concerns *both* the internal activities of the gathered Christian congregation *and* the ways the church interfaces with the world'.[38] It is this 'and' that I find problematic, for what this 'and' suggests, as Romand Coles has put it, is that 'there is a people called and gathered *prior* to encountering others'.[39] But is this not to construe *encounter* with 'the world' as somehow less constitutive of the people of God than the church's own internal and primordial identity as a *counter-polis*?

Second, this concentric structure instrumentalizes doxology. Take, for instance, Yoder's statement, 'Worship is the communal cultivation of an alternative construction of society and

---

36 Yoder, *Nevertheless: Varieties of Religious Pacifism*, rev. ed. (Scottdale: Herald Press, 1992), p. 136.

37 Wannenwetsch, *Political Worship*, p. 268.

38 Yoder, RP, p. 361.

39 Hauerwas and Coles, *Christianity, Democracy, and the Radical Ordinary*, p. 212.

history.[40] Against the important insight, traced out above, that doxology is our 'unhanding' of history as the mode of our participation in the politically subversive apocalyptic historicity of Jesus, we have here what seems to be a constructive-historical *implementation* of worship. Here, in articulating the church's culture-critical aspect, Yoder appears to be lapsing back into (though inverting) the kind of 'Troeltschian' privileging of the inner cultus of which he is otherwise often so critical, by seeking 'to pull up for analysis the kind of political commitment a particular cult form implies'.[41] But this is certainly to eschew the notion of doxology as a pneumatological happening that occurs at the point of encounter with Jesus in his 'independence' from both church and world and rather to view doxology first according to the gathering of an internal cultus, one *function* of which is commitment to a certain mode of political 'construction'.

Third, this instrumentalization of worship tends to lead (especially in such followers of Yoder as Hauerwas and Reinhard Hütter) to a direct correlation of the work of the Spirit with the Church's practices of worship, whose primary function is to make of the Christian community a 'habitable world'.[42] Now this correlation certainly runs the risk, which Rowan Williams has warned against, of conceiving the church as the 'domicile' of the Spirit, rather than more truly as the *sign* of the Spirit's work in the world.[43] But my main concern is this identification of the Spirit-inspired practices of the church as constituting its own kind of 'domicile' – a 'habitable world', in itself. Not only does this reduce the work of the Spirit to the mere ordering of our habits, insofar as worship is the *habitus* through which

---

40 Yoder, PK, p. 43.

41 Yoder, PK, p. 43.

42 Hauerwas, WGU, p. 214. Cf. R. Hütter, *Suffering Divine Things: Theology as Church Practice*, tr. D. Stott (Grand Rapids: Eerdmans, 2000), esp. pp. 95–145. For a critique of both Hütter and Hauerwas on this point, see Healy, 'Practices and the New Ecclesiology: Misplaced Concreteness?', pp. 296–303.

43 Williams, *On Christian Theology*, p. 124.

'we find ourselves grafted into the story of God',[44] but in so doing it abstracts from the Spirit as the life-giving *newness* of God's grace amidst the contingencies of ongoing (secular) history and so circumscribes the very 'excess' of Jesus' own apocalyptic historicity, conceiving that excess, in some sense, as the 'product' of the church.

This circumscription of the Spirit demonstrates most clearly the way in which the church-as-*polis* alternative, like its 'Constantinian' inverse, is itself 'incapable, not only accidentally but constitutionally, of making visible Christ's lordship over church and world'.[45] This is not least because it presumes a stable 'centre' to the church's identity, according to which Christ's lordship is discernible as operative in a mode of ecclesiological (and so pneumatological, political, and liturgical) 'gathering' that occurs *in advance of* encounter with 'the world'.

Put simply, the church conceived as *polis* shortcircuits the work of doxology, by way of a more fundamentally *missionary* failure. By way of addressing this failure, I should like to suggest an alternative conception of the church's engagement with the world, articulated in terms of what one might call an *apocalyptic politics of mission*.

I have already indicated the ways in which we need to break with Troeltsch's modern historicist assumption that mission has to do with Christianity's 'universality' as a world-historical 'religion', as well as Hauerwas's 'metanarrative' concern for mission as a mode of re-narrating the world in relation to 'the church' as 'the story of Jesus', insofar as both of these paradigms, in their own way, provide an account of Christian identity that is functionally 'ideological' or 'absolute'. What I am suggesting rather is that mission has to do fundamentally with the lived embodiment of Christ's reign as enacted in the apocalyptic historicity of Jesus of Nazareth. Insofar as mission implies first a 'sending', it is the sending of the Spirit by which we come to participate in – are 'gathered' into – the priestly work of

---

44 Hauerwas, AC, p. 108.
45 Yoder, RP, p. 61.

God's perfect *agape*, the 'self-giving way of love' by which alone Christ reigns and is confessed as 'Lord'. So mission, one might say, is the *form* in which Christ *gives* himself in the 'historicity' of the Spirit: to be given over to participation in the apocalyptic politics of Jesus, *through* whom our own historicity is opened to the excess of God's *agape*, we must have been given over, *in* the Spirit, to a work of love by which we are *bound* to the ongoing contingencies and singularities of history precisely in their being 'unhanded' by Christ to the reign of God's love. 'Mission' thereby names the ongoing enactment of Jesus' non-territorial, subversive, apocalyptic historicity in the world.

My point is that the apocalyptic historicity of Jesus is that of a singular political act whose inbreak occurs as an irreducibly *missionary* exigency. What this means is that there is no 'church', no real Christian existence even, prior to or apart from this mission. It is important to recognize that this point is made by Yoder himself in much of his early writings on 'mission', which lead up to the publication of *The Politics of Jesus*. In one crucial essay published in 1969 and reprinted in 1994,[46] Yoder suggests that the problematic of 'history' as bequeathed to us by Western Christendom is itself symptomatic of a fundamental 'compromise' of the church's political mission. As Yoder understands it, the only way properly to conceive the church politically is to conceive the church *as* mission:

> The political novelty that God brings into the world is a community of those who serve instead of ruling, who suffer instead of inflicting suffering, whose fellowship crosses social lines instead of reinforcing them. This new Christian community in which the walls are broken down not by human idealism or democratic legalism but by the work of Christ is not only a vehicle of the gospel or only a fruit of the gospel; it is the good news. It is not merely the agent of mission or the constituency of a mission agency. *This is the mission.*[47]

---

46 Yoder, RP, pp. 65–101.
47 Yoder, RP, p. 91 (emphasis added).

The important thing is the way in which Yoder here refuses to instrumentalize mission by making of it a 'religious' or 'narrative' function. Rather, in this passage and throughout the essay as a whole, Yoder seems to be appropriating the important Barthian insight (reiterated throughout *Church Dogmatics* IV/3) that *mission makes the church.*

However, in order more adequately to appropriate this insight that 'mission makes the church' and that the church is political only as irreducibly 'missionary', it will be necessary to move decisively beyond the church conceived politically as 'counter-*polis*'. One should rather argue, in a manner akin to that of Herbert McCabe, that the 'church' is not so much an 'alternative society' or even an 'alternative to society', but a kind of subversive *challenge to society* or to 'politics' as such.[48] From the apocalyptic perspective, one might thus think of political worship (or Christian 'discipleship') not so much as the 'construction' of a counter-history or counter-society to that of 'the world', but rather as a way of living 'independently' (as did Christ) of those anonymous and autonomous ideological forces – the 'powers and principalities' – that hold 'the world' under their sway. As the work of the Spirit, such an 'independence' would need to occur at a point of *missionary encounter* between church and world and from within a *complex liturgical space* opened up everanew by the apocalyptic historicity of Jesus of Nazareth.

Liturgy and Diaspora

Having made the case for moving beyond church-as-*polis* to a more constitutively missionary conception of *ecclesia*, I want in this section to articulate more precisely the manner in which 'mission makes the church', by rethinking what is meant by 'liturgy' as a particular kind of *work*, which I will call the work of 'exile' or 'diaspora'.

---

48 H. McCabe, *God Still Matters* (London: Continuum, 2002), pp. 87–91.

Liturgy

The ongoing importance of Jesus' historicity – his apocalyptic singularity – for the church finds expression for Yoder in the central role given to doxology and more particularly to 'liturgy'. Indeed, liturgy is central to doxology because it marks the church's inextricable connection in time to the narrative particularity of Jesus.[49] Here Yoder is recalling the Barthian insight that 'church order' is liturgical in that 'it celebrates and remembers the particularity of Jesus Christ'.[50] It is important that Barth stakes this claim within the context of a discussion of the Holy Spirit that culminates in the key insight that the church is 'ordered' by 'public worship', which constitutes its 'prophetic mission' in the world.[51] Indeed, liturgy is central to the ordering of the church insofar as it is through the power of the Spirit that the church is given 'its concrete form in its coming together' in its confession of and directedness to the lordship of Jesus Christ.[52]

I want to intensify Barth's position here by stressing all the more the historicity of the Spirit in relation to the apocalyptic singularity of Jesus. It was said in the previous chapter that Jesus is 'Lord' of history insofar as he in his very historicity *gives himself* – his very 'identity' – to be received everanew in the recognizably singular and contingent diversities of ongoing history; it was also pointed out that the Spirit is the one in whom this giving and receiving occur. Hence the paradox we find especially at the heart of John's Gospel, for example: Jesus, precisely as the *bearer* of the Spirit, is 'identified' in his reception of and his being received by 'another' and thus by innumerable 'others'. For it is the peculiar work of the Spirit

---

49 Yoder, RP, pp. 110–11. It is interesting to note that in this context, it is precisely the narrative particularity of Jesus which Yoder suggests prohibits conceiving the church in terms of 'an ontology being realized'.
50 Yoder, FTN, p. 28.
51 Barth, CD IV/2, pp. 698–726.
52 Barth, CD IV/2, pp. 704–9.

to witness always to another – *as other* (that is, not merely to himself-as-other, as in the Hegelian *Geist*).[53] To say, then, that the Spirit is the one in whom we worship is to say that liturgy is to be especially conceived as a twofold 'work' of the Spirit internal to the apocalyptic historicity of Jesus of Nazareth. The work of the Spirit is first of all that operation by which Christ himself – in his coming, his death, resurrection, ascension, and promise to return – is given to be received as other and to receive the witness of the other. And second, the Spirit's work is that by which we ourselves are given to receive and be received by the other and so to be *gathered* with the other in Christ as a sign and gift of the coming Kingdom.

To deepen this point, I suggest supplementing this understanding of liturgy with Michel de Certeau's brilliant analysis of Jesus as 'La rupture instauratrice'.[54] Certeau stresses the historical 'singularity' of Jesus as an 'inaugural rupture' opening a space of encounter within history that is alone the 'condition of truth' of this event itself.[55] This space of encounter operates according to what Certeau calls the 'not without', meaning that the 'truth' of that which we call 'Christianity' occurs *neither* apart from encounter with the singular historicity of Jesus himself, *nor* apart from the plurality of others to whom Jesus is identifiably bound in the kenosis of his 'person'.[56] Thus Jesus is 'named', in his singularity, *as* Other: 'Jésus est l'Autre'.[57]

---

53 For this way of putting things, see Wannenwetsch, *Political Worship*, p. 322.

54 See M. de Certeau, *La Faiblesse de croire*, ed. L. Giard (Paris: Éditions du Seuil, 1987), pp. 183–226. See also Certeau, 'How Is Christianity Thinkable Today?', in *The Postmodern God: A Theological Reader*, ed. G. Ward (Oxford: Blackwell, 1997), pp. 142–58. All translations from the French editions of Certeau's work are my own.

55 Certeau, *La Faiblesse*, pp. 213–15.

56 On the logic of this 'not without', see Certeau, 'How Is Christianity Thinkable?', pp. 146–7.

57 Certeau, *La Faiblesse*, p. 225. One would do well to remember here that it is the Spirit that is given the work of 'naming' in Scripture. It is by this Spirit, this 'other', that we name Jesus as 'Lord' (1 Cor.

It is important to emphasize, however, that Jesus is 'Other' for Certeau only as the possibility of a *praxis*; Jesus *bears* (as Jesus 'bears' the Spirit, one might say) in his Otherness a *work* that speaks of the possibility of 'other places to come'.[58] It is precisely by way of this work, a work of perpetual 'encounter with others, elusive brothers', that 'God shows himself greater'.[59] Jesus, that is, *gives himself* as the 'work of an excess'.[60]

If, with Yoder, we think of this work, by which God shows Godself 'greater', to be the very 'excess' of the Spirit by which Jesus is witnessed to everanew as the 'more' of history itself, then we might say that this 'work' internal to Christ's historicity is our very own 'encounter with others, elusive brothers', by which alone we are 'Christian'.[61] We might thus speak of the 'space of encounter' opened up by the inaugural rupture – or apocalyptic historicity – of Jesus as the space of a praxis by which we are delivered over to the believing testimony of another; one is 'Christian' only in being continually *converted* by and to the other's witness to Jesus.

But this is no small observation – it might be rather that the whole weight of my argument turns on this one point. For the apocalyptic Christology we have been seeking to articulate only exists because of this work, this liturgy, this *missionary* exigence that is borne by Jesus in his very historicity. In other words, an apocalyptic Christology is only possible *as* this praxis of missionary encounter with the other by which we are together given over – converted – to the 'more' of Jesus' life, the shape of whose pneumatological excess we cannot possibly control.

Here a very critical point emerges, which is that the litur-

12.3), and it is by this same Spirit that we name God as 'Father', and specifically as the Father of Jesus (Rom. 8.15; Gal. 4.6).

58 Certeau, *La Faiblesse*, p. 225.

59 M. de Certeau, *L'Étranger; ou, L'Union dans la différence*, 2nd edn (Paris: Desclée de Brouwer, 1992), p. 69.

60 See Certeau, *La Faiblesse*, pp. 277–86.

61 Cf. Certeau, *La Faiblesse*, p. 305: 'No person is a Christian alone, for himself, but in reference and connection to the other, in openness to a difference called and accepted with gratitude.'

gical act occurs primarily as a movement of what Jean-Yves Lacoste calls 'la dépossession messianique'.[62] Such 'dispossession' is the experience not only of a kind of death to the historical and spatial territorialities according to which we might schematize in advance how 'Jesus' will present himself in a given context (though it is certainly that). But more concretely it is the experience of the church's 'non-possession' of itself, of its own 'identity'. An important lecture by Rowan Williams on 'Mission and Christology' makes this point well: If 'mission makes the church' (my phrase), then 'Jesus' cannot be delivered to us through a given institution, a single historical narrative, or a set of achieved practices and habits, but only received everagain as the gift of another, at once unpredictably new yet recognizably strange.[63]

It is this missionary space of encounter opened up by the singularity of Jesus which impels one to move beyond speaking of 'the truth given sacramentally in a Church that remains a particular society'.[64] Named as it is by the following of that one whose very life and calling indicate a 'going beyond', a perpetual 'movement of listening to and following the Father',[65] Christianity as such can no longer claim to be 'the centre of the world and the place of the true'.[66] Marked by the excess in history that is Jesus' ongoing historicity, 'church' no longer names either a stable site of production, nor does it possess a proper place of its own.[67] Rather, as that work which binds us

---

62 J.-Y. Lacoste, *Note sur le temps: Essai sur les raisons de la mémoire et de l'espérance* (Paris: Presses Universitaires de France, 1990), pp. 177–80.

63 R. Williams, *Mission and Christology: J. C. Jones Memorial Lecture* (Church Missionary Society, Welsh Council, 1994).

64 Certeau, *L'Étranger*, p. 41.

65 Certeau, *La Faiblesse*, pp. 281–2.

66 Certeau, *L'Étranger*, p. 37.

67 As Certeau notes in several places, the implications of this are profound: 'If one accepts that there is no longer any Christian place, and hence neither are there any tasks which are proper to it, then Christian experience can no longer be a system or a language.' Certeau, *La Faiblesse*, p. 278. In denial of this loss of a proper place,

everagain to the particularity of Jesus, liturgy is precisely the practised *loss* of a historical 'place' or 'identity'. Genuine liturgy thus occurs by way of what Certeau calls a 'movement of perpetual departure', whereby a faithful mission might be enacted precisely *because* there is no longer a hierarchized body – 'Christendom' or 'the West' – which presumes to mark off the boundaries for measuring the advance and retreat of that mission, that action.[68] The liturgy of Christian mission is thus a way of thinking the church itself as a mode of dynamic participation in Christ's own apocalyptic singularity, which, precisely as a work of 'losing its property', might give the church to appear as an executed 'cut in the social body', as a living in the '"moment" of the break' with every identifiable social institution and site.[69] Such is the Spirit's own apocalyptically irruptive work, by which we are called everanew into subversive openness to that reality which arrives as always in excess of every social 'site' as such: the 'original revolution' of God's reign that is Christ's cross and resurrection.

---

ecclesiological discourse is bound to refer itself to an imaginary which attempts to 'locate' the particularity of Christianity's praxis with respect to a universalizable discourse of meaning. For example, Certeau argues against the identification of a given social body as a *habitus*, insofar as such identification falsely reasserts the 'strategic' logic of identity, territoriality, and propriety, by constructing a 'socially constituted system of cognitive motivating structures' that locates the practice of that social body with respect to a 'place of its own'. Similarly, Certeau critiques the referral of practice to an overarching 'narrative' structure for the way in which such appeals to narrative almost inevitably promote a mode of practice that 'is continually concerned with marking out boundaries'. M. de Certeau, *The Practice of Everyday Life*, tr. S. Randall (Berkeley: University of California Press, 1984), see pp. 76, 57–8, 124–5. It should be added then that 'church' so conceived (qua *habitus*) would thus make of the discipline of ecclesiology and the theorization of ecclesial practices themselves mere ideological substitutes for the risk of action by which one enacts faithful obedience to Jesus-as-Other.

68 M. de Certeau, *The Mystic Fable*, tr. M. Smith (Chicago: University of Chicago Press, 1992), p. 299.

69 Certeau, *La Faiblesse*, pp. 296, 279.

Diaspora

So far I have been arguing that liturgical practice is not first of all for the sake of locating and performing a *given* political identity. Rather, liturgy is the 'apocalyptic ricochet', we might say, of the 'inaugural rupture' that is Jesus Christ; it is that action by which our bodies themselves are made to be a work of that irruptive and dynamic movement of the Spirit by which we are bound to Christ's own historicity, opened everanew by Christ's rupturing arrival to his coming and coming again. But does this make it impossible any longer to think 'church' qua *ecclesia*, as the *gathering of a people*? Is it really possible to go on speaking of 'Christian community', of a *communion*, a *bondedness* which we might still call 'church', if the missionary movement to which Christ calls us by definition requires our being stripped of any such community's apparent *givenness*, disappropriated of any presumed *identity*?

Certeau himself has been accused of such 'ecclesiological nihilism'. But it might be that this 'missionary movement of perpetual departure' points us in the direction of an altogether different conception of *ecclesia*. This possibility is broached in a passage near the end of *La Faiblesse de croire*. Speaking of the manifest impossibility 'of identifying faith with a site [*lieu*]', Certeau suggestively writes:

> We today are more radically obliged, by the grace of history, to take this lesson seriously. It concerns the Church itself, which loses its property [*ses biens immobiliers*]. The Christian 'new Israel' seems to rejoin the old Israel in exile and in the diaspora. Like the Jews deprived of a homeland [*pays*], without their own [*sans propre*] and therefore without history (there is history where there is a place [*lieu*]), after the destruction of the Temple, believers are delivered up to the road with texts for baggage.[70]

If we are to go on speaking of *ecclesia* at all, it will have to be in terms of an 'exile', a 'diaspora' – terms which are distinctively

---

70 Certeau, *La Faiblesse*, p. 296.

Jewish and, perhaps especially for that reason, irreducibly political.

Here it is helpful to reinvoke Yoder in supplementation of Certeau, on the basis of his later thesis that Christian apocalyptic requires thinking ecclesial existence as the *prolongation* and *intensification* of Jewish diasporic existence. Yoder's argument for the normativity of Jewish 'diaspora existence'[71] is

---

71 I am acutely aware of the tendentiousness of Yoder's claim to diaspora as 'normal Jewish existence', which taken in itself is highly problematic. Peter Ochs has registered a deep criticism of Yoder on this point, particularly as regards the complex status of 'Israel' in relation to 'the land'. I think Ochs is right to suggest that Yoder has played up the 'normativity' of diaspora for Jewish 'existence' in such a way as to overgeneralize its normativity for historical Jewry, *tout court*. See Ochs, 'Editor's Commentary', in Yoder, JCSR, pp. 203–4. More right still is the suggestion of Daniel Boyarin (who is otherwise in deep sympathy with Yoder's revisionist reading of the Jewish-Christian relation) that Yoder is perhaps not quite careful enough to refuse to define an 'essence' to Judaism as a religion. See Daniel Boyarin, 'Judaism as a Free Church: Footnotes to John Howard Yoder's *The Jewish-Christian Schism Revisited*', *Cross Currents* 56.4 (2007), pp. 6–21. Cf. Boyarin, *Border Lines: The Partition of Judeo-Christianity* (Philadelphia: University of Pennsylvania Press, 2004). In contrast, it should be noted that Boyarin himself has in another context submitted his own proposal for 'diaspora' as 'constitutive' of Jewish identity, as has his fellow Jewish theologian Marc Ellis. See D. Boyarin and J. Boyarin, *Powers of Diaspora: Two Essays on the Relevance of Jewish Culture* (Minneapolis: University of Minnesota Press, 2002); M. Ellis, *Practicing Exile* (Minneapolis: Fortress Press, 2002). This is of course not the place to sort through this multi-layered discussion, and my intention at any rate is not to determine the 'essence' of Judaism, much less to determine the final status of 'Israel' as such. Rather, my concern is with the particular importance and centrality of diaspora for what it means to 're-Judaize' Christianity. That is, whatever one might finally decide regarding the status and identity of 'Israel', as both a 'people' and a 'land', it remains the case that the 'Jewishness' of Christianity, as oriented by and towards the historicity of Jesus of Nazareth, can only truly be conceived according to the terms of a 'diasporic' peoplehood. I would argue, following Boyarin, that this is the only possible way in which to think Christianity in Jewish terms without at the same time falling into the trap of supersessionism.

meant, as Chris Huebner has shown, to emphasize the sense in which Judaism from Abraham onwards 'understands its people-hood as a gift over which it is not finally in charge'.[72] There is an evidently positive *Jewish* case to be made (and thus not simply a reductively 'anti-Constantinian' case) 'against "taking charge" of the course of history'.[73] For Jewish existence is decidedly *not* dependent upon instrumentalities of 'survival' or 'preservation', insofar as the Jewish people is a people continually formed and reformed by its ongoing receptivity of the evernew grace of God. Jewish diasporic existence is thus inherently 'nonconcentric', meaning that, as opposed to the kind of 'political' body that lives from and requires the positing of a primordial centre, the diasporic Jewish body is one that emerges as its people move out into and encounter always foreign social contexts and settings.[74] Such encounter, in fact, really is prior to any identifiable 'gathering' as a people, such that in the mode of Jewish diasporic existence a certain receptivity to otherness emerges even prior to its filling the community in the shape of institutions, disciplines, and practices.

It is according to this mode of exilic existence that Yoder conceives the *politics* of diaspora. One sees this in Yoder's emphasis upon the prophetic command of Jeremiah 29.7: 'But seek the welfare (*shalom*) of the city where I have sent you into exile, and pray to the Lord on its behalf, for in its welfare (*shalom*) you will find your welfare (*shalom*)' (NRSV). It is by way of this Jeremianic vision that Yoder in his later work moves beyond those concepts required to maintain the identity of Church-as-*polis* (especially the concepts of cultural-linguistic narrativity and intratextuality, as examined and critiqued in our analysis of Hauerwas). For example, Yoder emphasizes the way in which the political vision of *galuth* is a vision that

---

72 C. Huebner, *A Precarious Peace: Yoderian Explorations on Theology, Knowledge, and Identity* (Scottdale, PA: Herald Press, 2006), p. 125. This particular paragraph is much indebted to some of the wording used by Huebner in his discussion of Yoder on this point.

73 Yoder, JCSR, p. 191.

74 Yoder, JCSR, pp. 188–9, 190–2.

is 'at home in no one semantic world, in no one social world',[75] such that the fundamental 'challenge to the faith community' is now so to embody the truth of the gospel 'that the world can perceive it to be good news *without having to learn a foreign language*'.[76] To live diasporically *for the nations* is for the world itself to hear in the Jeremianic command, as it is lived out, 'the invitation, as good news, to participate ... in the cosmic meaning of the sovereignty of their risen Lord'.[77] On this reading, the diasporic challenge to Christianity is a call not to conceive Christ's lordship over history first in terms of his headship over the Church-as-*polis*, but rather, inversely, to insist that Christ is 'head of the Church' *only insofar* as he is first 'the Lord of history'.[78] In other words, rather than referring the world back to an identifiable 'home' into the practices of which one could then be habituated (where such habituation becomes a kind of 'entrance requirement to the world to come'),[79] *galuth* names the common mission of Jews and Christians to an exilic existence as envoys of God's coming messianic reign.[80]

Here we come to the main point which I am wanting to stress: conceived as a work of 'exile' or 'diaspora', the liturgy of mission decisively reorients the question of Christian political action with respect to the eschatological New Jerusalem. There are two 'sides' to this point, which must be held together in tension.

Jewish diasporic existence, as well as the missionary call to 'seek the peace of the city', are to be interpreted in light of the prophetic-eschatological insistence that it is according to the coming messianic-apocalyptic inbreaking of the New Jerusalem that God's liberative action is said to be *for the nations*. Because Jerusalem is 'built to be a city where people come to-

---

75 Yoder, JCSR, p. 183.
76 Yoder, FTN, p. 24 (emphasis added).
77 Yoder, FTN, p. 5.
78 Yoder, RP, p. 149.
79 Yoder, JCSR, p. 152.
80 Yoder, JCSR, pp. 183–202.

gether in unity' (Ps. 122.3 [author's translation]), it is a city
that we are to relate to here below as that city which is 'beyond
us' or 'above us' – 'to come'. Yoder speaks to this when he
describes the important function the *earthly* Jerusalem plays
within Judaism as more than a 'place':

> What matters is *why* Jerusalem matters as more than a
> place or a population. The answer to that question must be
> a statement not about the city but about the God who some
> three millennia ago chose it for a special function . . . [Jeru-
> salem] could serve as David's capital, and then as a site for
> the Tabernacle, and then for the Temple, precisely because,
> although encircled by Judah, it had belonged to none of the
> tribes. The Lord's choice of Jerusalem left behind their tribal
> judges' seats and their local holy places. Even on earth, extra-
> territoriality was part of his self-definition.[81]

Jeremiah's acceptance of *galuth* as mission thereby functions
as an extension of established Israel's own non-sovereign, dispossessive relationship to the city on earth. To 'seek the peace
of the city' in a foreign land is not then to sanctify its given
structures and polities, but rather to live in that city by way of
positive relation to that which is in *excess* of it, namely, that
'"higher" or "future" city of peace' by which the liberation not
only of Zion but also of *all* the nations is to come.[82] To live in
this way is to 'relativize the given in favour of the gift'[83]; it is
to live relative to and in subversion of the given mechanisms of
political power by way of that mode of action which is uniquely
receptive to the peace of that eschatological city which occurs
always in excess of so-called 'politics' as such.

The other 'side' of the present point has to do with the
apocalyptic-historicist claim that Jesus is the Messiah in whose
person the reign of God has been inaugurated. Yoder rightly

---

81 Yoder, JCSR, p. 161.
82 Yoder, JCSR, p. 164.
83 Yoder, JCSR, p. 162.

points out that such a claim is 'meaningful only in a Jewish frame of reference. To use the name *meschiach* for the person in whom the new age begins is only possible in a Jewish setting.'[84] Whatever else Christian assertions concerning 'the Messiahship of Jesus, his Lordship, and the presence of the Holy Spirit' might mean, such meaning flows out of the fact that these assertions were for the earliest Christians first of all a confession that Christ's apocalyptic inbreaking does not signal a surpassing but rather an *intensified mode* of Jewish diasporic existence. Christian existence is no less determined by its orientation toward the New Jerusalem, the coming reign of God. The difference is that for the Christian the descent of the New Jerusalem is bound up with her expectation of the 'return' or 'coming again' – the *parousia* – of the one she calls Messiah. Thus, the re-Judaization of Christian existence situates one firmly within the tension of the 'already-not yet', the 'open finality', of Christ's apocalyptic historicity. Yoder highlights this tension well in a provocative passage about 'messianic fulfillment':

'Fulfillment' is a permanently open border between what went before and what comes next. Whenever a Jew says that the Messianic age has not yet come, he or she is saying as well that it might come. That means that such a Jew can never say *a priori* that anyone's statement that the Messianic age has come is unthinkable, but only that it is not yet demonstrated. Fulfillment must also be an open border from 'this side'. Christians must continue to be claiming as Paul did that Jesus whom they follow is to be interpreted to Jews as the one to whom they still look forward.[85]

Thus it is that the Christian messianic vocation is not to return to Jerusalem but to scatter into the world and 'make disciples of all nations' (Matt. 28.19) while awaiting Christ's return.

---

84 Yoder, JCSR, p. 32.
85 Yoder, JCSR, pp. 97–8.

Holding the two sides of this point together, one might state more directly the importance of the Christian messianic claim for its participation in the Jewish politics of diaspora: the call to the life of exilic dispossession is a call to a political act of subversion which occurs not simply by *awaiting* but also and especially by *embodying* the interruption of the coming reign of God. For the Christian community to join with Israel in the diasporic work of mission is to insist that the work by which we 'seek the peace of the city' and according to which we await the New Jerusalem to come is no less a concrete flesh-and-blood reality than the singular event of Christ's cross and resurrection. For it is only as such that the Christian is given over to the excess of God's perfect *agape* that is the Spirit's work in history. At the same time, to make the Christian messianic claim is to insist that Israel's obedience to Jeremiah's command to seek the peace of the city was itself always-*already* an embodied sign of the coming reign of God. So it is precisely by way of the reality of and her participation in Christ's apocalyptic historicity that the Christian joins with Israel in *embodying* the coming of God's reign as a mode of apocalyptic hope. For only as it joins Israel in diaspora does the Christian 'not yet' become something other than a theological dilemma concerning the 'delay' of the *parousia* and become rather the condition for the political cry of 'come', a cry for the messianic inbreaking to occur everagain, for the Spirit to gather us everanew, in the very contingencies of our own ongoing histories, into the reality of the 'already'.

So to sum up this important section: I have sought to propose here an alternative thematic, that of 'mission', as more adequate to the apocalyptic politics of Jesus than the 'counter-*polis*' model which has dominated much of 'postliberal' theo-political thought since Barth. I have tried to do this by arriving at a particular understanding of what *leitourgia* means, as the customary term to describe the 'work' of the church in the world, in relation to the apocalyptic historicity of Jesus of Nazareth. Drawing upon the work of Michel de Certeau, it was suggested that 'liturgy' is the work of a dispossessive dispersal by which the Christian community emerges as a mode of concrete reception of Jesus-as-Other. Here, however, Yoder's appeal to the Jeremianic vision of *galuth* proves to be an important supplemental rejoinder to the analysis of Certeau. For here the Christian mission is understood against the backdrop of Jewish apocalyptic eschatology, such that the event which constitutes the church in diaspora is not simply the 'permissive' event of Jesus' withdrawal or his absence at the origin, but his promise to come, to 'return'. As such, it is precisely as Jesus is 're-imagined through the medium of Jewish experience' that the otherness according to which he is encountered in history occurs as a sign and a hope of the eschatological vocation of God's people.[86] As such, it becomes possible to reimagine 'church' itself 'through the medium of Jewish experience', as a people of exile, a people whose exile occurs now as the grace of a promise, the infusion of an apocalyptic hope according to which alone our missionary encounter with the other is an *embodiment* of an altogether different political act – namely, our ongoing *conversion* to the coming reign of God.

Conclusion

'The hope in which the Christian community has its eternal goal', Barth famously remarked, 'consists . . . not in an eternal church but in the *polis* built by God and coming down from heaven to earth.'[87] Barth is right. But the point of apocalyptic is that such a coming is not just history's eternal *telos*, but a concrete messianic *irruption* of history itself. As rooted in the ongoing reality of this irruption, the work of exile is constitutive of that mode of *action* by which we are finally delivered over to 'doxology', insofar as it is that action which lives from and towards the priority of God's Kingdom. It is as such that the diasporic liturgy constitutes the real *challenge* to 'politics'

86 Williams, *On Christian Theology*, p. 102.

87 K. Barth, *Against the Stream: Shorter Post-War Writings, 1946–52* (London: SCM Press, 1954), p. 19.

as such, by exploding 'the limits that our own systems impose on our own capacity to be illuminated and led'.[88] For it is precisely as such that we are bound to Christ's historicity in a mode of singular action by which we ourselves are graciously set free (by the historicity of the Spirit) to act 'independently' of those powers and principalities by which such 'limits' – *controls* – are maintained.

So, to conclude the present task, I want to make three observations that I think are implied by the missionary orientation to the apocalyptic historicity of Jesus, as a way of gesturing towards the *ecclesial* shape and content of this apocalyptic political action. First, a diasporic politics of mission requires that we radically reconceive the terms according to which we think 'church' and 'world'. The heart of the question of mission has to do with coming to 'see the church in relationship to the world rather than defining ecclesial existence "by definition" or "as such"'.[89] Whatever we thus mean by speaking of the church as an *ecclesia*, we can no longer simply mean by this a 'gathering' which occurs exclusively or even primarily in terms of 'centred' spaces of a formation that occurs *prior* to the movement into that which is 'outside' or 'beyond'. Bernd Wannenwetsch reminds us that the Christian use of the term *ecclesia* in its earliest form – as *ekklesia tou theou*, 'the assembly of God' – was most likely prompted by the use of the phrase *qᵉhal el* in apocalyptic Judaism to refer to 'God's End-Time gathering'.[90] The immediate referent of the *ecclesia* is not then that church which would tarry along here below as a counter-*polis* to the cities of earth, but rather that eschatological city in the fullness of whose coming there will no longer be even a church, but rather the manifestation of that 'new humanity' from all the nations in and through whom God's own life will be all in all.[91]

One might illustrate this point by referring to another set of writings addressed to a people in exile, the epistle to the

88 Yoder, RP, p. 129.
89 Yoder, RP, p. 78.
90 Wannenwetsch, *Political Worship*, p. 138.
91 See McCabe, *God Still Matters*, p. 91.

Hebrews. For the author of Hebrews, the promise of the city that *is to come*, the New Jerusalem, is a promise whose 'firm foundation' goes along with the awareness that here we have 'no abiding city' (Heb. 13.14). At the same time, this concrete exilic existence of the people of God in diaspora is understood as their already 'having come to the city of the living God' precisely by way of their having come to *Jesus* (12.22–24), himself being 'the one who is sent', *apostolos* (3.1). Thought in these terms, the church-world relation is to be significantly reconfigured. The true 'gathering' happens where Christ in his apocalyptic historicity breaks into the world in all its contingency and singularity and secularity, and opens it to that mode of life which is in excess of the powers and principalities. This 'worldly' site of inbreaking itself becomes the site of 'calling out' and 'gathering', a site that is politically a non-site, always 'outside the city gate' (13.12–13). Thus, Yoder can describe the 'distinctness' of that peoplehood constituted by Jesus' 'independence' as a distinctness that is 'not a cultic or ritual separation, but rather a nonconformed quality of ("secular") involvement in the life of the world'.[92] For the *ecclesia* is 'called' and 'gathered' not by the invocation of some ambiguous beyond, but precisely by the pneumatic call of this very *world* as it is being transformed by the occurrence of that which is, eschatologically speaking, an event *neither* of the church *nor* of the world in any strict sense of those terms, namely, the irruption of God's Kingdom. The dispossessive truth of this apocalyptic irruption is that there is no *ecclesia* as such that can by-pass 'the secular', the coming of the Kingdom qua *saeculum* which is itself the work of the Spirit. There is no *ecclesia* apart from our being bound by the Spirit to *this* world, for only as such are we truly *gathered* into the apocalyptic 'sending' that is Jesus himself.

Second, as bound up with the world in this way – as the *saeculum*, the becoming-time, or as Barth phrases it, the 'coming-to-earth' of God's eternal Kingdom – the politics of

---

92 Yoder, PJ, p. 39.

diaspora relativizes, by subverting, the given structures of power according to which the earthly city operates. As such, diasporic existence occurs as a very particular kind of exile *from* the given power structures of the world *in solidarity with* those marginalized and oppressed by those powers.[93] Thus, at the heart of Jeremiah's diasporic vision we find a joining of the apocalyptic hope of a redeemed humanity with a concrete embodiment of God's redemptive solidarity with the widow and the orphan, the poor and the oppressed, as a challenge precisely to the idolatry of all established ideologies (whether religious or political, Jewish or Babylonian). As Yoder suggests, Jeremiah's acceptance of *galuth* as mission points us toward the coming New Jerusalem precisely insofar as this promised coming 'points us away from possessiveness and toward the redefinition of providence so as to favour the outsider'.[94]

Thus, the apocalyptic politics of diaspora operates in a mode akin to what the theologies of liberation have taught us to call 'the preferential option for the poor'.[95] And yet what 'the

---

93 On this point, I have found the work of Jewish theologian Marc Ellis to be particularly helpful. See M. Ellis, *Revolutionary Forgiveness: Essays on Judaism, Christianity, and the Future of Religious Life* (Waco, TX: Baylor University Press, 2000), pp. 125–42; Ellis, *Toward a Jewish Theology of Liberation*, 3rd edn (Waco, TX: Baylor University Press, 2004).

94 Yoder, JCSR, p. 162; cf. p. 163.

95 On the importance of apocalyptic for rethinking the Christian 'option for the poor' today, see D. Tracy, 'The Christian Option for the Poor', in *The Option for the Poor in Christian Theology*, ed. D. Groody (Notre Dame: University of Notre Dame Press, 2007), pp. 119–31; J. M. Ashley, 'The Turn to Apocalyptic and the Option for the Poor in Christian Theology', in *Option for the Poor*, pp. 132–54; Ashley, 'Apocalypticism in Political and Liberation Theology: Toward an Historical Docta Ignorantia', *Horizons* 27 (Spring 2000), pp. 22–43. On Yoder's suggestion that 'exile' provides a 'wider setting' for liberation theology, as also another way of understanding the 'option for the poor', see J. Yoder, 'The Wider Setting of "Liberation Theology"', *The Review of Politics* 52 (Spring 1990), pp. 285–96; Yoder, 'Exodus and Exile: The Two Faces of Liberation', *Cross Currents* 23.3 (1973), pp. 297–309.

poor' names here is not the *object* of the church's outgoing, but rather the very 'non-site' of the church's gathering, the non-site of eschatological transformation. For insofar as it is precisely to the poor that the coming of the Kingdom is promised, as it is in and with the poor – those 'outside the city gate' – that Christ is crucified by the powers and resurrected to a life lived independently of them, so it is in the lives and bodies of the poor today that Christ's cross and resurrection is manifest and celebrated as the *sign* that God's Kingdom has come in Jesus.

It needs to be made clear that the 'option for the poor' does not here mean (as it does, for example, in certain political theologies of liberation, or, more fashionably, in certain post-nationalist political theories like that of Michael Hardt and Antonio Negri)[96] the privileging of 'poverty' as the generative site of some alternative political 'potency' or 'power', by which the power of 'the poor' might then be deployed on behalf of some 'world revolution'. 'The poor' is not simply a useful category, deployable as a way of 'holding open' history for the sake of some immanently conceived future transformation. Rather, 'the option for the poor' is our mode of participation in *the apocalyptic transformation of history itself* – the 'original revolution' that is the perfect *agape* of Jesus' death and resurrection.[97] As such, 'the church' is not first a people that *then* chooses to act in degrees of 'solidarity' with the other (the poor, the destitute, etc.), but rather *ecclesia* occurs as that people which emerges to view as a dynamic movement of *becoming with* the dispossessed other in *identification with Christ*. (In other words, the church does not simply 'exercise' *an* 'option for the poor'; *ecclesia* happens *as* that very option.)

Such participation in and identification with Jesus Christ ensures that the Christian 'option for the poor' can only occur

---

96 M. Hardt and A. Negri, *Empire* (Cambridge, MA: Harvard University Press, 2001), see pp. 156–9; Hardt and Negri, *Multitude: War and Democracy in an Age of Empire* (New York: Penguin, 2004), see pp. 129–38. See also A. Negri, 'The Political Subject and Absolute Immanence', in *Theology and the Political*, pp. 231–9.

97 Yoder, FTN, pp. 165–79.

as the *singularity of a decision – une option singulière*, to steal a phrase from Certeau.[98] That is, the option for the poor, and thereby the visibility of *ecclesia* itself, is irreducible to what Yoder calls 'sloganeering professions of loyalty to liberty or justice, peace or plenty'.[99] Instead, it requires that we discover everanew within the ongoing contingencies and particularities of history that *action*, that *praxis*, that *work of service* which is the sign of the inbreaking of God's grace and of our own conversion to God's *agape*. Only in this way is Jesus continually identifiable for the world, for only in this way are we given over – in the contingencies of our very histories, as was Jesus in his – to the 'more' of the Spirit by which God reaches 'beyond available models and options to do a new thing whose very newness will be a witness to divine presence' – the presence of Christ's own 'perfect love'.[100]

It is precisely by way of this option for the poor that the church appears as a political *challenge* to the powers of this world, for here the 'gathering' of the Spirit accords with the very 'logic of singularity' by which Christ himself operates 'independently' of those powers. Yoder puts it thus:

> The first word in the reaffirmation of the human dignity of the oppressed is thus to constitute in their celebrative life the coming Rule of God and a new construal of the cosmos under God. To sing 'The Lamb is Worthy to Receive Power' ... is not mere poetry. It is performative proclamation. It redefines the cosmos in a way prerequisite to the moral independence which it takes to speak truth to power and to persevere in living against the stream when no reward is in sight.[101]

The 'challenge' is not that of an alternative political power, but the 'moral independence' of a lived *doxa* – the cruciform,

---

98 Certeau, *La Faiblesse*, p. 256.
99 Yoder, FTN, p. 242.
100 Yoder, OR, p. 49.
101 Yoder, AE, p. 53.

subversive, and suffering love that is God's *agape*. The 'praise of the poor' marks the real political challenge which we name 'church', for such praise is *living* poverty in a mode of celebratory performance, proclaiming it *already* to be a sign within the fallen world of a new world whose 'fullness' – *pleroma* – is *not yet* as 'to come'. To sing about the resurrection of a slain lamb is to find oneself caught up into the life of that One whose love is always and everywhere a decision *for* poverty and powerlessness, exile and dispossession, and *against* the domination of the world by the manipulative fantasies of power and control.[102] Of course, the praise of the poor will always be met with contempt by a world designed for the purposes of controlling it; but the martyrial reality of the poor (their 'witness') is that the suffering entailed thereby is the surest sign that this life of praise – and the death to which it leads – cannot be so controlled. And this because such praise frees us to live cruciformly as a way of living from and embodying *resurrection* – the work of the Spirit by which one is delivered over to the other in the mode of God's *agape*. It is here that the 'the given' of 'politics' as such is relativized in favour of 'the gift' of that eternal *polis* to come, for it is here that we are given over to the very bodily transformation that is the concrete *sign* of God's coming reign.

Third: we speak finally of Christian 'community', of 'corporate life', of *koinonia*. If mission is constitutive of a 'new humanity', a new 'fellowship' in which the established boundaries and partitions that divide us and oppress us are perpetually transgressed, then the 'church' that mission makes is only ever visible qua some kind of 'social body'. But such a body can only emerge to view *as* a work of dispossession; such is the only possible notion of *communion* for any vision of humanity that converges on the historicity of Jesus Christ and lives by the excess of the Spirit. As a people in exile, we will need to

---

102 See Williams, *Christ on Trial*, p. 45: 'Christ will always be in exile, a refugee, in a world constrained by endless struggles for advantage, where success lies always in establishing your position at the expense of another's.'

reconsider what it might mean for the 'Christian community' to be and become 'the church of the poor', in line with the familiar Jewish image of exilic Israel as 'the congregation of the poor'. I suggest that we thus think of the church as a kind of 'dispossessed sociality', in two senses.[103] On the one hand, the church is only ever visible as a *people* of dispossession, a *sociality* of shared poverty whereby shapes and structures of communion emerge in which the gift of the coming new humanity is shared and celebrated as sign and as promise. On the other hand, the church in mission is precisely that people which exists without a centre in their own achieved 'sociality'. As given to a people under exile, the sociality granted to the church is indeed without controls; it is a sociality received as gift only insofar as it immediately *loses itself* in the dynamic movement of mission, a movement in which, just as Jesus himself is received in the other, the *koinonia* that occurs as the Spirit binds us *to* others in Christ is itself received everanew in ways which we can neither determine nor predict. Undoubtedly, this 'dispossessed sociality' registers as something of a paradox: without the vision of a concrete sociality, it makes no sense to say that 'mission makes the church'; and yet where this sociality is assumed and referred back to as first of all a *given datum* (a 'society' or 'polis' as such), I have argued, we are no longer genuinely speaking of either *mission* or *ecclesia* – the *people* of God. What this finally means is that the 'people' that we are to be as 'Christian', and the 'sociality' which we are to become, must themselves emerge, like doxology and the liturgy of mission itself, as *action* and as *gift* – as *signs* of that Kingdom whose coming we cannot control.

A dispossessed sociality. A sociality of dispossession. This is what the liturgy of Christian mission commits us to. And yet, there is no way theoretically to anticipate what this sociality will look like; as Yoder puts it, 'The only way to see how

---

103 For this concept of 'dispossessed sociality' and the idea of 'engaged action', and for some of the ways of putting things in this and the next paragraph, I am indebted to conversations with Josh Davis and Craig Keen.

this will work will be to see how it will work.'[104] Such a sociality is only discoverable as we are *bound* everanew to the world via that pneumatic gathering which constitutes our participation in that ongoing Christic inbreak that is God's apocalypse. Constituted by mission, 'church' is entirely the operation of God's apocalyptic *action* in Christ, and its 'peoplehood' the diasporic *work* of the Spirit. As under exile, such a peoplehood is bound to appear as tenuously ad hoc, its fleeting presence being only 'for a time', and so at best politically *irrelevant* and at worst dangerously *ineffective*. And yet such might be the surest sign that one has, by God's grace, been delivered over to that mode of engaged and embodied action whereby alone we pass from ideology to doxology.

---

104 Yoder, PK, p. 45.

Index of Names and Subjects

Jesus Christ *continued*
ascension of 7, 91, 144, 148,
151, 153, 156, 177
and Church 2, 15–16, 20, 21,
107–9, 111, 120, 121–2,
123, 129, 172–3, 176–80,
187–8
cross and resurrection of 1–2,
7, 14, 15, 21, 71–2, 87, 96,
97, 102, 103, 124, 133, 136,
138, 139, 141–4, 145, 147,
148–51, 153–8, 159, 165–6,
167, 177, 180, 187, 192, 194
as event 4, 13, 70, 74–9, 80,
91, 93, 109, 130, 181
historicity of 1, 5, 13–14, 15,
21, 57, 70–1, 72, 73–9, 80,
83, 84, 86, 89, 90, 91, 93,
103, 104, 106, 111, 114–15,
125, 126, 127, 133, 136, 139,
141, 142, 144–54, 156–8,
178–80, 189, 194
apocalyptic 14, 92, 116, 128,
129, 130–2, 134, 135–7,
145–6, 150, 151, 154, 155,
157, 158–60, 161, 162–8,
172, 173–5, 176–8, 180,
186, 187, 189, 190
and history (relation to) 7, 10,
13–14, 20, 21, 73–9, 80, 83,
87, 89–91, 92, 94–5, 96, 97,
99, 100–16, 116, 126, 130,
138, 143, 145–6, 149, 151–2,
154, 156, 176, 177
cosmic 13–14, 20, 53, 55–6,
60–1, 63, 75, 76, 77, 78,
90,132, 134,
136, 163
psychological 54–7, 63, 90,
136
social 54–6

incarnation of 53, 73, 91, 132,
145–8, 150, 151, 153, 155,
157, 158, 165–6, 167, 177
independence of 13–14, 93,
104, 116, 131, 132, 134,
142–6, 170, 172, 190 *see
also* Yoder: independence
as Jewish 6, 13, 75, 91
and Kingdom of God 14, 49,
72, 73, 79, 89, 90, 92, 97,
102–3, 105, 106–7, 127,
132, 143–4, 145, 154–5, 157,
161, 163, 165–6, 190–2
as Logos 21, 54, 91, 134, 147,
151, 158
lordship of 1, 5, 7–8, 10, 11,
14–15, 53–7, 63, 72, 75, 77,
79, 80, 89, 90, 91–2, 95, 96,
97, 99, 100, 102, 105, 110–
13, 119–20, 121, 125, 133,
136, 141, 151, 152–3, 167,
168, 170, 173, 176, 184
mission of 2, 14, 16, 105, 133,
141, 147, 173–4, 190
parousia of 14, 88–9, 91,
123–4, 125, 153, 177, 186,
187
participation in 14, 15, 16,
98, 154, 157–8, 159, 161,
162–3, 167, 168, 172, 174,
192
and powers 7, 10, 13–15, 130,
137, 139–43, 145, 175, 192
presence of 14, 15, 77, 86, 87,
88, 89, 90, 91, 106, 111,
153, 154, 157, 166, 192, 193
as priest 15, 55, 152
as prophet 15, 55
and reality 13, 14–15, 70
and resurrection 91, 143,
148–9, 151, 153, 160, 194

Index of Names and Subjects